INDIAN WOMAN

INDIAN WOMAN
THROUGH THE AGES

V. JANAPATHY

GYAN

GYAN PUBLISHING HOUSE
New Delhi-110002

INDIAN WOMEN: THROUGH THE AGES

Price: Rs. 495/-

ISBN 81-212-0758-4

Published in 2002 in India by
Gyan Publishing House
5, Ansari Road, Daryaganj
New Delhi 110 002
Phones: 3261060, 3282060, Fax: 3285914
E-mail: gyanbook@vsnl.com
Web site: http://www.gyanbooks.com

Laser Typeset at: Sai Graphic Design, New Delhi
Printed at: Mehra Offset Printers, New Delhi

Contents

Preface

Status of woman is a topic now drawing the attention of one and all in the Indian Society. When a traditional society is taking the shape of a modern society and its basic philosophy and life style are undergoing drastic changes, what should be the role of a woman? What will be a woman's contribution to the society?

These are some questions which need to be answered. The image of Indian woman is undergoing considerable change, from mere passivity to positive self-assertion in view of her education, employment opportunities, break up of joint families, rapid industrialization and urbanization. No doubt, the freedom movement and the period immediately succeeding independence, brought many a women into the political arena. Women are climbing mountains and Himalayan peaks and are shining in traditionally men's occupations as scientists, administrators, also as judges and lawyers as well as in white collar jobs proving their mettle and merit.

Women-carriers of Change

Though women are the carriers of social change, "most of the men do not want to give up their traditional superior position in the family and moreover women themselves do not want a change in their attitude—our Indian society is extremely status-conscious and status-bound" as Smt. Phulrenu Guha, head of the committee on the Status of Women in India, puts it very aptly.

In today's world, where people are facing vast challenges, Indian men are not less inhibited by superstition and old attitudes.

Indians, having great respect for tradition cannot easily get rid of age-old ideas or welcome a drastic change in thought or deed. As Mrs. Indira Gandhi, in her message to the Mexico Conference in 1975, put it "Men and even women are imprisoned by fear of change".

Women's Equality, a Myth or Reality

Equality of women is an idea of recent origin and emerged only from the beginning of the 19th century, when the individual gained more importance over his status in society. Then what is this equality and what for? Is it simple confrontation? Is it exchanging fields of activity, such as women taking to jobs and men working in the kitchens? Is it oppression again or domination of women over men in the process of decision making? None of the above propositions seem to define equality. There cannot be equality of sexes *per se.*

In the truest sense, it is nothing but equality of opportunity to develop one's own capabilities to the extent possible, without any fear of oppression or exploitation by another person. Our concept of freedom is very different from that of the westerners. As a matter of fact, when we look upon the arguments on the status of women, for and against, over the past century and a half throughout the world, we notice a glaring truth. Many revolutions, slave revolutions have been fought and won. But, the revolution on the basis of sex still remained unpersuasive. What is it due to?

Certain Misconceptions and Presumptions?

A woman, with a clear vision, a sense of responsibility and dedication, with a capacity to see things and to judge for herself with an intellectual acumen, is definitely an asset to her husband and to the family. No one can deny this fundamental truth. But there were times, when Indian women were simply confined to the four walls of the house and even her appearance in public was considered to be disrespectful. Education was denied to her and she was ordered to lead a life of bondage. Almost all religious leaders preached that women should be meek and submissive. But our ancestors allowed a talented woman to exhibit her talent in public though they prescribed several 'dos' and 'don'ts' for her, that she should live within a limited sphere and should confine her activity only to the family fold.

Family System—The Basis of Society in India

The family is the unit of Indian society and the centre of family is considered to be the woman in principle *Jayae-Dastam* (wife is the home) is a Rigvedic expression, which shows how domestic life is interwoven with the life of a 'woman'. She is called by several names 'Speech', 'Learning', 'Prosperity', 'Calamity', all take feminine forms as per our mythology. The whole universe is depicted as *Prakriti* (*stri*) and the concept of motherhood- *Na Matuh Paradevta* (there is no greater goddess than mother)- speak of the glory attributed to a women. There is a *Lakshmi*, *Saraswati* or *Sakthi* in every family as a woman is kept on high pedestal notionally. Family bonds are strong. 'Marriage' is an important event in every women's life and this institution of marriage gives her a status in the family as 'wife' and also as 'mother'. Kalidasa, the great Sanskrit poet says in Raghuvamsa *Kanyayam Kula Jeevitham* (It is the maid that brings name and fame to the family). Of quoted sayings like. *Janani Janma Bhumishta Swarga dapi Gareeyase* (The mother and motherland are greater than *Swargaloka*). This speaks of the glory attributed to 'motherhood' or *Matru Bhavana* by Hindu Devotions. One of the fine concepts is that of Siva depicted as *Ardhanareeswara* (one half man and the other half woman). Thus we see that a *Devi* is adored and worshipped.

Complexity of the Situation

So far as the ideology is concerned, it is very generous in outlook. But, in real life, Indians have not given to woman what they have given to *Devi* in the 'Cosmos'. Laws laid down in the authoritative texts were different from what were practised. Thus a wide gap developed between the principles and social traditions. There is no scriptural sanction for some of our customs like *Sathi*, 'pre-puberty marriages', and 'dowry'. There is a world of difference thus, in precept and practice.

When we trace the cultural evolution of society, we find that there was a gradual transition of sacred laws of the Aryans or Law givers as taught by *Apastamsa, Gautama, Vasistha* and *Boudhayana*; An 'illegal child' was unknown to ancient texts. These *Maharisis* have recognised fourteen kinds of sons like *Kaneena*, (born to a *kanya*), *Gudhaja* (born secretly), *Kshetrya* etc. Such being the elasticity or Catholicism of our *dharmastrakaras*, very mean and petty-minded concepts have crept into Indian lives perhaps on account of wrong interpretations of our customary laws. The culture which had imbibed several tribes and kinds of people into its fold, have been crippled into a small network surrendered by narrow casteism and inequality. It is this inequality added with malpractices like polygamy, *Devadasi* system, *Sati* (burning of the wife on the pyre of the husband while alive) that have lowered down the status of woman. As times went on, several contradictory opinions, currents and cross-currents of thoughts found place in the course of thousands and thousands of years. Due to the upheavels brought about by different rulers, the Indian society lost its original salient features. Altogether a different society developed wherein false and ambiguous ideas ruled and gained importance and the broad universal outlook, that once prevailed, strangely disappeared, especially in the matter of giving a status to women.

The Great Land of Manu

Manudharma Sastra is considered to be the authoritative text, on the basis of which, the Britishers established and developed the law courts in India. It appears to be a hotch-potch of several contradictory opinions. In one place, Manu says *Yatra Naryasthu Pujyanthe, Ramanthe Tatra Devatah* (Where women are adored there gods rejoice) yet in another place he says, *Na stre Swatantrya Marhati* (A woman is not entitled for freedom) This has created so much of confusion and ill will. Several misapprehensions and misrepresentations were made. Several writers have criticised Indian culture on the basis of this text. But on clear analysis of this text, clause by clause, it appears that 'Manu' is not a "Person", but a "Post" like a chairman. We find that several Manus like Vaivaswatamanu, Bhrugamanu were there and then kings appointed them as "Heads" of commisions and authorised them to make laws required by conteporary society. What we now call *Manudharma Sastra* is a compilation of all of them. My personal discussions with Sri Vinoba Bhave, also a great Sanskrit Scholar, were very useful in arriving at some conclusions on 'Manu' and his *Dharmasastra*.

I am neither supporting nor criticising this text. I am only trying to place before the reader, my analysis of this *dharma sastra*, which had been responsible for creating so much of havoc in lowering down the status of women. But, the ultimate goal of our ancient law-givers appears to be the well-being of society at large. In Indian culture, the individual is made secondary and the collective welfare of the society is considered primary, by our law-givers. Our *vedas, upanishads*, our *puranas* and all our religious concepts reveal this fundamental idea. When once we understand this basic truth, we can easily understand the rest of the inner thought, underlying our tradition and culture. Our ethical values are moulded in such a way. The entire background of Indian context is unique and has a strong basis. So, the status of woman cannot be a separate topic, isolated from the main framework of society. Both the issues are interlinked with each other.

There is a school of thought, which says that woman's status has deteriorated on account of the male domination. No doubt there are several structures and systems in society that are not allowing a woman to have her rightful place in society. Any number of barriers and taboos are obstructing a woman's progress to the fullest extent. So, the great land of Manu is not able to see the bright side of the argument that a woman has a role in the outside world also and in decision making at various levels-may be at family level or the governing level. The role of a woman in the family and in the society has to be framed, judged and defined from a much more wider perspective, than mere confrontation level.

No Ideological Resistance

Though medieval times made women to live in seclusion and men dominated the society, there was no ideological resistance from men at any time of history. On the other hand, in times of crisis, women were encouraged to participate and to lead as well. Independence movement is a clear evidence of this fact. When a national upsurge was there, women joined in huge numbers and voiced their protest. They picketed before liquor shops, went to jails and bore the brunt of the tyranny of the British rulers. This was possible because men encouraged their wives and sisters to participate in the freedom struggle. In fact, it was the *Brahmos*, on account of the influence of freedom struggle, that started schools for girls. It was the National Congress that started the women's movement and it was customary to hold a women's session in every congress session. We don't find such a situation in any corner of the world. India was the country that could see a woman as a prime minister for the first time. Unlike in other more advanced foreign countries, Indian women got the 'right to vote', immediately after Independence, without any struggle. This right to vote has given Indian woman a status. Even in the so called developed countries, women could get such a right to vote only after some struggle. Pandit Jawaharlal Nehru, no doubt, the first prime minister and architect of modern India, gave a new importance to this thought of giving freedom to the Indian women much against the will of several conservatives. On account of his initiative several acts were passed.

Past History and Present Set-up

On a birds eye-view of past history we can only draw some conclusions, as historical proof is not available. Only some religious texts and mythical tales exist. So, we can broadly divide our past into different ages—pre-historic age, the classical age, the medieval age, the British period and the renaissance or the independence movement and the modern age. The Rigvedic woman could be a *Brahmavadin* and appeared in *Pandita Parishads* and was honoured as an intellectual. But, on account of changed values of life, the medieval woman was merely confined to the four walls of the house and education was completely denied to her. During Muslim period, even child marriages became customary. Again, schools were started and women were allowed to participate freely during the period of independence movement. Of course the modern period is able to see the other side of the picture of renaissance as regards woman but with a difference. The basis of society is being displaced, rather disturbed, which may turn out to be dangerous for its very existence. Of course, there were upsurges, pitfalls and again upheavels which is natural for any society moving towards progress and that too during the course of some thousands of years. so, in Indian society, the status of woman kept changing from time to time. There is also another point to be considered. A sweeping generalisation cannot be made as regards the status of women in our society. Laws are customary. A girl brought into Khasi family in Meghalaya is a wife to all the brothers as Draupadi, whereas, there are different customs and traditions, as regards marriage, divorce, property rights etc. On an impartial analysis, we find that a woman among the toiling masses is more free than a middle class woman. But still the domination of man is there everywhere in all communities. Man's right to have the upper hand in all decisions is not denied. A woman is being exploited in several contexts. Still atrocities are going on unabated, dowry is prevalent in almost all classes in some form or other, though education at all levels is made available to girls also.

Of course, there is some change in the process of thinking of parents. But yet, we are groping our way in transition. Today's society is in an unsettled atmosphere. The old values' have not totally deserted us. The 'New' ones give us a blurred vision. So, my attempt in this booklet is to show how the values that have changed and that are undergoing change, form a basis for the incoming generations.

This volume is a culmination of my efforts spread over six years in collecting, analyzing and presenting data. I hope it would be helpful to the researcher and the general reader in framing a serious thought on salient points of Indian culture with regards womanhood. I tried to give a glimpse of our past history, as well as our ideology and tried to highlight some important aspects, wherever necessary.

"Blessed be God, who made me a man and not a woman", thus runs a Hebrew Prayer. Times have come, When woman have to prove that "blessed be God who created woman, to make man's life fuller and richer". Any serious thinker or reformer would have to struggle hard to fix up modernity, which runs against the current of practices and thoughts of yesteryears, something new cannot be built up overnight. Basis will be there always! No-one can deny the fact that Indian woman lives in Kavyasas a mother and a sublime soul. But that is all fiction and is different from fact. We do not have authoritative evidences to show her status in any age. We have to simply draw conclusions from the writings available.

Status of a Woman within the Home

One of the indicators of a woman's status is her participation in the decision making process in the home and her husband's participation in her household activities and their mutual sharing of leisure time activities. A woman's status in the community in which she lives is also dependent on the nature of community and is a variable factor to a great extent. Literacy level of a woman also helps her to find a status. Her access and exposure to mass media and her awareness of problems around her also gives her a higher status, when compared to others.

A healthy atmosphere should be developed in society, wherein due impetus is given to women's problems. The culture and religions of India, place women in Indian society at varying and different platforms. In fact, a woman in India has yet to seek identity as a human being with equal status in the family in which she is born and in the family to which she is given in marriage. Marriage is must in any traditional family. *Kanyadaan* is a traditional custom by which a girl is married and it is this custom that had lowered down the status of woman initially. A girl was given a right to choose her husband (*swayamvara*) or life partner only notionally in the ancient times. Infact only the father selected the boys to be invited for such *swayamvara* and tested their valour. So marriage as a necessary event in life is an acid test for a woman and her future depends on the decision to marry. Maternity is another important event in woman's life. Nature has endowed on woman 'Motherhood' by which she brings forth progeny and gives shape to new human beings. But this richness itself becomes a curse to her if she is unmarried. Her dignity and self-respect become questionably, in some pockets of society, though some welfare services are available.

In conclusion, it can be said that women are not treated well in their families and also in the society at large. Main reason for this is, lack of facilities for education. The woman is not still considered an asset in middle class families. At the lower level exploitation, both mental and physical is the watchword. Impact of science and technology is not visible and media have failed in presenting a proper image of her. To improve the situation, voluntary organisations have to champion the cause in the best possible manner. Many deserve my heartfelt thanks for bringing out this book. I owe my gratitude to several eminent scholars and personalities, who helped me in analysing the situation as per our texts. This book is meant not only for the feminists but for all those interested in women's development. I hope it would catch the eye of the public, for eliminating the maladies.

Introduction

Data available in history of religions suggest that women have not been excluded from religious rites nor relegated to an inferior status. In early times, mother-right and matriarchy preceeded patriarchy, in the development of human societies. The status of women in early agricultural societies was comparatively high. Women were considered to be not only creators of life, they were also the providers of food, and helpmates of men. They were considered to be the supreme symbols of fertility itself. Thus there was widespread worship of mother Goddess in the form of many powerful deities. The civilisations of Babylonia, Egypt, Phrygia and Phoenicia from where it spread to Greece and Rome paradoxically exhibit these alongwith a legal position of women's complete subordination to the authority of father or husband. The Greek, Roman and Indian pantheon in particular are replete with female deities. We find in both primitive and ancient religions, the presence of women as magicians, healers, visionaries, seers, prophetesses and priestesses.

In earlier times, when religious practices were less formally organised, it was easier for women to hold positions of religious authority. Female temple priests and attendants were known in many religions, for example, in Egypt, Sumeria, Babylonia, Greece and ancient Japan. Roman religions knew the *vestals*, the consecrated virgins charged with the care of the perpetual fire in the temple of goddess 'Vesta'. We find the phenomenon of temple prostitution also.

Of great renown are the *Sibyles*, the prophetesses and fortune-tellers, who were considered to be the mouthpiece of a particular god. They were pictorially depicted in Christian churches from the 11th Century onwards, the most famous example being Michelangelo's paintings in the Sistine Chapel in Rome. Female visionaries played on important role in Germanic religion and the women oracles of Greece were equally well known, especially the famous oracle at Delphi.

No one can deny the influence of woman directly or indirectly, ever since the days of Mother Eve. Whether living in isolation or having a freer life of the western world, woman had played an important role in the march of events in any country and exercised a subtle power in all things, great or small. To appreciate or assess their position properly is an uphill task. There are a variety of myths that exist about Indian women; some of them are our own invention and some by the westerners.

Tilling the soil was the beginning of the Earth Goddess cult. The religion of all such societies was connected with the earth, fertility cycle of procreation etc. From the Mediterranean to the Pacific, the *Mother Goddess* was the eternal symbol of life. The Rigveda reveals "a stage showing that Aryan women of the higher and better classes, enjoyed equal freedom as men did, in all matters, social and religious. It was this feeling of equality and freedom that evoked the highest virtues of the Aryan womenhood and lifted society to a high status of culture (Abhinash Chandra Das, p. 106 *Rigvedic Culture*) In Vedic literature, we come across a ritual, recommended for ensuring birth of a scholarly daughter (*Brihadaranyaka Upanishad*-IV 4.18, Poona, 1918).

In Vedic period, daughters, like sons, were initiated into learning, self-control, and discipline (*Atharva Veda*, XI. 5.18, Poona, 1918, 1956, p. 10). Many women rose to become Vedic scholars, debators, poets and teachers. Some remained unmarried and indulged in a life-long pursuit of knowledge and were known as *Brahmavadins*. Women were married at a mature age and enjoyed full freedom to select their husbands. From the solemn promises made by the bride and groom at the time of marriage, it appears that monogamy was prevalent. Women were partner in all the activities of their husbands – both temporal and spiritual. They were free to attend and visit public assemblies and social gatherings (S.R. Shastri – *Women in the Vedic Age*, Bombay, 1960, p. 20). They were participants in agriculture and cooperated with men in manufacture and use of arrows, cloth and other articles of public utility. (Prof. Griffith gives a graphic description of a "Home" as found in *Adharva Veda*).

When Buddhism flourished in India, women were assigned an honourable position in social life. They were admitted into *Bhikshuni Sanghas*. Some of the *Bhikshunis* achieved great distinction as poets and biographers.

In Jainism women were given absolute rights over property.

"In spite of the unrivalled culture and high ideals of society that ancient India placed before us, we have to bear witness to the tragic fact that we have fallen ever so far from that happy estate and perhaps in no sphere of life has that fall been so great as in the case of woman" said Raj Kumari Amrit Kaur, writing her foreword to Gandhiji's book entitled *Women and Social Justice*. *Grihya Sutras* were all centred on the birth of a son for performing funeral rites for a man after his death. Hence, the very meaning of a woman's existence began revolving around giving birth to sons only. Woman's existence merged with that a man through marriage ceremony.

Prohibition of remarriage, lowering down the age of marriage, allowing man to have more wives, led to deterioration of woman's position in India. Women's status was not so bad even when Buddhism was dominant in India. The right of admission to religious order generated self-confidence among women. Even Amrapali decided to join this religious order giving up the life of a courtesan. Women were also educated. Birth of a girl was not considered to be a calamity. (Horner L.B., *Women Under Primitive Buddhism*, p. 104).

However, towards the latter half of the eighteenth century, position of Indian woman came to be deteriorated.

Gandhiji's greatest contribution to the movement for the emancipation of women lies in his insistence on the participation of women in politics. As a result of participation in public life, Indian woman realised the need of living like a conscious human being and trieds to free herself from the shackles imposed on her by society. Mrs. Pearl Brick, wise authoress of *Good Earth* has said without women in Public Affairs, men have made a world in which Science is over-developed in comparison to human relations. It is time for women to influence the social values, as she alone knows cost of producing life and preserving it with care and affection. (Neera Desai, *Women in Modern India*, p. 140).

Status of Women in Indian Society (From Pre-historic to Modern Times)

"A living tradition influences our inner faculties, humanizes our nature and lifts us to a higher level" said Dr. Radhakrishnan, our philosopher, politician and President of India. Very true! our tradition was rich in content and its influence continued till today. In India, the image of a woman is visualised as *shakti* (Energy). She is described in all our ancient texts as the force behind creation and divinity.

> "*Yatra varyasthu pujyanthe*
> *Ramanthe tatra Devatah*"
> (where women are adored, Gods rejoice)–is the Vedic expression.

"Speech", "Learning", "Prosperity" and "Calamity" take feminine forms as per our mythology. Several ideologists, foreigners, philosophers and eminent personalities have studied Indian woman "from several angles and wondered at the Indian ideology" says Dr Anne Besant (Lecture No. 4 – Ancient Ideals in Modern Life).

In several words like "Jaya", "Patni", "Mahila", "Stree", "Ardhangi" etc., a woman is exalted to the position of glory and grace.

For the philosophers, she is "*Yogamaya*", "*Muktikanta*", "*Kundalini*"; for the poets, she is "*Ushabala*", "*Vanalakshmi*", "*Sandhya Sundri*, "*Annapurna*", "*Raja Rajeswari*" and she is "*Ushas*", "deity of beauty" for the artist and the painter. The concept of "Ardhanareeswara" (God dividing Himself into two halves) is unique in Indian philosophy.

When we look at our literature, sculpture, arts or mythology, we find that our ancestors felt that woman is "Replica" of the universe. The whole aesthetic sense in the art of creation and the sublime perfection of mind are associated with woman and this philosophy of *Soundarya Tatwa* kept "woman", on a high pedestal in Indian concept. So, '*Aptruna*' (man without woman) is not considered to be "*purna purusha*" (Mahenjodaro Civilization: Pridhvi Mata.

From the ruins of Mahenjodaro and Harappa, it is evident that a great culture flourished on the banks of Sindhu river before the advent of Aryans. Researches made by some indologists and also foreigners revealed the great fact that this culture which was prevalent in Indus Valley, was purely native and also paved the way for future generations, in the fields of art and culture. A famous indologist and student of Dr. H.D. Sankhaliya, a specialist on Indus Valley civilization tells us that "Indus Valley Culture" was vedic according to the seals available there and it was also evident by Harappan civilization. Of course, there is some controversy about this statement, but one thing is clear from the "woman images" available, Sir John Marshall, who carried out research on Indus Valley civilization, says that "they are indicative of *Mathru Bhavana* and these was a perfect culture with deep roots.

Figures of Terrakota – Mahenjodaro

People who lived in Mahenjodaro were all Hindus and worshippers of Siva and also his bull. They were also worshippers of "Kali" – a female deity. Foreign experts like Keith and Macdonald say that Siva was not the god of Aryans and the word 'Rudra' is mentioned in Vedas. So, this Rudra may be the same Siva. (Sir John Marshall – Indus Valley Civilization) when this theory is accepted, the words "uru", "kishi" available on the seals are also to be accepted. 'Urukshiti' is found in Vedas, which is supposed to be the name of a place in Mesopotamia. This may be the spot on which *Yagnas* were performed. So, it can be said that Mahenjodaro depicts Vedic culture and it had been ruined by Aryans.

Whatever may be the controversy on this Aryan, Non-Aryan argument, the word 'Urukshiti' which appears in *Rigveda* is used as a synonym for "Agni" (Fire). So, it can be gain said that Indus Valley Civilisation depicts Vedic culture dating back to two thousand five hundred years.

Dr. Winternitz, an authority on Sanskrit literature, says that Vedas belong to the later period of Indus Valley Civilization. The above explanation is meant to suggest that there was a matriarchal society before Aryans came and brought their culture into India. (There is also a theory that Aryans did not come from somewhere else, they are natives of India only and they spread their culture to other areas of the world.)

Aryans are supposed to be more civilized. But matriarchal society prevailed before their advent and it was not in any way inferior to that of Aryan culture. In its original form, it belonged to India. It is called Indus Valley Civilization. Sir John Marshall, with his team of experts conducted very useful surveys and arrived at such conclusions. Some are now calling it Dravidian culture. Anyway, Indians gave importance to *Matru Murthy*. Man who lived by hunting before he learnt agriculture, looked after his cattle and felt happy. He worshipped nature as "mother" and imagined her to be *sakti* which is all pervasive, universal mother.

Egyptians called her "Isis", Romans called "Siris", Greeks "Dmetr" and Indians "Pridhvi". Matru Devata of Mediterranean culture was perhaps the origin of this worship. This generous mother is "Bhumata" which can be seen giving Yield and which Greeks called as "Giya", Romans "Tellis", Indians "Pridhvi". It is a wonder to note how and why our ancestors entertained the idea of "mother" and "motherhood" as the origin of all. In course of time, it might have been this universal motherhood that led to the worship of women deities.

Indologists have expressed that the figurines taken out from the excavations of Indus Valley suggest that people who lived in the Valley worshipped *prakriti* (nature) as the main deity. Similar figurines were available in Mesopotamia, West Asia, Asia minor, Syria, and Palestine. So, it can be presumed that "Devipuja" was prevalent in Indus Valley Valley and from there, it spread to Nile river. Sir John Marshall says that, "like in India, in no other country '*aradhana*' (worship) of *prakriti mata* was there. Perhaps on account of the matriarchal system prevalent such a worship of "mother" had a beginning." (M & I Vallevy Civilization, Vol I, p. 51)

Many of the terrakota figurines tend to prove that "Mother deity" was worshipped. Her features are high head decorations, profuse garlands over the neck, and a belt for the waist. This sort of figurines are in standing posture. Some figurine show the hands as hanging. In some other, they are lifting hands and touching the forehead as if saluting. Aryans recognised this *Matra Murthy* as the wife of *Siva*, the un-Aryan God and took her as one among other deities. This sort of Aryan and un-Aryan synthesis was achieved to some extent by *Puranas* and also by *Tantra Sastra.*

Village Deities

Village deities like "Pochamma", "Poleramma", "Pothapatemma", "Mysamma", "Mahankalamma" are still popular in the villages of India by different names and they are considered to be different shapes of *Durga Devi*, the consort of *Siva*. Mode of worship is also different between Aryan Gods and non-Aryan Gods. In course of time, as a replica of synthesis of these two cultures, several *Janapada Gadhas* were evolved and they are popular among the village folk even today.

Kumari puja (worship of a girl) is one such mode of worship even today in India, and *Kumari* (a *Kanya*) is supposed to be *Sarva Devata Samanya Swarupa* (figure of all devatas put together) and her worship, it is believed, would take away all the sins. Sir John Marshall (Vol. I. p.51) says that the Great Mother Goddess of Asia Minor, Ishtar of ISIS, appears to be definitely associated with vegetation cults, forges connection of Indian Durga Devi with vegetation (R.P. Chanda, Indo Aryan Races, pp. 1313.

It being a matriarchal society, this sort of worship of village deities was conceived and made popular; so, he further says, it can be presumed that these village deities, gained much importance among in Aryans. Even today, some of the tribal communities have not yielded to purely Hindu or Aryan influence and they worship only mother goddess, *Amba, Mata, Ambamayi, Mahamaya, Jagadamba, Devi* are some of the names by which the goddess is known. In Gujarat, names of 140 deities are mentioned. In Telugu, "*Ankamma*", "*Mahalakshmamma*", "*Peddamma*" "*Marvullamma*", are some of the names by which she is called. In Dravidian land "*Mata*", "*Renuka*", "*Mahoramma*", "*Korranye Ayye*", "*Akkalu*", "*Karu-Mariamma*" are some of the deities among the famous ones.

Villagers believe that if the goddess is worshipped and a line is drawn, she would protect everyone within the precincts of that line. This is called "*polipettadamma*" or setting of "*poli*". In the four corners of the village, in ancient India, it was a custom to instal these deities. Even today, we can see people offering "*Bonas*" (offering of food) and performing "*Jatharas*" (festivals) in the villages to these deities annually, praying for health and prosperity. Some of the seals found in the Indus Valley are yet to be deciphered and a day may come, when more facts about the pre-Aryan times are brought to light giving us more facts on women of those days.

Eminent historians tell us that some more Mahenjodaros and Harappas are hidden in Andhra Pradesh in our remote villages. When they are brought out to light, the treasure trove might reveal, many more facts. In this context I would like to mention about the pre-historic skull that was discovered in Yemmanapalli village in Adilabad district (News from *The Hindu*). Many more such wonders might be hidden somewhere.

Ravindranath said "There are some who believe that the past is the bankrupt time leaving no assets for us only legacy of debts..... It is well to remind them that the great ages of renaissance in history were those when men suddenly discovered the seeds of thought in the granary of the past."

A.L. Basham in his *Legacy of India* regards Harappa as another "capital" of the Indus Empire. There is enough evidence to show that the great Indus Civilization left many indelible imprints on the latter day cultures of the sub-continent". It is also clear that the maternal remains of that Indus Valley Civilisation was in certain respects superior to that of Aryans.

"For the position of woman in pre-Aryan times, we have no written literature nor archaeological evidence. If we think that Indus Valley Civilisation is pre-Aryan, then we have to deduce the position of woman from the material evidence found at Mahenjodaro and Harappa", etc. Thus wrote Sri H.D. Sankhaliya, Professor of Deccan College, P.G. and Research Centre, Poona, an authority of Indus Valley Civilization. When I approached him for his opinion on pre-Aryan society and the status of women in it, he aptly pointed out that we have no written literature or direct evidence to prove anything about the then society, which is supposed to be matriarchal.

Hopkins in his "Religions of India" speaks of matriarchy, creeping into Hinduism from the Southern Wild Tribes. Hall also establishes that matriarchy was not a feature of Aryan society. Prof. Paton takes a different view from Hall. He says that some believe that "Woman Goddess" was given more importance because she is associated with upbringing of her children.

However, it can be presumed beyond doubt that this pre-Aryan culture, in its original form belonged to India and Indians. Our scriptures, our classics, our epics and our *dharma sastras* speak of Aryan culture. Thus, in course of centuries wide gap between precept and practice developed and altogether new ideas crept in the very thinking process of Indians.

It is said that, the culture of a nation is judged by its attitude towards woman. We Indians never subscribed to the view that a woman is an evil force or a destroyer. There is an interesting story about creation of a women. The "heat of the sun", "the pleasant cold in the moon", "the hastiness of the earth", "the limitlessness of the sky" "the depth of the sea" are all put together and "a woman is evolved" out of all these qualities.

So, the whole world is imagined to be the "vilasam" or "grandeur" of mother earth, which is a noble concept. All our rivers are also named and worshipped as "women deities". For example, Ganga, Yamuna, Saraswati, etc. Houses are supposed to be abodes of Kalalakshmi, Mahalakshmi, Anandalakshmi, etc.

When life span is divided into four Ashramas, Grihasthasrama is described to be full of aesthetic sense and feminine beauty and is idealised as a source of inspiration.

In all *purushardhas*, it is enjoined that man should follow "*woman*" in pursuit of happiness, *moksha* (salvation) and also in discharging his duties in the mundane world.

Look into this sloka:

> "*Surya Devi, Ushasa guru*
> Yocha Mana Marceyah
> *Vayosha Yakhyethu Paschat*"

> meaning, just as Surya Deva, the Sun God is following *usha* (the dawn) in his travel, man in the world should follow woman in the performance of religious duties.

Though there are no evidences to show, that there was worship of "shakti" in Indus Valley Civilization it might have started from beginning of Mathra Aradhana (Mother worship). There are some resemblances of our sakti puja with some of the traditions of religions in West Asia.

Our Mundakopanishad tells about Sapta-Matrukas like "Kali", "Karali", "Manajava", "Sulohita", "Sindhumnaparna", "Sphulingini" and "Vignaruchi". In Sapapata Brahmana and Sankhyayana Grihya Sutra, there are evidences to show that these 'Devi Puja', with the names of "Sri", "Bhadra Kali", "Bhawani" and "Durga". Even at the time of puranas (Markandeya purana), there was worship of Devi. So, it can be concluded that Aradhana of Devi which started in early times, is going on till today.

Ours is a culture of synthesis and of human values. Prof. A.L.

Basham in his *The Wonder That is India* mentions "in no other part of ancient world were, the relations of man and the woman and the man and the state, so fair and humane" ... to us the most striking feature of ancient Indian civilisation is its humanity". The Indian orientalists saw an ancient Hindu civilization in which Brahmanical authority was paramount.

Our ancient society and law were founded on certain social and sociological concepts and was an admixture of religion and ethics. The sources of our humanitarian values are the four Vedas—Rig, Yajur, Sama and Adharvan "Vedo Dharma Moolam" say our ancient *rishis*. They were revelations of the sacred law. Our Dharma sutras, our Puranas, our Upanishads are speculative and mystical scriptures which are known for their doctrines of universal reality. Our epics also are of great importance and it is no exaggeration to say that there is no Indian, who does not know about the stories of *Ramayana* and *Mahabharata*. In all the texts mentioned here, anecdotes of women find an important place and through them we get glimpses of the then sociological order and the status of women. Texts like Kautilya's *Arthasastra* say so much about women of those times. It is a wonder to note that Kautilya used the intelligence of women in state craft. He appointed women as supervisors of some other women, who were working for the government. He used to get reports from them from time to time. Women were running rest houses and were offering hospitality to "outsiders" who came into the city for the first time.

The other secular text, apart from all other religious texts and Ardhasastra was Vatsayanas *Kamasutra*, which gave a new twist to the life of a civilized man (a nagarika). Vatsayana gave the idea of "Vilasini" for the first time and could draw a line in between two categories of women — the wife and the woman who gives pleasure. He also mentioned about the sixty-four arts practised by men and women in his times. This was a wonderful text, which was translated into several other languages like Spannish, Italian and English.

The third text that spoke of a woman, Vasantasena, a courtesan, was Mrichchakatika by Sudraka. It is surprising to note that Varaha Mihira, the great astrologer wrote about women in society in his times and the status given to them.

Thus all our ancient texts speak of society, its customs, norms and laws, that helped an individual to interact with others. On a bird's eye-view of all our texts, we get an idea about our rules, our guidelines and our beliefs and sentiments, which formed the basis of our values. More importantly, the all include women in there scheme of things.

Secular Sanskrit literature provides us with ample data for the study of ancient society and culture of India. Sudraka's *Mrichchakatika* or *Clay Cart* is notable for its depiction of the city life and social conditions of those times.

The *Pali* works and *Jataka* stories tell us a lot about society and culture of ancient India. The works of Jains also provide us a lot of information about our ancient civilization and culture and also women in that era.

Foreign sources of information on the ancient history corroborate with our evidences called out from epigraphic, numismatic, archaeological and literary sources. Some hearsay references recorded by the Greek and Roman historians, particularly the observations of Herodotus and Ktesias and the first hand reports of the officers of Greek Army, who invaded India at the time of Alexander (326 to 323 BC) give us ample information on ancient India. These reports were later on supplemented by the Indica of Megasthenes, who visited the court of Chandra Gupta Maurya. Besides these Greeks, we have the first hand diary records of the Chinese pilgrims, who visited India on religious mission after Buddha. They are Fa-Hi-ian, Hiuen-Tsang.

Right from the *Rigveda*, the earlier literary monument, down to 12th century AD, notable historical works like *Rajatarangini* by Kalhana and dynastic chronicles like *Ramacharita* of Sandhyakaranandi were produced.

Vedas, though primarily religious, give us a clear picture of the life of Aryan people with their religion, literature and culture. They speak of the social practices of people. Epics, particularly the *Mahabharata* give us a total picture of Indian civilization in all its aspects. The *Arthasastra* of Kautilya, a work on polity, yields loads of information on the social and economic life of Mauryan period. From *Grihya-sutras*, smrithis and puranas we get a codified picture of socio-cultural activities of our ancient society.

Kings of ancient India, maintained official records and chronicles and they also give us glimpses of our ancient life. Dharma sutras or Smrithis deal with social topics in a detailed manner and systematise their beliefs, their sins and *prayaschita*, the duties and the status of women as regards property etc.

Apart from these texts, *gathas* or proverbial sayings of ancient

India, which have also come down through ages, are of great importance.

Thus, the culture and antiquity of a nation can be assessed through its literature or written texts that document a civilization. But in India, learning was by way of *'smrti'*. The words that were heard were repeated and memorised. Later texts and mythological traditions that were built up in course of time, laid the basis for the history and culture of society, which is extremely complex.

Socio-Economic Conditions in India by 18th Century

By eighteenth century, India, which was once upon a time shining as a beacon light in the whole of Asia, lost its glory both socially and culturally. The country that taught lessons to countries like Java, Sumathra and Indo-China, itself lost its prestine glory and became rigid and short-sighted.

The rule of Moghuls came to an end. There was political uncertainty everywhere. There was no single principle which could unify the warring forces. Child marriage were rampant. *Sati* become customary. *Purdah* was observed by not only Muslims but Hindus also. Education was denied to women and it was felt that a woman well versed in Art or Music is unfit for family life. It was considered disgraceful to declare that one knows these arts.

The salary of a school teacher was in the range of Re 1 to Rs 15 only. Schools were run in open air. Above all these things only children coming from *Devadasi* families were attending schools and education was considered necessary for them and not for other family girls. Socially speaking, it was common to have many wives. Even when the first wife was alive, man could get freedom to marry a second time, without any legal sanction. Society never looked down on him. Nobody felt that injustice was being caused to women. Children belonging to different wives, though belonging to the same family, turned out to be a big burden on society. Needless to mention about children born illegally. They were more problematic to society.

Prostitution became common and an order of the day. Such houses were many in every town and city. To maintain a prostitute was a symbol of the dignity of man. *Devadasis* were dancing in temples in the mornings and evenings before God. Government was granting them land and maintaining them. So, women was considered as a toy of pleasure.

Indian Society at the Beginning of the 19th Century

Infanticide was more in North Western Province and in Oudh of Rajasthan. Jats, Gujars, Ahirs, Tagas and Kories were killing their girls. In Punjab Bedis, Sodhis, Brahmins, in Rajasthan, Khatris, Pathans, in Kutch and Kathiawar districts, Juregas and Jaitwals, Thakoors, were resorting to female infanticide by giving them opium. Rajputs were placing girls in mudpot, while alive and placing them underneath the earth. In some places, cow dung was placed in the mouth of the girl child or she was immersed in cow's milk. So, the birth of a girl was not welcome.

(British social policy and female infanticide in India – Doctorate Thesis – By Lalitha Parigrahi).

Montgomary got prepared a list of communities, who were committing infanticide. Kharnas, Kavurs, Malhotras, Seths, Kakkars, Aroras were among those resorting to this atrocious custom. Even some Muslims and Sikhs were observing this infanticide as customary. The problem was so hidden that Britishers could understand this after about one hundred years.

Reformist Movements

Rajaram Mohun Roy, the founder of the *Brahmo Samaj* was one of the most remarkable man of his times. The *Brahmo Samaj* launched a progamme of social reforms including the improvement of the lot of women, education and providing reformative literature. To start with, the Normal for girls and the Victoria Institution for Women, trained women in needle work and taught them English and Bengali. After completing the course, those who were taught, went round teaching other women. In the Bama Hitaisini Sabha, women took part in debates and read papers. A summary of these discussions were published in a monthly periodical the 'Bama-Bodhini Partika'. For organising charity, pandit B.K. Goswami gave valueable medical aid to sufferers.

The reform relating to education of women and raising the marriageable age were welcomed. But, remarriage of widows did not catch on, it did not receive social consent. Polygamy declined.

The Prardhana Samaj

The *Prardhana Samaj* was inaugurated by Dr. Atmarann

Pandurang in Bombay in 1867. The spirit behind it was Kesavachandra Sen. Others who gave the organisation strength, were R.G. Bhandarker and M.G. Ranade.

The *samajists* were more significant as reformers rather than as followers of any particular faith. They laid stress on abolition of caste, *purdah*, child marriage and introduction of widow remarriage and education for women.

Arya Samaj and Dayanand Saraswati

While other reformers of the 19th century, imbibed western ideas and tried to interpret Hinduism, Swami Dayanand Saraswati (1824-83) did not know English and accepted the authority of Vedas. Arya Samaj also took up reform movement and the cause of women. It was quite successful in its mission.

Mrs Anne Besant's *Theosophical Society*: Theosophists believed that all religions are derived from one source – all human beings have their origin in the divine and that there is a life after death. Indian branch of *Theosophical Society* was opened at Adyar, Madras. Mrs Anne Besant, who came to India in 1893, activated it and many prominent Indians became its members.

Reforms in the 20th Century

Though Indian National Congress was a political party, reforms were associated with it in the 20th century. At its 10th session (1896) the Indian National Social Conference has emphasised women's education without which, 'progress of society is not possible'. It also formulated certain objectives to achieve this, like training of good teachers, publication of text books and courses on Home Science.

The guiding spirit of the Social Congress, was justice M.G. Ranade. When he passed away, Sri Narayan Chandavarkar, also a judge of the High Court, Bombay led the movement. The Social Reform Association was organised as a Central Association. Under his able guidance, its activities were spread throughout the country. The Hindu Social Reform Association was vitalised by C.Sankaran Nair and Mrs Anne Besant.

Reform in the 20th century, as in the 19th century was focussed on the conditions of women, improvement of the lot of the depressed classes and other matters like removal of social evils.

Spread of Education Among Women

With the spread of education among women, they began to take an active part in social reform. In 1903, a women's section was added to the Indian National Social Conference and a women's conference was held in 1909 under its auspices. The Servants of Indian Society was started in 1905 by Gopal Krishna Gokhale and it did valuable work in improving the outlook of men and women.

Dr. Ravindranath's Visvabharati, the Seva Sadan and the Bharat Stri Mandal organised by Sarala Devi Choudharani in 1910, were some of the other effective agencies that worked for reform of society. Maharshi Karve's women's university, which was started in 1916 at Poona by Dhondo Keshav Karve, whose 1st Vice-Chancellor was Rama Krishna Gopal Bhandarker, a renowned scholar, made a big contribution towards women's education. A number of girl's colleges in Gujarat and Maharashtra were affiliated to it.

Women's education made some progress in the first twelve years of the twentieth century. Almost five percent of girls of school-going age were getting educated in 1912, when compared to 1902 in which the percentage was only 2.5. In 1921, less than one woman in fifty in British India, could read and write. In the years before independence also progress in women's education was maintained to some extent. In Bombay, the number of girls studying in men's colleges, rose from 382 in 1927 to 704 in 1932. Vidyasagar College in Calcutta opened a women's section, which enrolled 110 girl students. The universities of Benares and Aligarh started separate departments for women.

Legislation

Measures of legislation also were there though not many in British India in the 20th century. Bhupen Basu moved special marriage bill in 1911 and Vithal Bhai Patel moved a bill to validate inter-caste marriages in 1918 but they could not go through as there was no official support.

A civil marriage bill was passed in 1923 but in a very modified form restricting it to Hindus only. Attempts were made in the Assembly by Indians to put forward a bill to sanction divorce and to make Hindu marriages monogamous, but they were all defeated. In 1927, Har Vilas Sarada introduced a bill for preventing child marriages. This was passed in 1929.

In 1929, an Act was passed that gave the son's daughter, the daughter's daughter, a sister and her son, their natural place in the order of inheritance. In 1937, the Hindu Women's Rights to Property Act was enacted, which gave Hindu widow a share in her husband's property and the right to demand partition.

National Movement and its Impact

Social reformers continued their effort to improve the status of women. In addition, the national movement gave them an opportunity, to leave *purdah* and to come out in public. Mahatma Gandhi's efforts were particularly fruitful in this respect. Gandhiji believed in the emancipation of women. Speaking at an annual gathering of the Bombay Bhagini Samaj, he said 'woman is the companion of man, gifted with equal mental capacities. She has the right to participate in very minutest detail in the activities of man, and she has an equal right of freedom and liberty with him." He appealed to women to take up the work of picketing before liquor shops and spinning *charkha*.

Though Act of 1856, had legalised marriage of widows, in practice very few widows married again. So, reformers started to open Widow Homes. Prof. Karve's institution served as a model.

Another sphere in which the reformers failed was to find any success in reducing marriage expenses and restricting dowries.

Summing up

For total emancipation of women what is needed is not the change imposed from above or merely talked of. It should come from within, from the depths of the heart or from the spontaneous reaction to a gievn situation. This cannot be borught about, according to me, by mere preaching. The very thinking process should undergo a thorough change. This book has been written to draw the attention of society towards women's issues and to speed up their progress in order to bring them on par with men in the shortest possible time.

PART – I

Ancient Times

CHAPTER 1

Women in Mohenjodaro and Harappa Civilisation

From the ruins of *Mohenjodaro* and *Harappa*, it is evident that a great culture flourished on the banks of Sindhu river, even before the Aryans came! The researches made by some indologists and also foreigners revealed that this culture was purely native and also paved the way for future generations, mainly in the fields of art and culture.

A famous indologist by name Sri S.R. Rao tells us, by reading some of the seals available, that it was 'Vedic culture' that was prevalent there. Of course, there is some controversy about this but one thing is clear. From the 'woman-images' available, Sir John Marshall says 'that they are indicating *Mathru Bhavana* (Mother's concept) and there was a perfect culture with deep roots.

Figures of terracota from Mohenjodaro civilization tells us that people who lived in there were all Hindus and worshippers of *Siva* and also his bull. But foreign experts like Keith and Macdonald hold that *Siva* was not the God of Aryans and the word '*Rudra*' is mentioned in *Vedas*. This *Rudra* may be the same *Siva*. When the theory is accepted, the words *Uru*, *Kshiti*, available on the seals are also to be accepted. *Urakshiti* is found in Vedas, which is definitely supposed to be the name of a place in Mesopotamia 'Rushayas' may be the spot on which *yagnas* were performed. So, it can be said that Mohenjodaro depicts vedic culture and this had been ruined by Aryans. Whatever may be the outcome of this Aryan, non-Aryan controversy, in *Rigveda*, the word *Urakshayas* is used as a synonym for *Agni* (fire). So, it can be again said that it was Vedic culture dating back to two thousand five hundred years.

Matriarchal society was prevalent there before the advent of Aryans. It was a civilization, which was not, in any form inferior to that of Aryans and that it was in its original form, that belonged to India." If we accept this basic theory that Indians gave importance to *Matru-murthy*, the rest of the things can easily be understood. Aryan culture started with *Vedas*. Their society is, in nature, patriarchal. So that means, Aryans have introduced their new ideas, replacing the hitherto prevalent matriarchal system.

During Rigvedic period, the dominant mode of worship was through prayer and offering of sacrifices. People worshipped Gods, not for spiritual salvation but for *praja* (children), *pasu* (cattle), food, weather, health etc. Man who lived by hunting before he learnt agriculture and tended his cattle and produce in the field, felt immensely happy. He wished and worshipped for the welfare of his family. *Viswa Matru Bhavana* was developed. *Puja* for *prakriti-mata*— was performed—ancient man worshipped nature as 'mother'. Archaeologists, have proved beyond doubt, from the excavation of the ancient world, that the ancient man worshipped *Matru-Murthy*, imagined her to be the *Sakthi*, which is all pervasive – universal mother.

Egyptians called her *Isis*, Romans *Siris*, Greeks *Dinetr* and Indians *Pridhvi*. This *Matru Devata* of the Mediterranian culture was the origin for the worship. This generous mother is *Bhumata*, which can be seen giving yield, and Greeks called her *Giya*, Romans *Tellies*, Indians *Pridhvi*. It is a wonder to note how and why, our ancestors entertained the idea of "Mother" and motherhood, as the origin of all. In course of time, it might have been this 'universal motherhood' that led to the worship of women deities as per the dictionary of Folklore and mythology and legend which says "The Great Mother evolved through the centuries into the totemic mother, the mother and God."

But this sort of *Matraardhana*, is not to be found in Vedas. They worshipped *Varuna*, *Indra*, *Pridhvi*, the wind, the sky, the rain, maruts etc., but not *Matru Devata*. Indologists have expressed that from the figures taken out from the excavations of Indus valley, it is evident that they worshipped *Prakriti* (nature) as the main deity. Similar figures were available in Mesapotamia, West Asia, Asia Minor, Syria and Palestine. So, it can be presumed that *Devi Puja* was prevalent and spread from Indus valley to the Nile river.

Sir John Marshall says that "like in India, in no other country, *Aradhana* (worship) of *Prakriti Mata* was there, perhaps on account of the Matriarchal system prevalent such worship of mother had a beginning (M & I.V. Civilisation Vol. I, p. 51). This might have led to *Sakti-Puja* which came later on." Many of the terracotta figurines go to prove that 'Mother deity' was worshipped. Her features are high head decoration, profuse garlands over the neck and a belt for the waist. This sort of figurines are in standing posture. For some, the hands are hanging (PL VIII p.2) Some are lifting hands and touching the forehead as though they are saluting (PL.VIII 2 Vol. M.S. *Excavation at Harappa* Vol. P.LLXVII 59).

Aryans also recognised this *Matru Sakti*, as the wife of 'Siva', the Anaryan God and took her as one among other deities. This sort of Aryan and Anaryan synthesis was achieved to some extent by *puranas*. So also by *tantra sastra*.

The village deities, popular in several names, were considered to be different shapes of *Durga Devi*, the consort of *Siva*. Mode of worship is also different between Aryans and non-Aryans. But, as a replica of synthesis, of these two cultures, several *janapada gadhas* (folk stories) were evolved. *Kumari puja* of Aryans is one such, carried on till today and *Kumari* is supposed to be *Sarva Devata-Samanyya Sivarupa* and her worship would take away all the sins.

Village Deities

Sir John Marshall (Vol. I, p. 51) says that the Great Mother Goddess of Asia Minor, Ishtar of *Isis*, appear to be definitely associated with vegetation cults, forges connection of Indian Durga with the vegetation (R.P. Chanda, *Indo-Aryan Races*, p. 1313).

Because it was a matriarchal society, this sort of worship of village deities was possible, it can be presumed, he further says. These villages deities gained much importance among Anaryans. Even today, some of the tribal communities have not yielded to Hindu or Aryan influences and they worship only mother Goddess.

Amba, *Mata*, *Ambamayi*, *Mahamaya*, *Jagadamba*, *Devi* are the names by which the Goddess is called. In Gujarat, names of 140 Deities are mentioned. In Telugu land, *Ankamma*, *Mahalakshmamma*, *Poleramma*, *Pothapatemma*, *Mahankalamma*, *Peddamma*, *Mavullamma* are some of the names by which she is called. In Dravidian land, *Mata*, *Renuka*, *Mahoramma*, *Korranya Arya*, *Akkalu*, *Vanam Mariamma* are some of the deities that are famous.

Villagers believe that if the Goddess is worshipped and a line is drawn, she would protect every one, within the precincts of that line. This is called setting of *Poli*. In the four corners of the village, it was a custom to install these deities. Till today, we can see offering of *Bonas* (offering of food) and performing *Jatharas* (festivals) in the villages to these deities.

Fertility Cult

Wil Helm Wundt in his *Elements of Folk Psychology* says that our ancestors gave a safe place to mother Goddess in their religious procedures because of the fertility cult. This sort of *Srujana Saktyaradhana*, was prevalent in all ancient societies. The figurines of Mohenjodaro, speak of this cult. There is the proof of a leaf germinating from the womb of a woman, who is naked.

In Andhra Pradesh, several such stories were taken out from excavations in several places like, Rangapuram, Eleswaram and Sangameswaram and Alampuram. Local people call these deities as *Renuka*, *Nagma Kabandha*, *Bhudevi* etc. *Nagnakabandha* in the southern part of Alampur temple of Mahabubnagar district is very famous. Dr. M.L. Walts, who conducted the excavation at *Harappa*, said that this *Nagnakabandha* is exactly similar to the *Matru Murthy* taken out from *Harappa*. Holding mangoes in both the hands, these images appear to be symbolic of *Sujana Sakti*.

Some Historical Evidences

Apart from terracotta figurines, some earthen round blocks were also available from Harappan excavations. One of the blocks, a woman lying with her stretched legs and a new leaf coming out from her womb is there (Colebrooke – *Religion and Folklore of Northern India* pp.46-7). So, he establishes that our '*Srujana Saktyaradhana*' has got links with *Bhumaata* and this is the clear evidence of that belief. Another golden image was taken out in western India; wherein, the mother holds a bunch of grapes and a child is hugging her. This appears to be representative of motherhood and mother deity (B.M.P. Vol. XXVII MOS 3-4) (1963 – pp. 130-31).

Sir John Marshall opines that the circular rings available from Taxila of the 3rd century, may be symbolic of fertility cult. On these rings, very finely and efficiently carried images are found, indicating fertility. The rings from Mohenjodaro and Harappa are also with same faith and this presumption is reasonable, says Sir John Marshall (JM-Vol. II – p. 62).

Some images are holding babies in arms, some are pregnant and some other are mother deities. These might have been carved; perhaps, to indicate the importance of prayers offered to have children, says

John Marshall. (P1.XIV 20; Pl.XIV 24, 29 & 30). *Purnakumbham* (the round *kalasa* with water) is suggestive of the womb of the mother. Offering of this *kumbha* is considered to be auspicious by Indians and they considered it as reminiscent of *Srujana Saktyaradhana*. From this *Aradhana* concept, the right of the mother might have been formed. (W.R.H. Rives. "Mother Right" *Encyclopedia of Religion and Ethics* p. 851/VIII). From the above discussion, it is evident that it was matriarchal society in the ancient past. Women were the original agriculturists.

Mother's right is nothing but calculating kinship, and property through the mother. To understand this mother's right or to know about the history of or the origin of the matriarchal system, we have to know the fact that several matriarchal society have mixed to form the caste system, says Ihrenfils. Our people believe that *Prudhu* or *Bhumi* appeared in the form of 'cow'. It is a Hindu custom to worship the tail of the cow, even today, that it is auspicious. In Mesapotamia, Min-Khursang's (deity) symbol was considered to be the cow. (Horn Blower – His article on pre-dynastic rights of women and their successors in Jown Egi Arch. May 1929 pp.-29-4-See also Hall & Wolley. Vr. Excavations Vol. I, pp. 14/3). Horn Blower says further that *Hathar*, the diety worshipped by Egyptians left her symbol, the cow. *Sakti puja* was not there before Aryans and this worship of deity was not mixed with the worship of Siva. But Aryans also worshipped Devi.

Our Rishis called her *Aditi*, *Ushas*, *Saraswati*, *Pridhvi*, *Ratri*, *Purandhri*, *Ila*, *Dishana*, *Vak* etc., (*Devi-Sukta* – R.V. XI 25 – *Ratri Sukta* R.V. X 12). Even today, we worship her by several names as *Uma*, *Ambika*, *Durga*, *Kali* etc. Mundakepanisha tells about the worship of *Sapta Matrukas* by name *Kali*, *Karali*, *Nanojava*, *Sulohita*, *Sudhumraparni*, *Spharlingini*, *Viswaruchi*.

Sankhyana grihya sutra speaks of *Devi puja*; *Satapata Brahmana* speaks of *Sri*, *Bhasakati*, *Bhavani*, *Durga*; *Markandeya purana* describes how *Devataradhana* was done. So, it can be presumed that the *Aradhana-Raodhati* (Mode of worship) of Devi, which started in the remote past, continued in consequence in other ages also and we do it even today.

One point clearly comes out that woman was respected and honoured, not only by Indians but by several others ancestral societies also. It was a matter of deep conviction for them that *Mata* would bestow prosperity, well-being for the family and she was worshipped. Barth says *Saktipuja* is as ancient as India (Barth, op.cit., p. 200. It is noteworthy that many primitive tribes worship *Sakti* almost exclusively (Hopkins, loc. cit. p. 537).

Some of the seals found in *Indus valley* are yet to be deciphered and more facts are likely to come to light about the pre-Aryan times when these re deciphered.

In the end it may be said that status of women was quite high in the ancient societies as is proven by various materials recovered belonging to those times.

CHAPTER 2

Woman in Cultures of Ancient World

Several great cultures flourished in the ancient world. Indian culture could imbibe new ideas drawn from other cultures like Sumerian Scythian, Greek, Iranian, Mongolian and Babylonian cultures. Because it is an admixture of different cultures, it could take lead in policy of tolerance and understanding. It could widen its horizon because of its association with other similar cultures, though changing its outside colour but keeping its original intrinsic worth. In no other country, such mixture of cultures took place as in India.

The cultures mentioned above lived for a period but perished because they were not deep-rooted or they could flourish only for a breif period due to their short-sightedness. They could not lay down any universal ideas or could not frame any basic values of philosophy. So, people of latter generations could not honour the past. As times moved, past values perished.

But in India, the continuity of thought could have greater influence on the minds of latter generations. Because of their universal approach, our ancestors could impart some great dictums, which are applicable to all times and climes.

Now let us peep into the great cultures comparatively.

Mesopotamian Culture

Modern country called Iraq, which is in between Tygris and Eufratus valleys, gave birth to a great culture.

Greek historian, Hirodotus wrote that he never heard of this Mesopotamian culture, which was born in a desert. So also Babylonian scholar named Birosin wrote that he heard of this Sumerian culture by 250 BC in Puranic stories. Until about a hundred years ago nobody knew about this great culture. All were simply staring at the 'figurines' left by the Sumerians, not knowing what they were. But German scholar by name George Frederick could decipher the meaning of those figures for the first time.

After the First World War, Professor Worly employed some

scientists to make a deep study of Iraq. They could trace out some temples, some living houses, some sculptures and could arrive at a decision that "Mother Goddess" image was found and so concluded that Sumerians honoured "woman" as a "mother". The woman figure found on earthen pots was made with hand very artistically. So also, some other "woman figures" were found separately. Archaeologists decided that these figurines belonged to 8,000 years back and they had a look on the future.

The historical text of Sumerians is *Gilgamesh* and it is very famous like our *Ramayana* and *Mahabharata*. This was found in the Royal palace. In 3000 stanzas, there is description of Mahapralaya. On 12 plates, their history is written. Their religious leaders could predict future. It was Mesopotamians, who thought of God and the necessity of having a "temple" for him for the first time, in the world. There were '*Devadasis*' working as servants in the temples. It is also mentioned that any father was proud of dedicating his daughter to the temple as a *Sevika*. By celebrating the great event of dedication to the temple, he used to invite all to witness the festival.

They had several moral laws by that time. Their marriage system was strong and also complicated. What all was given by the father to the daughter at the time of marriage, was in the name of the girl only. She, along with her husband had to decide how and who should inherit this. A woman had some authority on the children also, along with her husband.

When husband was not there, she used to protect the house and the property. She had the right to appoint a slave or dismiss him/her. She had also control over the business transactions of her husband. Some women could even rule! There is mention of '*Shub-Ad*', who was a queen! But Sumerian 'man' had the upperhand. He had the right to sell a woman as a slave. When he could not repay debts in some contexts, man could hand over his woman to others.

As regards rights to property were recognised, two kinds of standards were formed. It was not a crime for a man to live with another woman. But if a woman resorted to the level of living with another man other than her husband, she had to face the punishment of sentence to death.

The chief function of a woman's life was to give birth to children. When she could do that duty, she was discarded and man was permitted to marry a second time to another woman. But women belonging to higher castes wore costly jewellery, and spent luxurious life and used costly perfumes. This was evident from the material found out from their tombs.

Egyptian Culture

It reflects mostly the culture of early man during the stage when he was learning to till the land and live on agriculture, after leaving his forest life and tracts. In the ancient period, family was the rust of society and the woman, may be a mother or wife, was the pivot of the family. She had considerable status and recognition. In a way, it can be said that it was similar to a matriarchal society. Inheritance of property was traced through the mother. We know Egyptian Pharaohs married their own sisters and step-mothers, as they were unwilling to give their property to a woman's sons who comes from a different family. In some instances, one used to marry all the sisters in the family. Even fathers used to marry their own daughters.

Women were allowed to look to their affairs and their property independently. She used to go out without anybody's help and return safely unmolested. She could even look to her business or industry. If she participated in dinners openly with men, it was not considered to be any wrong. She had the right to donate her property to anyone she liked. She had the upper hand in the house. So, some of the historians have depicted Egyptian woman as dominating man and he was only a tool in her hands. Egyptian *pharaohs* had big *zenanas*. Their wives, their sisters, step-mothers, and the women captured in wars, women gifted by foreigners and servant women also were living in the *zenanas*. Some hundreds of people, were living, thus, under the patronage of the king. Officials working under the king, were having as many women as they could afford to maintain. But the ordinary man had only one woman.

Family Life

It appears that their family went on smoothly in spite of their strange customs. Divorce was unknown to them. Even the modern civilized societies may not afford so much freedom to woman as the Egyptians allowed to their women. We find women images of their sculpture, who are drinking happily and enjoying life comfortably. Egyptians of those days, painted woman images even on their mud pots. It appears that family life went on according to a particular discipline and in obedience to a code of rules and customs, so, there was peace in their society.

There is another strange custom among them. Diodorns and Siculus report that after marriage, man had to obey his wife's orders. In a way, it appears that man entrusted all his responsibilities to his wife and lived a leisurely life.

Max Muller, surprised over the family system of the Egyptians, says that "people living in the Nile Valley gave such freedom to their woman as any other race had not given even to this day". Woman used to take initiative in marriage affairs. Even a dancer could find entry to the company of high class citizens. They never gave respect to character or obedience. They were hot blooded. A woman was ready for marriage by the age of ten years.

'Daughter of Ahamasi' is famous as a great ruler in Egyptian history. Her valour and bravery are well known. Egyptians of her times imagined her to be the replica of God's capacity. She used to give *darsan* to people in a man's dress, with a long beard. The country was very peaceful during her reign. She ruled very efficiently for 22 years. People were very happy under her rule. Her real name was 'Nilocriss'. With her ended the dynasty of pharaohs (Gin).

'Se be knopur' (12th dynasty) and "HataSepsut" are two other queens known in Egyptian History. They used fine needles, 4,600 years back and they respected their women.

Egyptian women painted their lips. They used nail polish for their nails, like our moderners. They applied oils to their head and to their skin. They used green colour for the lower eyelid and black colour to their upper eye lid. Perhaps, they felt the eyes would look bigger by doing so. In their tombs, pencils, small wood pieces and sticks, cosmetics in kits of elephant cave were found out.

They felt perhaps that they should be hidden in the tombs happily not only during their life time. All the favourite articles belonging to the dead person were kept in the grave alongwith the dead body.

Babylonian Culture

Culturally speaking, these Babylonians and Sumerians are the same. But, Babylonians had some more peculiar characteristics. They believed in Tantras, in the existence of devils and their influences.

Their moral standards were low, when compared with others of those times, in accordance with the opinions expressed by ancient writers of those days. Babylonians were people who had hanging gardens and this was considered to be one of the seven wonders of the world. But, they gave their women a lower status, when compared to Romans and Mesopotamians.

No doubt, woman had a right to have property of her own and had a right to sell it also. Some were even running shops and were doing business efficiently. Women of higher castes were confined to the four walls of the house. But women of toiling classes were going out and earning and were thus eking out their livelihood.

Babylonians also worshipped a Goddess called *Ishtar*. So, it can be deduced that they also showed some respect to women.

In principle, a man had to live with only one woman. Absolute fidelity was expected in the relationship of man and wife. If a woman exceeded her limits, she was thrown in water or if the man wanted to take pity on her, he used to throw her into the streets naked. But if the man went to another place and never returned for a long time, his woman was free to live with another man thus finding a way of life. But there was a condition laid on her, that she should live with her husband if he comes back.

Parents used to fix up marriages of their children. In some cases, a girl was purchased for the sake of marriage. According to Herodotus, the historian all eligible brides were brought to a place, like in a market, and men used to select a girl wanted by them. A good-looking girl could fetch more money. A girl thus purchased, became his wife automatically. Perhaps, this custom was prevalent among some communities or in some areas.

There was *purdah* system among higher communities and when they had to go out, eunuchs were to accompany them.

But women used to enjoy property in their name as a right. Houses and slaves also were considered to be property in those days and some women had these two in their name. There is mention of notaries and they had some special rights. Women could go to courts of Law and argue.

Divorce was unknown to Sumerians. Legal system was changed to suit to the convenience of women. If a man wanted to divorce her woman, he had to maintain her and her children.

There are descriptions of "Semirabin" a Babylonian queen, when we read Sumerian literature. There are many stories and legends about her in propaganda even today. It is difficult to decide which if it is correct and which is not. But, according to Greek historians, the credit of preparing the hanging gardens goes to her. They could find out a sculptural plate in 1909, in which she was described as the queen belonging to "Shangi Adad Royal Palace". She had a special place as such. She is also referred to as the bold woman who stood fast, when there was agitation and change of her government. She also led the invasion against Indo-Europeans and also Chaldians.

This is on one side. On the other side, women were sold as slaves. A woman slave was cheaper also. Depending on her age and her capacity to work, her price was fixed. Unable to repay debts, man used to send his wife and sons to work in the house of the debtor, until the debt was repaid.

Children born to slaves, those captured in war as captives, those punished under any crime, those who were voluntarily offering their services as slaves, were considered as slaves. Thus slave trade was carried on freely. Herodotus mentions that every girl was going to the temple of *Millitta* and offering herself to the guest. It was a common custom among Babylonians. All the girls in the village used to gather as a crowd in the temple. Girls of rich people with *purdah* in carts, wearing costly clothes used to come to temple.

When all the girls stood in a row, guest selected a girl of his choice and it was considered that she is dedicated to *Millitta* for that day! Till her marriage was performed, she need not come to the temple again.

It took a lot of time for girls who were not good-looking, it seems. Some kept waiting for 4-5 years for such dedication.

Thus there were several strange rituals among Babylonians.

On the one hand, there was respect for woman and on the other hand, there was the evil practice of lowering her status in many ways. This may be because of economic levels prevailing in society and this reflected on status of women.

Assyrian Culture

Assiria was a military kingdom. So, they encouraged women to give birth to more children for the sake of the country. According to their moral standards, abortion was a great sin.

Assirians always wanted only success and they lived only with this strong desire. So, they lived very ambitiously and their culture also was nearer to animal instincts. There was the system of marriage among them. But, in fact buying of the girl is only marriage. In many cases, she continued to live in her father's house only. Husband was a 'guest', who used to visit her now and then.

Assirian woman enjoyed even lower status than a Babylonian woman. No woman was supported to appear in public. She cannot go out into the street without a veil. She should be loyal and sincere to her man. The king had a big *zenana*. Women living in such *zenana* were living in *purdah*, completely isolated. She had to respect man's superiority or control over her.

But, it appears, even in their history, there were some women, who came to higher levels of authority, through marriage or deceit.

Persian culture

Herodotus, the great Greek historian says that "a house filled with many children filled with joy" was their ideal. There was a custom among them to have many wives and 'keeps'. It was a common custom among them. Brothers used to marry their sisters, fathers their own daughters, mothers their own sons.

Women of some classes were going in *palanquins* with curtains. Lower classes allowed their women to move about freely. They had no *purdah*.

Scythians

They had Mongolian blood and European blood, mixed up. They were all warriors. They had terrible beards. It appears to be their speciality. Their custom was to keep their women behind curtains.

They always were indulging in invasions. It was these strong men who conquered Assirians and made them weak. They loved warfare and in fact, for living only they fought. They drank the blood of enemies. To quench their blood thirst only, was their hobby. They used to wear garlands of heads of dead persons, around their waist as a decoration.

A woman was only a plaything in their life. Because all these nations lived in the present and adopted a particular attitude towards life and their women, they flourished at a particular time and then perished. They lived in the utopian ideas. They framed and lived in a periphery of their joy and pleasure, and framed their policy and cultures and social norms according to their whims and fancies, they no basis for a universal outlook or culture for strong societies, that they could love forever.

Woman in Greek and Roman Times

Among the Homeric Greeks, marriage had two distinct objects in view: preservation of a pure line of descent and protection of the property rights of the family. Hence wife and the mother were furnished with the greatest responsibility of continuing in sacred traditions of the family. If she preserved, she added to the glory of the family. If she violated, the prestige of the family suffered. So, as a consequential development, there was no divorce and no polygamy.

Women of Homer's time had no rights in the modern sense of the terms. Dr. Mitchell Corrol in his *Greek Women* (1908, p. 29) says "throughout the whole of life, their position was subject to the will or the whims of men". After marriage, woman merely passed from the tutelage of her father to that of her husband who had absolute power over her.

Education of girls in those days was of the simplest character. As they grew up, they learnt simple things of life, from her mother– like needle work, piety towards gods, and efficiency in the management of the household work. Most prominent feature of Greek polity was the city state (H.G. Wells: *Outlines of History*, 1920, p. 153).

The characteristic feature of Greek polity was that citizenship was limited to heredity and every legal measure was taken to preserve its purity. To preserve the purity of citizenship, writes Mitchell Coroll "every precaution was taken that the daughters of Athens should not be wedded to foreigners ... and therefore the marriage of an Athenian Maiden with a stranger or of a citizen with a foreigner was strictly forbidden and the offspring of such union was held illegitimate (Lecky: *History of European Morals*, 1910, p. 287).

Thus owing to the Athenian conception of the city state, the natural functions of woman were domesticity and companionship. So, Athenian man looked to his wife merely for the care of the home and bearing and rearing of children. "There was the cordial recognition, writes Lecky, in his "History of European morals" of two distinct orders of womanhood – the wife whose first duty was fidelity to her husband – or the mistress, who subsisted by her fugitive attachments."

This evil was worn which ate away the cord of the social life of Athens and caused the unhappiness of the female sex. Thus one class of women consisted of high-born matrons of Athens, glorifying in their birth right and rulers of the Home, the other the resident aliens of the female sex, the unmarried, who could live as 'companion' of the great men of the city. In the peaceful atmosphere of the Home, Greek wife was expected to live in absolute isolation. She was married usually when young. She never attended any functions, received no male visitors, except in the presence of her husband.

Commenting on this secluded life of Greek women, Lecky writes "Living as they did almost exclusively among their female friends, deprived of all the educating influence of male society, having no place at these public spectacles, which were the chief means of Athenian culture, their minds must necessarily have been exceedingly contracted". (Lecky, *History of European Morals*, p. 287).

J.H. Breasted severely comments on this seclusion of Greek women from public life. "The Greek citizens always kept their wives in the background and they were no more than mere housekeepers. They had no share in the intellectual life of men, could not appear at their social meetings where serious conversation was carried on, nor were they permitted to witness the athletic games at Olympia. Their position was even worse than in the age of tyrants." (*The Conquest of Civilisation*, 1921, p. 362).

In general, she was a perpetual tutelage. Her parents disposed her of her hand, to her husband and her days of widowhood to her sons.

In Iphigenia in Tauris, Iphigenia laments over the low position accorded to woman. "The condition of woman is worse than that of all human beings. If a man is favoured by fortune, he becomes a ruler and wins fame in the battlefield and if gods have ordained him misfortune, he is the first to die a fair death among his people. But the joys of woman are narrowly compassed; she is given unasked in marriage by others often to strangers, and when destruction falls upon her home, she is dragged away by the victor, through the smoking ruins, through the corpses of her dear ones". (Bebel, *Woman*, p. 19).

Quite interesting are the views of Simonides regarding Greek women. He says "women are the greatest evil God has ever created.

Even if at times, they appeared to be useful, they turn into a torment for their owners.... Men are so preposterous that each will praise his wife, while speak ill of his neighbours' while nobody sees that we are in the same predicament, for as I began by saying this is the greatest evil God has created." (Quoted from Weith–Knudsen, *Feminism*, p. 178).

So, we see that the old Greek conception of woman was anything but lowly. It was she who, according to them, was the cause of family feuds that led to wars, as is evident from Iliad and caused unrest and discontent among men. It was 'she' who was held to be responsible for the good or bad conclusions of men's undertakings.

A man with a quarrelsome or ugly wife attributed his failure to his wife. Idleness and greediness are considered to be her special vices. The wife who violated her marriage vow was punished with most terrible disgrace. The man who ventured to marry her was punished with disgrace and was disenfranchised. A man could divorce his wife on the slightest pretext.

The son inherited the property out of his full rights as a continuator of the family. It was the religious character attached to the property that vested the whole property rights in the son, to the exclusion of the daughters.

The rule of the family worship was from male to male. The daughter was not qualified to continue the paternal religion since she might marry and thus renounce the religion of her father.

(Furtel De Coulanages, *The Ancient City*, p. 94)

Roman Culture

The two characteristics of the Roman Republic were:

(a) The authority of the state.
(b) The integral root of the family.

The most constituent feature was the despotic powers of the Pater Families, the father of the household. He was the owner of the whole family estate and the lord of the wife's body and spirit, of his children and their children and of its servants and slaves all of them owed implicit obedience.

The right over men included:

(1) The right of chastisement.
(2) The right of life and death.
(3) The right of sell or send as hostage against debts.
(4) The right to betroth, give in marriage and divorce.
(5) The right to despose of at will.

Not only of the family wealth but any money the sons obtained independently.

Thus the Roman family of the ancient times was a common slavery to the head, i.e., the Pater Families, sanctioned by religion, law and morals. The position of the Roman woman is not described but can be imagined.

Roman religion did not place the woman in a high position. The wife took part in all religious acts but she was not the mistress of the hearth. She herself did not become an ancestor. In death as in life, she was considered to be only a part of her husband. Roman Republic had divided society into two classes – the patricians and the plebians. Woman belonging to neither class had any legal part either in state affairs or any public functions, excepting those of a religious nature. "Her duties were confined to Home .... the only advantage which a patrician women could possess were her natural pride in privileges of her family and whatever was reflected upon her by her relatives. (Rev. Alfred Brittain, *Roman Women*, 1908, pp. 40-41).

The husband was all powerful in the family. Nobody was recognised by law. The power of the husband over the wife was called *manus*. The wife was placed in the same category with the children and the slaves. They were all *mancipia* under him. The husband was in one sense a state in miniature. He ruled over his family. It was he who answered to the state for his wife, and children and slaves.

Legal subordination of woman was recognised by the Romans in the legal principle that she belonged to the family and not to the state. No one thought that woman possessed any claim or right to independence of individuality. She was always under a master – her father when she was a girl, her husband when she was married and her nearest male relative if she was widowed. Compared with her Greek sister, Roman woman enjoyed more social, if not more legal, freedom. Unlike the sister in Greece, she was never secluded; she was not limited to one part of the house, nor was she excluded from free social movement. "Unlike the Greek, the Roman women walked abroad, frequented the public theatres, and took their places at festive banquets with the men. (Rev. Alfred Brittain, *Roman Women*, p. 127).

So also, she received relatives and paid visits, shared meals inside and outside the house, attended religious ceremonies, and could even appear before a Court of Law, and indeed with her husband's permission, go to circus and theatre. The only thing required of her was that she should not go out unaccompanied. In the home, she was the mistress of the whole household economy, looking after the instruction of the children, taking care of them and governing the domestic slaves.

But, all this independence was nullified by the marital position in which law placed her. Roman marriage was only a *marriage de convenance* having very little affection in it.

Edward Carpenter (*Civilization, Its Cause and Cure*, 1906), says, "In the Roman antiquity, marriage seems, with some brilliant exceptions to have been a prosaic affair—mostly a matter of convenience and house-keeping—the woman having little of the ideal attached to the relationship of man and wife."

Men regarded marriage as a device for securing heirs of unquestionable legitimacy for their gods and wealth. So Romans regard wives as their personal property, the bearers, wet-nurses of their sons and heirs. Romans recognised two distinct kinds of marriages – The strictest and in the eye of law more honourable, which placed the woman into the *manus* or hand of her husband and gave him absolute authority over her person and property. The less strict form, left her legal position unchanged. The first one, was more in vogue during the days of Republic. Look into some of the laws that Solon pronounced. "A woman should not wear costly dresses but this does not apply to women living like prostitutes. She should not wear gold on her body over and above half of an ounce. She should not go beyond one mile from Rome, may be in a cart. She should not travel to any part of the city. Home is her only place. She had no right even to sign as a witness. So, she was dependent on husband for everything.

I happened to read a text book in Calcutta in Tagore's library, wherein two photos of classical Greece attracted me. One was a weaving scene at home – two women were sitting near a loom. Most

Roman houses were small workshops, where household necessities were produced from raw materials.

The other photo was about "measuring sandal". A shoemaker places his customers' foot on the leather and cuts the sole. The writer says that many Greeks went barefoot indoors and during summer.

There is a mention of the quiet lives of wives and mothers. Among the various cosmetics used by Greek women were scents, white lead to whiten skin and alkanet root to redden the cheeks. The playwright Menander writes, "The loom is woman's work and not debate". When the husband entertained guests at dinner, women remained in their own quarters on the second floor, dreamily watching the street traffic through windows. When there was no guests, man and wife shared company. Thus in segregated relationship ordained by society melted the family love. That again and again is picturised in their vase painting and sculpture.

Women were expected to prepare meals, run their households and stay out of sight. Fathers arranged marriages for their adolescent girls. Wives lived under the total control of husbands. They received much male advice on the subject of staying at home and being silent. So Athenian society was organised pre-eminently as a man's world.

But there were women among their intellectuals. Safo was a great poetess. Aristotle accords her status equal to that of Homer, Plato recognised her as the "10th Goddess" of Greeks. Her poetry was published in nine volumes and was full with love and was very appealing to heart. She was also running a school for girls. "Ode to Aphnodite" was the text, she left to future generations.

Janthippi was wife of Socrates. She is known as a termagant woman. But she was a shrewd woman. The great Socrates, a philosopher was damn afraid of her. When he was talking of his philosophy she poured water on him with pots, the story tells.

So, when we sit on judgement about the culture, studied above, it is clear that the material remains of Indus Valley Civilisation, reveal that Indian culture was far more superior in all aspects to the other ancient cultures. Indian woman's civilisation was highly developed and she had a "golden throne" (Kanakapur *Sinhasana*) she won laurels as a scholar, participated in discussions as a fully grown individual and had full freedom to select her husband.

CHAPTER 3

Pre-Vedic Period

Tradition, Modernity and Status of Women

Yatra Naraysthu Pujanthe Ramanthe Tatra Devatah.
(where women are adored, there Gods rejoice)
(Mann Samhita III 56-57, 85)

In India, the image of a woman is visualized as *Shakti* (Energy). She is described in all our ancient texts as the force underlying creation and divinity. In several words like *Jaya*, *Patni*, *Mahila*, *Stree*, *Ardhangini* etc. woman is exalted to the position of glory and grace.

Vedic expressions like *Jaye Dastam* the woman is the house (The woman could make home even if she sits under a tree) indicate the recognition given by our ancestors to womanhood and her place in life. Dr. Mrs. Anne Besant says in her lectures that "the traces of womanhood as found in Indian culture are not to be found anywhere in the world". Women are described to be perfect caricatures of womanhood in Indian literature. "Speech", "Learning", "Prosperity" and "Calamity" take feminine forms as per our mythology. Several indologists, foreigners, philosophers and eminent personalities have studied Indian womanhood from various angles and wondered at the Indian ideology.

Ancient Ideals in Modern Life

The Indian woman had been an object of interest to the westerners and also to her own countrymen. She had been the subject of countless works of art and literature through the ages, from the ancient epics and cave paintings to sculptural wealth.

The Vedic period gave India a golden age and the great compilations of learning by women seers called *Brahmavedins*. In due course of time, a system of metaphysical doctrines developed and several principles based on *dharma*, purity and sacrifice came into being, embodied in 'Smrithis', pushed women to the secondary level, and with 'Smrithis' regulating everyday life, lowered down her status still and made her almost a non-entity, depending on man entirely, out of all this evolution of society during the course of some thousands of years, joint family system, which is the bedrock of Hindu social organisation, came into existence and roles of man and women were clearly defined, as a result of which women became confined to certain activities. The patriarchal system completely dominated the society, which we can study in later chapters.

For the present, while we confine our study to the classical age. We find that before the invasion of Aryans, there flourished great civilisation which was matriarchal in nature and was destroyed by Aryans as evidenced by Indus Valley Civilisation.

The culture of a nation is judged by its behaviour and attitude towards women, says a French writer. We Indians, never subscribed to the view that a woman is an evil force or a destroyer. Our *Maharshis* viewed a woman's place from a broader perspective.

The Mother Concept—*Viswa Matru Bhavana*

Our ancestors imagined the whole universe to be a 'Woman'. They called that 'Shakti' as *Adiparasakti*, all pervasive and responsible for *Srishti*, *Sthithi*, and *Laya*. Her display of powers is found in all living creatures, they felt the heat of the 'Sun', the 'pleasant cold in the moon', 'the vastness of the earth', the 'limitlessness of the sky' are imagined to be her *vilasam* or grandeur. All rivers are worshipped as deities. For the philosophers, she is *Yogamaya*, *Muktikanta* and *Kundalini*. For the poets, she is *Ushabala*, *Vanalakshmi*, *Sandhya Sundari*, *Annapurna*, *RajaRajeswari*, and for the artists, she is *Ushas*, 'deity of beauty'. The houses are supposed to be the abodes of *Kalalakshmi*, *Mahalakshmi*, and *Anandalakshmi*.

A man without a woman is like a flower without odour' they felt and gave "Woman" a prominent place. When life span is divided into four *Asramas*, *Grihasthasrama* is described to be full of aesthetic sense and feminine beauty is idealized as the source of inspiration. When we look into our literature, sculpture, arts or mythology we can understand how our ancestors felt that woman is replica of the whole Universe. The whole aesthetic sense in art of creation and the sublime perfection of mind are associated with 'woman' and the philosophy of *Soundarya Tatwa* kept 'woman' on a high pedestal in

India. The concept of *Ardhanareeswara* (God dividing himself into two halves) is unique in our philosophy.

The above two concepts reveal that *patnee* is half of man and she is the custodian of what all man earns. In all the *Purusardhas* (*Dharma, Ardha, Kama, Moksha*) man should follow 'woman' in pursuit of happiness, *Moksha* and also in discharging his duties in the mundane world. In the realm of the kingdom of the house (*Griha*), the woman is the ruler (*Rajyalakshmi*).

Concept of *Dharma Patnee*

Look into this sloka:-

Vayosha Yakhyethu Sureeya Devi, Ushasaguru, Yochamana Mareeyah, Paschat.

Just as Suryadeva (the Sun) is following *Usha Devi* in his travel, man in the world should follow woman. In the performance of religious duties, man should take the help of woman—*Patnee Anyanavatch, Patneehpareemasyam, Patnee Swamini, Patniyaiyyanaya Maramsrothnee*".

The inner meaning seems to be that man should take the help of woman in attaining '*moksha*' (Salvation) also. The havis offered at the time of 'Yagna' performed by a man, should be touched by *Dharmapatni* then only it becomes pious or sacred. An *Apatneeka* (a man without a wife) is unfit to perform such religious duties. The ultimate goal of our Maharshi's appears to be the establishment of '*dharma*' and the welfare of the society at large. It was not an individualistic approach. The fundamental point is to be noticed before arriving at any conclusions on our ancient culture and also while fixing up the status of women in society.

Pre-Historic Background of Indian Culture

For the position of women in pre-Aryan times, we have no written literature nor archaeological residences. If you think that Indus Valley Civilisation is pre-Aryan, then you have to deduce the position of women from the material evidence found at *Mohanjodaro* and *Harappa* etc.

H.D. Sankhaliya, professor of Deccan College, P.G. and Research Centre, Pune is an authority on I.V. Civilisation. When I approached him for his opinion on Pre-Aryan society and the status of women in it, he aptly pointed out that we have no written literature or direct evidence to prove anything about the then society, which is supposed to be matriarchal. Hopkins in his 'Religions of India' (p. 54) speaks of matriarchy creeping into Hinduism from the southern wild tribes; Hall establishes that matriarchy was not a feature of Aryan Society. Prof. Paton takes a different view from Hall. Wilhelm Wundt says that "some believe that woman goddess was given more importance because she is associated with upbringing of her children." From the woman images available from the ruins of Mohenjodaro and Harappa, Sir John Marshall says that they are indicating *Mathru Bhavana* and there was a well developed and perfect culture even before Pre-Vedic or pre-historic period, so to say, with deep roots. Whatever may be the controversy on Aryan invasion, the then prevalent culture, call it Matriarchal or Dravidian or native, was destroyed to a great extent and Aryans introduced altogether a new culture, which was Patriarchal in nature. What I mean to say in this context, by this explanation is that pre-Aryan culture in its original form belonged to India and Indians. Replacing this system, Aryans enforced their new ideas. There were some clashes here and there, but it appears that there came about a synthesis of both these cultures in due course of time. All this did not happen in one day. It took some centuries.

Archaeologists have proved beyond doubt from the excavations, that pre-historic man worshipped *Matru-Murthy*, imagined her to be the *Sakthi*, which is all pervasive, universal mother. When the ideal is so superb, society began to think that the ideal woman is a meek, submissive person and a 'bundle of Sacrifices' (*Tyagamayi*, *Lajjavati*, *Sheelavathi*). When once a woman showed any resistance she lost all her respect. May be this fear of social norms that kept woman dumb and mute for long. Our Scriptures, our Classics and Epics and also our *dharmasastras* were written by men. They preached a different set of ideology for women-that was far, far away from the original ideas preached in vedic texts. Thus a wide gap between the precept and the practice developed. Certain religious concepts also kept woman far away from the mainstream of life. In course of some centuries, the woman remained confined to the four walls of the house.

REFERENCES

1. A.L. Bhasham: *The Wonder that was India*: Grovepress, New York, 1959.
2. Shakuntala Rao Sastry: *Women in Vedas*; Banarsidass Publication.
3. Tara Ali Baig: *India's Woman Power*; S. Chand & Co., New Delhi, 1976.
4. Committee on the Status of Women in India: Towards Equality Report of the Committee on the Status of Women in India Government of India, Ministry of Education and Social Welfare, New Delhi, 1974.
5. Das Gupta, Kalpana: *Women on the Indian Scene: An Annotated Bibliography*, Abhinav Publications; New Delhi.
6. Desouza Alfred (ed): *Women in Contemporary India: Traditional Images and Changing Roles*; Manohar Book Service, New Delhi, 1976.
7. Gupta Giri Raj (ed): *Main Current in Indian Sociology*, Vol. 2, *Family and Social change in Modern India*, Vikas Publishing House, New Delhi, 1976.
8. "Fear and Status of Women": *South Eastern Journal Of Anthropology*, Vol. 25 No. 1 pp. 81-95, 1969.
9. Hopkins Thomas et al: *Guide to Indian religion*, thesis of Dr. Nayani Krishna Kumari.
10. Devaki Jain (ed) *Indian Women*, Publications Division, Ministry of Information and Broad casting, Government of India, New Delhi, 1975.
11. Journal of South Asian literature: Special issue on "Feminine Sensibility" Vol. 12, nos. 3 & 4 1977.
12. Promilla Kapur: *The Handing Status of the Working Women in India*, Vikas Publishing House, New Delhi, 1976.
13. B.R.Nanda (ed): *Indian Women: from Purdah to Modernity*, Vikas Publishing House, New Delhi, 1976.
14. Sunday Reggy: "*Toward a Theory of the Status of Woman* American Anthropologist Vol. 75 no. 5 pp 1682-1700 1973.
15. Sardar, G.B.S. Mehta and Neera Desai (ed) Golden Jubilee Commemoration Vol. (1916-1966) Sreemathi Mathibai Damodar Thakrsey Women University, Bombay, 1968.
16. *Women in the Hindu Tradition*: Signs Journal of Women in Culture and Society, Vol. 3 no. 1, 1977.
17. *Womens Issues: An Indian Perspective*, Lakshmi Misra.
18. *Indian Women through Ages*; A.V. Thomas Paul; Asia publishing House, Bombay, 1964.
20. Altekar A.S.: *The Position of Women in Hindu Civilisation*, Motilal Banarsidas, Delhi 1962.
21. Mukherji D.P.: *The Status of Indian Women*, International Social Science Bulletin, Vol. 3. No. 4, pp 793-801, 1951.
22. Devi Mahatmya, quoted in Damidou, 1964 *op. cit*, p. 257.

CHAPTER 4

Vedic and Post-Vedic Period

The Period of Rigveda

Rigveda (4000-100 B.C. P.V. Kane) seems to be the first known literary treatise in which descriptions of women are found, who perform their duties early in the day while singing. Aryans laid down some decent norms of family life and a woman's life was interwoven with the family. She was given a high status of honour. Women could shine as poetesses, charioteers and also as dancers and musicians.

Girl Child was called *Duhtr*

Yaskacharya, the commentator writes that *Duhtr* means *Doore-Hita* (It is good to be distant). A girl child will not be useful in war. So, it is better to get her married after puberty and send her to a distant family. Though Patriarchal, Aryans seemed to have bestowed their love and affection on girls. The word '*Kumbhi Neerava*' indicates that girls were bringing water with pots. Milking the cows also was one of her duties. Taking yarn from the *charkha*, stitching, embroidery on clothes and above all keeping watch over the rice fields and chasing away the birds from the fields formed the important functions of a girl.

N.C. Sarkar in his text titled *Some Aspects of the Earliest Social History of India* (p. 104) says because it is the duty of a woman to bear children, our ancestors perhaps entrusted to her even from her childhood the job of milking the cows and rearing them.

Look at this:

Jamayo Adhveri Yatama
Viyate Ghratam (Rigveda)

This means, "Where there is sweetness of milk, there is the girl. Where butter flows, the *Duhtr* with her sweet smiles is present". Thus there are some beautiful descriptions of 'Duhtr' in Rigveda. Such a 'kanya' (unmarried damsel) was given in marriage to a deserving boy after attaining puberty.

Marriage was a Sacrament

'Kanya' was given as a gift to the bridegroom. Conceptually it is this *'Kanyadaan'*, that was responsible for lowering the status of woman. The Rigvedic Aryan, out of his immense love and affection for his daughter, never wanted to give her an identity or individuality. He wanted to make her more happy by giving her protection.

In addition to the father, brother *Brathru* also had some right over this girl and he was keeping an eye on her movements. The word 'BRATHRU' is used in all Indo-European languages. Because the brother is a well-wisher, knows the girl well and has to shoulder the responsibility of the family after the father, brother is given right over her, says Sri Sarkar. It was also feared that a girl without a brother may take to wrong path. In addition to the household duties, a girl was taught music and dance. Some who were well-educated also wrote hymns. Some were experts in music and instruments like, *Veena*, *Kandaveena*, *Talukaveena*, *Apasha*, *Talika*, *Richchna*, were played during festivals and girls were allowed to exhibit their talent in public places and gatherings. Some were famous dancers, others were experts in arranging artistic designs in front of the houses and some others very good at painting. Decorating the house with flowers was one of the favourite past times of girls, says Eanakshi Bhavani in her "*Women of India: Creative and Fine Arts* (Page 165).

> *"Asha yoshi vasu Naryasha Yata*
> *Prabhunuthe Janayanthe Vijinampa*
> *Upatayati pakshinam.*
> *Prabhunjathi, Jayanthee Vijinampa, "Utapatayati Pakshinam."*

Max Muller, the famous indologist concluded from the above *sloka* that "there were two kinds of women at the Rigvedic times—one *Sadyovadhu* the one married and leading a family life and the other Brahmavadin, welleducated and commanding respect in *Panditha Sabhas* and congregations. The intellect of the woman, capable of discharging of the duties was recognised and respected.

Status of Woman

From the evidences now available with us, we can deduce some conclusions. Girls were married after attaining puberty. There were instances of *Swayamvara* (choosing her husband) as is clear from the following sloka.

"*Bhadra Vadhurbhavati Yatsupesa;*
Swayam Samitram Vasute Kane chit (RV-IX)"

A girl had a right of protection in her fathers' family. So long she remained unmarried, she had this right. There are descriptions in Rigveda about women, who remained unmarried till old age and who stayed in the father's house. At the time of marriage, a girls' brother (*syalat*) had to give some gift to the boy, who married his sister. The expenditure incurred at the time of her marriage was from the family property. All the 'Money' 'Gifts' or 'Jewellery' received by a girl at the time of marriage belonged to her. What was given by the bridegroom was called *Streedhana* which she could keep exclusively for her. When there was no son for a father, a girl was entitled to perform funeral rights to such father. Freedom given to a 'Kanya' at the time of *Rigveda*. A *Kanya* (unmarried damsel) had full freedom to choose her life partner or to choose her pattern of life according to her desire. She was never behind purdah.

Rigveda says that a girl's aim was to win recognition in festivals like *Samana* and she was participating with full throated gusto (*Swayam Manaso* - RV). But what is this *Samana*? Commentators differ in their opinions. Yaskacharya says it is a *Homa*, whereas the foreigners say that it is a "Social gathering" (RV-1-1248), where poets and musicians participated for fame and name, women of all ages used to participate, with a view to choose their life partners. The *Samaroh* was being carried on from sunset till the fire was extinguished, which means till the next morning.

Sakuntala Rao Sastry in her *Women in Rigvedic Age* proves that women, especially youngsters used to decorate themselves and participate in such functions. Sayanacharya feels that such functions were held in vast areas, where horse races were held in one corner and dance or music competitions were held in another corner. (*Women in Rigveda*-Bhagavat Saran Upadhyay): Though marriage was considered a *Samskara*, it was not that compulsory for every one. They are descriptions of *Apala Atreyee* and *Ghosha*. There is also an episode that *Ghosha* married at a very late age as per Vedic index (Vol. 130).

Family Set-Up

Aryans, framed a family set-up on some sound lines with a view to lead a happy family life. Though traces of this we might still find around us, the basis for this is supposed to be the sacred marriage tie. As per R.C. Majumdar (*Ancient India*) the woman is the pivot in the family. Family life is interwoven with her. Expressions like *Jaye Dastam* (The woman in the house) echo this sentiment. The woman is kept on a golden throne so far her status is concerned during the Rigvedic period. She could exhibit her talent in public places but had to work within a framework of rules. But a man was *Neta* (leader) and woman *Neetha* (the lead). The word *Dampati*, indicates that the wife and husband constituted one unit. In one context, the husband, an idle monger bemoans that, he is responsible for the pitiable condition of his wife (R.V.X.34).

This relationship of wife and husband exists not only during life-time but extends to the other world (*Parloka*) also. There are some slokas in which there are prayers to *Devatas* to remove the differences between wife and husband. (Foot Notes: *Women in Rigveda*-Bhagawat Saran Upadhyay). As per the Hindu sentiment it appears that marriage tie was considered to be an indivisible friendly tie. The promises made at the time of marriage like "never leave my friendship, I will never leave your friendship" indicate that the tie of marriage was considered friendship for the whole life and was unbreakable.

Marriage—Procedural Details

Marriage, a sacrament, is described in 47 *slokas* and procedural details are given in 85th mandala (RV X.85-21.22). It was *Panigrahana* (giving and taking the hand). A *Salamkrit Kanya* (decorated damsel) was given as a gift to the bridegroom along with sacred water, amidst chanting of mantras. Praying to *Viswavasu* (who protects girls before marriage) relieves the girl from his authority and pass it on to the bridegroom was preliminary step. The bridegroom receives her with his right hand. There was no *Mangal Sutradharana*. Promises like "for prosperity I am receiving you! *Devatas* have given you to me. Live with me for life who is your husband for life" (RVXVI II.8) were made while receiving the girl. Usually marriage took place in the house of the girls' father. No *Saptapadi* as in modern times (moving round the sacred fire) was performed. After the marriage, the couple had to pray to *Devatas* to give long life and good children. They also took blessings of elders and left for the bridegrooms' house. A good feast after the marriage was compulsory. Friends and relatives of the bridegroom used to welcome the bride, addressing her on the following lines:

"You fortunate girl! live happily in the house with your children! Never look to your husband with Anger! Never entertain a feeling of enemity towards your husband! Be kind to animals! Have a generous mind! Lead a respectable life! Be a mother to all men in the family! Have devotion to all the *devatas*! Be a queen to your father-in-law and mother-in-law! Be a queen to the sisters of your husband! Be a queen to the brothers of your husband!" (RVX 85, 33, 42, 44, 48).

The above sentiments indicate that the entire running and image of family depended on the girl brought into the family by marriage and that she is going to be the queen of the house. From the above description, it can be also inferred that the girl brought into another family, is an expert in running the kingdom of the house and she is an adept in the craft of running the house. She was not a immature girl. So, it can also be safely concluded that, child marriage was not performed.

The Sloka *Stomam, Jushedham, Yuvaseva Kanyayam* (Just as youths accept the invitation of *Kanyas* O! *Aswini Devatas*, you accept our Prayers). That means the girl who wanted company of man, after attaining puberty, used to invite youth to marry. *Kalyani*, endowed with good qualities '*Sobhanarupa*' selected her lover amidst crowd of people is another description. But kanyadata had to give consent for the marriage. A girl had to be married to one who had good education, good character and who had relatives, but concept of *kanyadanam* though intended to do with some pious sentiment, made a girl to be given as a gift. Only the father had to perform marriage. The boy, who was selected with love was *Jamata*. The one married to a girl, receiving a *varadakshina*, if the girl was handicapped or sick, was '*Vijamata*' and he could not command good respect in society.

It appears that most of the women got married but some remained unmarried and stayed with the parents. Eight kinds of marriages like *Swayamvara*, *Prajapatya*, *Asura*, *Rakshasa*, *Paisachika*, were recognised. It is to be noted that *Rakshasavivah* (marriage by capture) also was recognised.

Certain Social Conditions

Children born got the name of the family of the father. But there were orphan children also. The word *Rahasu* indicates that there were children born illegally. Orphan children were taken care of by Indra (RV II -29-1). The episode of Paruchapa in *Rigveda* indicates that there was *Devadasi* system also. (RV-134-31-5-5 VIII-17). There is no mention of widow marriages clearly anywhere, but there is mention of a brother of a dead man telling his wife, 'O-woman come to the world where all live, the man standing next to you is dead; became life less: *Patneeva* was your duty. He did *panigrahana* and received you and loved you." (RV-18.8 and X. 40.2) Though monogamy was mostly prevalent, there were instances of polyandry (having more husbands) also (*Aswini Devatas* live with *Suryadevi* and *Rodasi* lives with *Maruts*).

Names of Brahmavadins Found in Rigveda

Names of 23 Brahmavadins are found in *Rigveda*. These women endowed with extraordinary intellectual qualities composed hymns. They are Gargi, Romasa, Ghosha, Viswavara, Atreyi, Lopamudra, Vasuhvepai Indrani, Apala, Sraddha (Kamayani), Vaivasvati, Yami, Powlami, Surya-Swasthi, Sikhandini, Oorvasti, Sachi, Devayani, Indradoota, Sarparagni, Vak(Juhu), and Godha.

26 *Slokas* of *Rigveda* were composed by these women and Gargi is the most famous among them.

Look into the Sloka of Indrani:

"*Sapatni, Mepara Dhatu Patamme Kevalam Kuru*"

Suktamly Apala is known as *Apalasuktam* where she interestingly depicts how a *Kanya* was suffering from skin disease and how she got rid of it by worshipping Indra.

Sayanachaya's commentary of Rigveda tells us that woman was 'Raja Mahishi' but look into this sloka:

"*Charitham Hiveri Vacchedi Rasnamaja Khalasya Parita Kamayam Sadyoja*
Ghamayaseem, Nischala Yodhare Hite, Nastha Vaipatya dhattam"
(RV 1. 115, 116).

It tells us that the leg of Nischala, wife of Khilarja, was broken in war. As that of a bird broken leg was refixed by *Aswini Devatas*. By this, we can conclude that women were experts in running chariots and in archery also. Indrasena, wife of Mudgala was an expert in running a chariot. Samuchi, Anudasu have made women expert in war. It appears that women had the upper hand in fine arts like dance, music. The word *Nruthu* indicates that women dancers were there and dance was considered to be a source of inspiration even in critical times. Family women also used to dance, covering their heads with white cloth (*Svetavasna - Avagunthana*) Some women took to dance as career in their life. Their deity was 'Ushas'. Dressed with colourful garments and decorated with precious Jewellery, Ushas was supposed to enter like the dancer entering the stage and there are several beautiful descriptions in *Rigveda* about her.

Even men used to dance, Sculpture and *Vastusastra* flourished in Rigvedic times. Twashta, Bubh were famous sculptors. Dwar, Pridhvi could add beauty to Ushas and Prakriti. In music field instruments like *Vani, Vema, Vamsa, Dhrutri, Bakura, Naali, Khonee, Karkaree, Aghat* were used. We do not have more details about them. Women of Rigvedic times were experts in weaving cloth. They used to prepare cloth required for the family *Vasah Valulpulee* (*Jaimini Brahmana*-Vedic Women) indicates women used to clean clothes. Women used to print and dye clothes. (*Raja Yatnee*-30 man 12). Savanacharya tells us that women used to put various designs and figures on walls and this was their exclusive talent.

When such is the picture of women in the practical world, several women deities were worshipped in the religious field. Deities like Aditi, Pridhvi, Ila Saraswati, Bharati, Cinevalee, Rakha, Sunrutha, Purandhri, Dhishana, Nirrithi, Asumathi, Indrani, Ushas, Rati, Sraddha, Amaravathai, Dampati, Aravathu, Aaranyani, Varunani, were worshipped for granting prosperity security and long life.

We don't find descriptions of such devatas in latter literature. On the whole it appears that during Rigvedic period, women were participating in every field of activity and they were recognised and honoured and some were even worshipped as *devis*. Nowhere in latter writings, we find such mention of women. As times passed on, original ideas changed and social pattern took a different shape. Several new ideas like *Suchi, Asuchi* Sacrifices, etc. crept into the thinking process of men and women and life for the women, became something new by the time *Adharyana Veda* was written. The dignity and the honour commanded by them during Rigvedic period disappeared and their functioning altogether took a different shape.

The Period of Adharva Veda

Pridhvi, the kind Mother-Earth is praised in Vedas, especially in *Adharva Veda*. The following lines would reveal the sort of reverence in which the earth has been held by our ancestors.

"She is great (*Mahi*), firm (*dridha*) and shining (*Arjun*)."

"May she, whose heart is in the highest heaven, be compassed about with Truth and everlasting glory. May she, bestow upon us lusture, and grant us power in loftiest dominion; kind, ever gracious be the earth we tread on, the firm earth, *pridhvi*, borne up by order, mother of plants and herbs, the all producer.

May that earth grant us breath and vital power! *Pridhvi*, give me life of long duration.

Be gracious onto us, O 'Earth! Let not the robbers find us! Keep the deadly weapon far away! Earth! May thy summer and thy rains; thy Autumn, thy winter and thy dewy frosts and Spring time-May thy years pridhvi! and orders seasons and day and night pour put for us abundance!

May she, the Earth assign to us opulence for which we yearn, O Earth my mother, get thou me happily in a place secure!" *(Adharva veda* 12-1-8). *Adharva Veda* is also called *Brahma veda* as *Adharvana*, according to our Sastras is, the son of Brahma. He is the great man who made *Agni* to come down from the sky!

Prof. Griffith says that the most fascinating description in this Veda is "the house and the woman living in it." The psychology of a woman about to deliver a child is described. The man who got married and is leading a family life, thinks of his baby to be born, while working in the field. He prays to God, that prosperity should be bestowed on his family and his wife and children should live long (AV. VIX. 11.3). In the 11th *sloka* there is a prayer that the baby in the womb of his wife, should not be a girl. In the eighth sloka, there is another prayer that the evil forces should not change the foetus into a female child instead of a male. *O Prajapathi, Anumathi, Cinewalee* make a girl be born somewhere else, but for me give a male child" is the actual meaning of that prayer. So, man imagined only a male child in the lap of his wife!

By that time, marriage became compulsory for every woman. From the prayers for a "good husband", it is evident how the importance of marriage increased! Not only that, for a girl who remained unmarried, life became unbearable. For her, *Yama Dharmaraja* was supposed to be the 'husband'.

"This girl may have a good husband! She may give birth to good male children" in another prayer. From the above lines, it can be presumed that getting married and begetting children was the purpose of the life of a woman!

Age of Marriage

Strictly speaking, age of marriage was not prescribed anywhere. When the boy and girl meet, exchange ideas and want to marry, parents used to fix up and perform marriage. From this statement, we may conclude that there were no child marriages. *Brahma* and *Gandharva* were the two types of marriages recognised. A young man used to make attempts to win the heart of a girl by *Mantras*, (AV. 8-82). A girl waiting for marriage, was participated in the festival of *Samana* and to get applause was a good certificate for her in the marriage market. Also, from the wealth she brought her value increased.

Marriage Procedure

The marriage procedure was the same, as in the Rigvedic period. The bridegroom coming to the bride's house, feast etc., taking the girl to his house and the elders blessing the couple are the same. The girl wanting her married life to be happy says "Let our eyes be sweet as honey! Our faces are gracious! take me into your heart! Let our minds be one." She also says "You belong to me entirely! Never speak of another woman".

Before the marriage, the procedure for bringing water for the auspicious bath of the girl is laid down in detail. There is description of one *Apala Atreyaan (Ide)* when the girl decorates herself to get ready to go to marriage *pandal*. The following *mantra* is cited: "You should be the mother of good children. You should bring luck and prosperity to your husband and you should behave in a submissive manner to him - then you will be leading to dignity."

This sort of sermon is not to be found in *Rigveda*. Standing on the rock, the girl wishes that her marriage tie should be pious and secure. This prayer also is not there in *Rigveda*. Perhaps this sentiment entered only after the entry of Agni in the 'the marriage ritual'. A boy receiving the girl's hand (*Pani grahana*) before Agni was a major event in ritual of marriage. Till all the vows were completed, a curtain was drawn between the girl and the boy. This custom is being carried on even now. Only when she becomes the legal wife, they are allowed to see each other. Another important stage is 'handing over' the girl to her husband, as formality (AV.XIV 1.58 & 59) by the girl's father.

Vows of Marriage

Several vows are made at the time of marriage, "Just as creepers embrace the trees, you also embrace me and my body. You yearn for my love. Your looks may be filled with love on me." (AV. V 5.8).

You should hug my hand and my heart.
You live under my control for ever.
(AV.VII 8.9 102, 129, 130, 131, 132).

From the above words, it is evident that man wanted his wife to be a meek and submissive one and also fixed up some norms for her behaviour after the marriage.

Importance of a Son

Remaining unmarried was considered to be a sin. Even after marriage, if there are no children, it was another sin. If all born are girls then it was a greater sin. A son is necessary for relieving parents from *Punnama naraka*, it was believed.

'*Aputrasya Gathirnasthi*' was the popular sentiment. Only a son was eligible to offer *Pitru Tarpan*. So, the importance of a son increased. To beget a son, man was allowed to marry any number of times. Accordingly polygamy became order of the day.

Widow Marriage

When a man died, it was a custom to burn all articles belonging to him, in all the ancient communities. The wife was also taken to the burial ground and was brought back after performing some rituals. She was even allowed to remarry. After giving a goat and five plates of food', a man could marry her. (AV. IX 5,27,28). Before burning the dead body a prayer was offered "O *Agni*! O *Jatavedas*, send him to his *Pitru Devatas*". So, strong were the feelings of the "other World" that people began to crave for salvation in the other World. But, on the whole, when compared to other ages, the period of *Adharvana Veda*, showed some tolerance in several respects. Courtesans had a place in society. The son born to an unmarried girl also was given legal status. But one prominent change came among the members of society. A woman, who was a partner in all activities of man's life during *Rigveda* period, merely remained within the four corners of the walls and her main purpose in life was to give birth to sons and to live under the control of man. Son's importance also increased, with, the onset of new ideas like *Paraloka*, *Punnama Naraka* etc. '*Yajurvedas*' are chantings of mantras. So, they are not studied in detail as they do not throw light on the society.

Society as Mentioned In *Brahmanas*

Brahmanas reveal that many of the religious ceremonies formerly left to the wife are now performed by the priests. She was not allowed to attend any assemblies or gatherings. Her position changed considerably, by the time of *Brahmanas*. Mainly the sentiments of 'piety' and 'impurity', '*suchi*', *asuchi* came into existence.

"A submissive wife, who could keep her mouth shut and dine after her husband", was now held up as an ideal. *Homas* and sacrifices that were performed by women are now performed by upper strata. A woman was considered to be '*Asuchi*' during certain days in the month and during such days she was not eligible to perform religious acts like *Homas*. Ordinary life was highly inter-woven with the religious acts and sentiments and mainly man's life was full of religious duties. *Brahmanas* mainly mention about the *Yagnas* and *Homas* and how they should be performed by man. But depending on these descriptions, we cannot calculate or assess the actual picture of the society.

"Dead people become devils and roam about in this World even after death, if they are sinners", it was strongly believed. If one commits a sin in this World, he will go to *Naraka* (Hell).

Thus some ideas about *Punya* and *Papa* (sin) came into in existence and people tried to live as per a set code of conduct.

Son's Birth–a Glad News

A son was considered essential to prevent parents from going to the hell and so, the son had to offer 'Pindas' such strong sentiments took roots. To please Gods of the other World and to have a happy life in the 'Paraloka', it was necessary to perform *yagnas* and *Homas*. But a strange part of such religious act was, to pray for a 'son'.

Aitraya Brahmana is the most important one among Brahmanas. From the story of *Sunah Sepa*, it is clear how people began to crave for the birth of a son (Ait. Bra. VII 13-16 or Harward Central Series Vol. 25. p. 299). A Raja by name Harischandra, belonging to *Ikshvaku* dynasty, had no sons, though he had a hundred wives. Parasara and Narada were two saints who were living in his Palace. One day, the Raja questions Narada, why people are crazy about a son and why a son is required. Narada says, it is a *Rinanubandha* between the father and the son, *Amaratva prapti* will be there, so a son is like a ship for the father's travel to *Amaraloka* (other world). It is an advanced idea.

It is one thing to pray for the birth of a son. But it is entirely different thing to take the birth of a girl to be a 'curse'. It was also customary to pray to Gods not to give a girl. *Taittareya Samhita* is full of such prayers to be performed on a full moon day, requesting Gods not to give a daughter. Narada advises Harishchandra, as per the *Samhita*, that if a man prays, chanting the following *mantra*, throwing (*darba*) into the air, a son would be born.

"A wife is a *Sahadharma charini*. A daughter is the cause for giving. But a son is like a torch in the *Oordhvaloka*."

The above *sloka* of *Taithareya Samhita*, resembles some of the *slokas* of Adharvana veda. In another place in the same *Samhita*, there is a prayer requesting *Cineevali* (Goddess) to give a 'Son' instead of a daughter. With the advent of such ideas which came into propagation, girls were not treated properly. Some *yagna* was performed by parents, only to have sons' and girls' birth was completely unwanted.

Prayers for the Birth of a Son

Zimmer Brooke opines that in Hindu society, to look down upon a girl child started with this strange idea. But Bothlink, another foreigner says, differing with the above idea, that "this custom was formed with the idea that girls go to a different house soon after marriage and not out of any ill will".

Maitrayani Samhita mentions that after *Yagna*, wife and husband perform 'Avabrudha Snana'. They put the mud pots there. They lift them to God 'Vayu' and they lift a son. (Mat. Sam. IV., 6,4,7,9).

The same idea is expressed in *Kadhak Samhita* also.

Wife More Important than Sister

In ancient community, sister, on account of blood relationship, was considered to be nearer to man, rather than the wife who joins him in life later on. The worship of Subhadra in Jagannadhaswamy temple of Poori (Orissa State) along with him, is a clear proof. But *Agni Maruta Sastra* changed the whole concept and gave important place to the 'wife'. For a *Yajamani*, when he is performing *pujas* to *Agni*, the wife sits next to him. So, though the sister is born from the same womb, she is next to the 'wife' in importance.

Idea of Dharmapatni

It is this *dharmapatni bhavana* that was mainly instrumental in bringing down the status of a sister. Because she is the wife, she is entitled to participate at the time of '*Aseervachana*' (Blessing).

"A pregnant woman is impure. If she touches, even food and water becomes *Asuchi* (impure). So, she must be made pure to perform Yagna's". The same idea was expressed in some Hebrew, and Jorastian religious texts also. "If a man has to do Agni, and his wife is pregnant, can he take food cooked by her - What has he to do" was the question. For purifying the food prepared by her, one *Achara Paddhati* (procedure) was mentioned. *Adharvana Veda* speaks of this procedure.

Status of Women

Women were restricted in their movements! They were not allowed to attend any gatherings or congregations. This sort of restriction was found, for the first time, in *Aitareya Brahmana* and *Mytrayani Samhita*. (Ait. Sram. IV 76-V., A.V. V.II. 45-8).

Maitrayani Samhita compares 'woman', with evils like 'drinking' and 'gambling'. (Mrit. Sam. VII 63). This *Samhita* also mentions that a woman is one of the 'evils'. A woman is not *Asatya*, *Anrutha*, but relates to '*Nirriti*' (*Nirriti* is a Goddess from whose evil influence one should be saved; prayers were performed to escape from her evil look). *Taitharya Samhita*, and also *Satapata Brahmana* have proved that, 'a woman is meaner than a bad man. (Tait. Sami. VI, 5,8,2, S.B. 1,3,1,9). This stage shows how a woman is made inferior to man in status. A lenient attitude developed and polygamy became common. A man was allowed to marry any number of times. In some *Brahmanas*, it is described that a king had four kinds of wives.

First wife was *Patta Mahishi*. She was the *dharmapatni* entitled to participate in all the religious acts done by him. *Parivartaki* was wife without children. *Vivata* was the most loved wife of the king. *Pingali* was the daughter of head of the *dashav*. These indicate a further decline of a woman's status.

Ritual of Yagas and Yagnas

The various kinds of *puja* (worship) done by the king under the auspicies of the *purohits* were many. Two of them were important. One was the *Aswamedha Yaga* and the other *Raja Suya*. Generally, they were performed to prove their superiority over the other kings.

A king who could perform these *yagas*, successfully, became *Sarva Bhouma*. But the last part of the *yaga* was to pray for the sake of social custom. When the horse died, they used to walk round the dead body nine times. All the wives and servants of the king had to do this. *Pattamahishi* had a peculiar duty. She had to lie down near the dead horse (Dr. Winternitz pp. 11, 12). Then the priests used to cover her with the pious cloth and to recite *mantras*, to give her a son, who is a hero. With this, the *yagna* ended.

Another *Vrata* wherein the wife participated was *Varuna Praghasa*. It was a custom to make the wife tell how truthful she was to her husband! Accepting her fault, if she had lovers, she had to leave the 'dry grass' on earth. After declaring in the above manner, he got the eligibility to participate in the *Vrata*. (Dr. Winteenitz p.11). Even in *Vajapeya Yaga*, wife had to be next to her husband. (Tait Sam, IXX Sat. Bra. V. Dr. Winternitz p.12). A man who wanted to perform this *Vrata*, had to climb on the chariot wheel of the highest pillar. Here the chariot is a symbol of *Surya Deva*. He had to adorn his wife with dry grass and say "Let us go to the sky" (introduction to *Tait. Samh*).

Bharya - Ardhangi

Here the idea is to make the wife an *Ardhangi* (a half) of him. Without her, he cannot go to *Swargaloka*. Without her, he is incomplete. So, to achieve the comforts of *Swargaloka*, it is essential to have a wife, it was felt.

Similar idea is also expressed in *Aitarya Brahmana. Kavshitaki Brahmana* also expressed the same idea. They used to believe that every married girl is protected by 'Gandharas' and they had some supernatural powers.

There is *Homa* which only the 'wife' could perform (Sant. Bra). But there is some controversy about this. *Satapata Brahmana* says that a "wife is half of the husband". But in another place, the same text says that, "a woman who does not counter her husband is worthy of praise". (Ait. Bra, III. 24).

Bride Price (*Kanya-Sulka*)

Maitrayani Samhita, and *Taitareya Brahmana* speak of 'selling of a bride'. *Jainaya Brahmana* speaks of giving the girl as a gift (the story of Chyanana).

In *Vajasaneya Samhita* the word *Kumari Putra* is used. But it cannot be defined as the son of an unmarried girl. There are descriptions of dancers here and there. So, they and their children also had some status in society, though it cannot be definitely proved. So, by the time of *Brahmanas*, caste system became very rigid and *varnasrama dharmas* were prescribed.

If a child was born to an uper strata man with a sudra woman, it was considered to be illegal but *Gautama* and *Boudhayana*, the law givers (*dharma sastra karas*) regularised such union also and gave a status to the children, born out of wedlock.

Mantra Brahmana

This is the most important of all the the *Brahmanas*. It speaks of marriage as a Sacrament and *Saptapadi* is introduced.

Unlike in Rigvedic period or the period of Adharva Veda, marriage ritual became very elaborate and *Mantra Brahmana* speaks of such details. It is not simply a compilation of *slokas*. Some believe that this formed the basis for the *grihya sutra* of Gobhila.

The first part consists of eight *suktas*. The first *sukta* speaks of 'the *Agni* prepared before any marriage. Inviting him as *Gowaha*, the goddess of love and praying to receive the bride is the preliminary step. Offering new clothes to the bride and blessing her to live for a hundred years is the next step. Man praying to *Agni*, This girl you have blessed me with, should give me sons and prosperity is an important aspect of this. (M.B. 1.1.7). To prepare *Garhapatya Agni* and to invite Agni Deva, Varuna Deva and to pray to them to protect the girl from death, is the next step. A *smarohanam* is the next step. Girl, climbing the stone, praying for confidence, security of the marriage tie, is the last Chapter. "Climb this stone! Be firm as a rock. Don't bend your head before your enemies." These are some of the ideas expressed by the *slokas*. *Laja homam*; is nothing but the girl praying for the welfare of her husband and her family and cooking food. (M.B. 1.2.2).

Saptapadi Introduced

'*Saptapadi*' is the next step. The bridegroom, holding the hand of the bride should walk round *Agni* seven times.

First step is for food.
Second step is for strength.

Third step is for Guna.
Fourth step is for friendship.
Fifth step is for the welfare of animals in the house.
Sixth step is for prosperity.
Seventh step is for the sake of the priests.

"You, who have walked seven steps with me, have become a *Sahadharma Charini* (follower) says the bridegroom. Then the marriage tie becomes sacred. (M. Brahmana).

"This girl is pious. Come and see her. Bless her." (M.B. 1,2,8 an exact replica of RV., X., 85.33).

"Don't look with evil eye. Don't bring death to the husband. Bring prosperity for the animals. Give birth to males". (M.B. 1,2, II. A.V.XIV.2.1 and RV.X. 85-4).

"Prajapathi should give us children; let us live together till old age". (M.B.)

From the above *slokas*, it is evident that the ideal of marriage tie was to have a partner in life. The next *sloka* is to give authority to the bride on the mother-in-law, father-in-law, the sister-in-law and the brothers-in-law. (M.B. 1,2,15).

There is another *sloka*, which is not be found in *Rigveda* or *Atharva Veda.*

"Let your heart be nearer to my vatras. Let your mind follow my mind. With a full heart, you, must follow my orders. Let *Brihaspati* give you amicability". (M.B.)

Like this, *Mantra Brahmana* eloborates the purpose of marriage. It is only in this text, that man wanted his wife to be a supporter in all his endeavours of life and in his ideals and practice of *dharma.* Some of the prayers in the third chapter are intended t take away the evil from the various parts of the body, in words, deeds and in behaviour and laughter.

"With this offering, I am taking away the evil from your eyes and your nervous system".

"I pray for taking away evil from your hair, from your look and from your talking".

"From your laughter, from your conduct, from your talk, the sin is taken away from this offering".

"I pray for taking away evil from your teeth, foot and gums".

"From your interior parts of the body and from your eyes, I seek to take away sin with this offering".

"If there are any sins committed by your people, with this offering, I try to take them away. The bride-groom prays and offers to Gods to take away the evil".

Over and above all this procedure is, seeing the star of *Arundhati*.

"The sky is permanent. The whole World is permanent. The mountains are permanent. Just like that the bride is also permanent, in the family of her husband". (M.B. 1,3,7).

From the above prayers, we can conclude that the girl was invited with some piety and goodwill into the family of her husband and marriage tie was considered to be sacred.

Social Set up at the Time of Grihya Sutras

The family was the unit of society even at the time of *Grihya Sutras*. There were joint families, small in stature at the time of *Vedas* and *Brahmanas*. But by the time of *Grihya Sutras*, large families came into existence and the eldest male member became the head of the family. The duties enjoined by him are such that, he had to look after the welfare of all the members.

He had to take food only after confirming whether all the elders, children and pregnant woman in the family have taken food or not. The sort of respect that the son had to show to this head of the family, is mentioned in these *Grihyasutras*.

After returning from a journey, the "manner" in which he has to talk to the family members, is also mentioned. First, he has to kiss the kids, then elders. This kissing also different for 'male children'.

In those days, it appears that they wanted more children and more males. Every son had to have his own "Agni" in his house and so, they wanted to have more such houses. This sentiment started with *Grihya Sutras* only. Respect was given to age. Responsibilities of the head of the family also were many.

The head of the family had to do five Agnis; called *Panchavaha Agnis* – '*Brahmagni*', '*Pitru Agni*', '*Devatagni*', '*Bhuta Agni*' and finally '*Aditi Agni*'. He had to do seven *Paka Yagas* in addition. So life became more complicated, with full of procedures and rules of conduct.

By that time, the caste system became more rigid. A *sudra* was confined to be unfit for '*Sanyasa*'. Two sects called '*Virnasitas*' and '*Anirva Sitas*' were formed even among *sudras*. Some with strange habits had to stay far away from the village. *Grihya Sutras* have enjoined duties, on man depending on his status, his profession. *Upanayana* was compulsory and *Ritu* was fixed as per one's age.

Marriage - Status of a Woman

Anuloma Vivaha – an upper strata man marrying a lower caste woman was allowed but not vice-versa. Such marriages were many. From the word '*Abhinada*', used by Ramini, it was presumed by scholars that there were lower strata wives also and they had a lower status than that of the wife who is a *savarna* (same *varna*).

In *Aswalayana Grihya Sutra*, eight kinds of the marriages are mentioned: *Brahma*, *Deviva*, *Praja Patya*, *Arsha*, *Gandharva*, *Asura*, *Pisacha* and *Rakshasa* are the eight forms but the first four forms are considered to be respectable, as per *Aswalayana*.

Parents offering the girl as a gift is *Brahma Vivaha* and this is what is practised even today by Hindu society, which considers marriage as a sacrament.

Daiva form is giving the girl to a priest, who is an intellectual and a learned man. *Praja Patya* is also *Brahmana* form but any guardian, can give the girl as a gift in the place of her father. In *Arsha* form, the bridegroom had to give a pair of cows, to the brides father, before receiving her hand. Of course, there was some controversy about this, among *Sutrakaras*. Some considered it as *Kanyasulka*, some said it was only nominal, customary gift and some said that there is no inner meaning in giving this gift. But this form of marriage was not prevalent in the *Grihya Sutras*. As per the writings of the Greek ambassador, Megasthanes, this form of the marriage won the appreciation of people in Mauryan times.

Gandharva is a love marriage, where one chooses one's own partner. Our *Sutrakaras* have not given the freedom to select one's own partner to the youngsters. They felt it was the duty of the parents. But there were occasions when youngsters selected their own partners and so, the *sutrakaras* made provision for such marriages also. They recognised such marriages because when once it is over it is a fact. To this extent, the broad outlook of *Sutrakaras* has to be appreciated.

Asura form of marriage is to pay for the bride and buy her. This was prevalent only among some communities. Aswalayana says that if marriage is performed as *Brahma* form ancestors of twelve generations would go to heaven. The last form though not much appreciated, was prevalent in society and it was also recognised.

In *Paisacha* or *Rakshasa* forms, some status had to be provided to the unfortunate girl, who was taken away by force while elders were sleeping. There were some, who considered it to be prestigious also.

Good Features of a Bride

The bridegroom was not allowed to see the girl before marriage and mediators fixed up marriages. The girl was not moving freely in the outside world and so, before selecting a bride, relatives of the bridegroom had to select her, after seeing her twice or thrice.

Sankhyana says this about the good features of a girl.

"Hair should be soft. The parts of the body should be strong. There should be two curves near the neck." Such girl would give birth to six sons, *Sankhyana* says.

"One looking like an animal, one who is cunning, one who looks harsh and one who is a dwarf, one who has bold head, one who has the skin of a frogor is unfit for marriage, says Samkhyana.

"One who has left her own people, one who has more friends, one who has more interest in worldly pleasures, one who is of equal age with the bridegroom is also unfit" he said.

When people come to see the girl, if she is "crying or sleeping", it is to be presumed that she is not willing for the marriage, Sankhyana said.

Judging the Future of the Girl

Aswalayana had enunciated certain principles for testing the good fortune of the girl. By that time, perhaps astrology was not much developed; so, they used to test her fortune in a strange way.

They used to collect mud from eight different places and ask her to touch it. The different kinds of muds were—

(1) Mud giving two crops in a year (perhaps to test whether she would give birth to children or not).

(2) Cow-dung (to test whether she has line of fortune for cattle or not).

(3) Pious earth (to test about her *Adhyatmaika Chintan*).

(4) Mud beneath flowing water.

(5) Mud from a place of gambling.

(6) Mud from the centre of four corners.
(7) Mud from barren land.
(8) Mud from the burial ground.

From the mud she touched, her fortune was tested. If she touched the first three she was selected provided that her looks and behaviour were good.

Age of Marriage

Grihya sutras clearly discuss about the probable age for marriage. Firstly, the bride and the groom should not be '*Sapindas*' or '*Sagotrikas*' (of the some *gotra*). The bride should be intelligent, healthy, of good conduct and must be from a good family.

They had to enter family life after their student days. But *sutrakaras* differ about the age of marriage of a girl. They have different opinions. One says that from the word '*Chaturdhakarma*' the duty performed after the three nights of sleep in the groom's house, that the girl should be of the age of puberty. Another says that she 'should be', a *Nagnika*. Who is a *Nagnika*? There was some controversy about this word. Some defined it as a "girl playing in mud" aged about six or seven. Some said it was girl of about sixteen years of age. But there is no evidence to show that the child marriages were performed at the time of *Grihya Sutras*.

From the language of *Grihya Sutras*, which is not as complicated as in Vedas, it can be presumed that, by that time, a society, which took a definite shape on account of a synthesis of *Aryan-Anaryan* cultures was there, though Vedic religion was practised in the South and North of the country. Some of the tribal communities did not forego their earlier customs, which they honoured. So, there might have been several occasions when tensions arose and there might have been much discussion on those rules that were to be followed. To solve such problems, *Grihya Sutras* were written by some intellectuals, to give guidelines for the normal routine life of a man to run his household. When viewed historically, these *Grihya Sutras* have come into existence one after another from 6th century BC till Buddhism spread. Some of them laid basis not only for life but also for *Atmasanthi* of the soul after death.

Most important of the writers are Apasthambha, Aswalayana, Sankhyana, Bhardwaja and Gobhila. They were not contemporaries and there is not much difference in what they said. Basic values laid down by each one of them were for the well-being of the society. Society went on changing and so, they had to base their principles, according to necessity and there appear to be some superficial differences here and there.

Procedure for Marriage

By the time of *Grihya Sutras*, marriage procedure became very elaborate. This is the actual 'Sanatanic' procedure, that is being followed even today. To invite *Agni* and to perform a marriage before him, became customary.

Marriage was usually performed in the house of the bride's father. When there was no father, it was performed in the house of the guardian of that girl. Most important aspect of marriage was 'giving the girl as a gift' to the bridegroom and the bridegroom accepting it. After reciting of Karma Suktam, the father or the guardian of the girl, would take a vow from the bridegroom that he would not do anything in the discharge of *Dharma, Ardha, Kama, Moksha* without informing her. (*Nati Charaami*).

'*Pani Grahana*' is receiving the hand of the bride and taking a vow saying "I am taking your hand into my hands. I am wishing for happiness. You live with me till I become old. Goddess like *Bhaga, Aryamata, Sarita, Purandhri* have blessed me with you. As the *Yajamani* of the house, I will do my *Dharma* along with you."

Our *Sutrakaras* have mentioned that the children to be born will depend on the way the bridegroom touches the hand of the bride. If he touches the 'top finger' firmly male children would be born.

In '*Laja Homa*' the main purpose was, to relieve the bride, from the evil looks of some Goddesses. This was done by the brother of the bride. When he pours corn into the hands of the bride, she would offer the corn to *Agni Deva*.

Rituals like *Agni-Paribhramana* (walking round the fire) and Asmarohana (standing on the rock), *Saptapadi* (making seven steps) are the same as in previous texts like *Brahmanas*. Blessings wishing for prosperity and long life were given by elders to the married couple, and after the feast bringing her to the husband's house and making her to enter the house (*Grahapravesa*) with prayers is another ritual.

Our ancestors seem to think of bridal dress also. Much importance is given to "new clothes". They were wearing two kinds of cloth – one 'Uttaryeya' (upper) and another 'Antareya' (inner) garment. They prescribed colours of the cloth also. They wished for long life, wealth and cattle.

Special Status to Wife

Their sentiment was that after *Saptapadi*, a firm relationship never to be broken is established. So, from marriage onwards, husband should take the wife's help in all his endeavours.

Apasthambha says, "The wife and husband are inseparable. They are a unit. They are one in the discharge of religious and secular duties."

"Without your knowledge, if your wife does anything, or if you do something without her knowledge, add all make it into one; you both must collectively create a world of your own", Gobhila also expresses similar sentiment.

"When the husband is absent, the wife can perform *puja* for the *Agni* in the house, because she is '*Ardhangi*'. Moreover, the house belongs to both."

Taithreya Samhita views this aspect in a different angle and says "The husband hands over his earnings to the wife. Because she is a partner, she must keep such wealth in the house and protect it." The same text, in another context tells, "wife is a friend to the husband. She is the wheel to the chariot of the house. Therefore, whatever man does, he must obtain the consent of her. Even for doing *Homa*, she has a share.

So, in all *Sroutha Karmas*, the wife should be present. The *Sutrakaras* prescribed. "Any pious deed can be performed by man only after consultation with the wife but not independently," they said.

Family Relationship

Man is made superior to all in the family and all the members had to obey his orders and live under his control. Nobody should be disobedient to him. He could even take away the right of inheritance, if he wished, for a son who was wasting money.

But Apastambha maintains that "the parents have no right to sell or gift away their children." "When the wife was alive, when she was willing to obey his orders and to discharge her responsibilities, when she unable to give birth to male child, the husband cannot take another wife." Apasthambha further fixes up punishment for a man who discards his wife. Such a man should be seated on a donkey and made to go to seven houses begging saying, "the man who discarded his wife has come, give him alms." So saying, he must be made to roam about in the villages. He should live for six months like that. That is the punishment for him.

When viewed critically, it appears to me, that our *Sutrakaras* made the marriage tie more indivisible, keeping in view, the welfare of the children. Parents had to give protection to the children and the latter had to touch the feet of parents and give respect to them.

In a family, much respect was given to 'Age'. The younger brother could not marry before the elder's marriage." In the event of death of the head of the family, ten generations used to observe ten days mourning. To develop a sort of affinity of family bondage, they prescribed several *sutras*. They gave more importance to the 'collective welfare' of the family members but not of individuals separately.

No Polygamy

Monogamy was observed by all, at the time of *Grihya Sutras*. From the description of *pujas* performed on *Amavasya* and the full moon day, it is evident that only man had only one wife not many.

Karwika Grihya Sutra says about *Pinda Pitrua Yaga* and tells that if there is a second wife, she should be given a second *pinda*.

In *Apastambha Grihya Sutra* and *Kausika Grihya Sutra*, also, several *vratas* by which, a wife (*Dharma patni*) who wants to govern over the rest of the wives, are described.

In *Aswamedha yaga*, there is mention of several wives. Rajas, nobles and rich men could have several wives but the common man had only one wife.

In a *vrata* called *Utsayana*, a man who had only one wife, was given an honourable place. A *Pativrata* had some supernatural powers, they also believed. Gobhila, in his *Grihya sutra* says in a *vrata* called *Pumsa vana* a woman dedicated to her husband only should pound the corn.

A woman had no right to have several husbands. *Taithreya Samhita* says "on a Pole, two wires can be fixed from both sides. A man can have two wives. But, how to fix one wire on two poles. A woman cannot be a wife to two men."

There Was No *Sati*

At the time of *Grihya Sutras*, the system of *sati* was not there. After the death of the husband, the wife was to lie down next to his dead body as a formality and later, she was asked to come home.

Even in *Dharma sutras*, there is evidence to show that wives lived after their husbands, because a provision was made, as per law, for their maintenance and some sutrakaras have given them the right of inheritance also. *Bhargava Grihya Sutra* says "After the death of the husband, the wife should light the pious fire (*Pavitragni*) in the house as a duty."

But, *Vishnu Dharma Sutra*, which came at a later stage, says that "After the death of the husband, the wife should lead a principled life or should die on the pyre of the husband."

From the above explanation, it can be safely presumed that no single set of rules was practiced at all times. Many additions and deletions kept taking place, so as to bring harmony among the members of society. Law was also not static; it kept changing from time to time, according to necessity. Some intellectuals suggested ways and means, by their texts and treatises and the society honoured them.

Widow Marriage

Boudhayana and Vasistha have given permission for widow marriage. Soon after marriage or soon after consummation of marriage, if the husband dies, such a girl, in prime youth, may be married again and they saw nothing wrong in it. But, for a woman who had given birth to children, this was not allowed.

Regarding property rights, Gouthama, in his *Grihya Sutra* says "that a women has got a right in the property of her dead husband. She has to share the property along with *Sapindas* and *Sagotrikas* of her husband."

Neoga System

If a widow wanted to have children, she could beget children through the brother of her dead husbnd. Sociologists of those times allowed this.

Gouthama says "A widow can have a son, but after obtaining

the consent of the elders. If her husband had no brothers, she can give birth to a son, through a *Sapinda* or *Sagotrika* or with a man having *Samana Pravara* and belonging to the same community of her husband. Some have laid down the rule that she can only beget children through her husband's brother and not with others. She could not have more than two children.

Boudhayana says that "a widow should not allow honey, mutton or liquor or salt near her." She should sleep down on the floor for one year after the death of her husband.

Moudgalya, another *Sastrakara*, also suggests that "a childless widow, can have a son after six months of the death of her husband through his brother."

Gouthama says "the child belongs to him, who gave birth to him or if the elders decide about the 'father', child belongs to him." This custom is still prevalent among *Tadas* of *Nilgiri*. If the child is a Khtraja, Boudhayana says "the child will have two fathers. So two *gotras* are there. So, he has to perform funeral rites to both the fathers." But this custom was not appreciated by society for a long time. It died a natural death. Apastambha, opposed this vehemently. During later stage, nobody reintroduced this custom or appreciated it, as per the evidence available. *Neoga* system was only prevalent during the *Sutra* period for a brief time and later sank into oblivion.

Purdah System

There was no Purdah for women, in the days of *Sutrakaras*. Women freely participated in all religious and social festivals of society.

Sankhyana says that "a bridegroom who is going to the marriage pandal, should take along with him some *Suhasinis* (married woman). It was considered to be a good omen, if an elderly married woman comes from the opposite direction or goes out on a good cause like marriage or travel.

Katyayana Grihyasutra says, that "when a marriage was being performed, four or eight women were singing in unison with man who were playing on *veena* and an expert dancer was dancing." From this, it is evident that family women also were experts and were participating and exhibiting their talent in fine arts in social gatherings.

When *Mahavrata* was performed there are descriptions that women played on instruments like flute and were merrily participating in festivals. From the writings of *Srouthа Sutra Karas*, we can know, that at the time of *Mahavrata*, *Aswamedha Yaga* or *Vajapaya Yaga*, women were allowed to freely participate. But one point is to be noted. This freedom was allowed only on special occasions and not in everyday life. In normal life, she was confined to her house only.

Courtesanship

There were courtesans in society even at the time of *Sroutha Sutras*. There is an interesting conversation between a student and a *Ganikee* at the time of a '*Mahavarata*'. Boudhayana says "A *Sanyasi* can have food from a courtesan." But Gouthama prohibited this.

Honouring the Guest Considered as a Yagna

Grihya Sutras say that honouring the guest (*Afidhi Yagna*) is one of the *Mahayanas*. It was not only a social custom but a religious duty, they considered. Chief among the guests are *Guru*, *Ritwik*, King, *Saataka*, Father-in-law and Son-in-law.

Atidhi (guest) may come at any time. As soon as he comes, *Sutrakaras*, have laid down that he should be offered 'water' for washing his feet, a '*Madhuparka*' and a mixture of 'Curd and Ghee'.

'Mistrust' should not be there towards friends, servants or even wives. They gave more importance, it appears, to bodily piety. They prescribed *Achamanam* (taking water inside) washing the feet for every small thing. They also accorded great importance to the "sense of morality and decency". One should have a pious body and a pious heart. For the welfare of mother and child, they observed some rituals before and after the birth of the child. *Sumanta-Nayanam* is one such ritual.

They used to give two names for the child. One among them was kept as a secret. The age of the child was calculated, not from the date of actual birth, but from the day of conception itself.

They gave recognition to self-respect and also respect for elders.

Education of Woman

Was there education among women? If it was there, what sort of education was given? We don't have sufficient evidences to establish any point of view.

But *Manava Grihya Sutra* says "One of the qualification for marriage, is education. This may be necessary for a boy or a girl. We have seen in the last pages of this Chapter, that Grihya Sutras have laid down the qualities for a good bride.

Katyana Grihya Sutra says that "a girl has *Brahmacharya* till her 10th or 12th year." Another *Grihya Sutra* gives in detail the procedure to be followed by the end of this *Brahmacharya*. *Devapala* critic says that the father should not keep a girl in his house after 10-12 years of age. That means he has to get her married and send her to the husband's house. Some critics said, "*Devapala*, perhaps means by *Brahmacharya*, not to have family life". But, according to some *Grihya Sutras*, *Brahmacharya* means not having family life, but having *Veda Pathana*. As per *Katyana Grihya Sutra* (vol. G. 2, 4), *Brahmacharya* was calculated, not from the date of birth but the date of *Upanayana*. So, Devapala's definition may be apt. Girls also might have had good opportunities for education, which means *Veda Dhyana* (study of *Vedas*) in those days. Yama, a *Dharma Sutrakara* says "even girls are eligible for *Veda Vidya*."

In addition to *Veda Vidya*, they were learning dance and music. As per Sankhyanan *Grihya Sutra*, there is description of a 'dance' which four or eight girls performed. *Katyayana Grihya Sutra* says that a girl was an expert in using the instruments like *Nadi*, *Tunuva*; *Mridanga* and *Panava*. *Apasthambha*, while describing the procedure of marriage says "women should be consulted." In his Dharma Sutras, he lays down that 'a women should have allround knowledge." (*Bahumukha Pragna*)

Descriptions of Women in Some Famous Ancient Texts and Writers

Brihat Samhita – Varaha Mihira

This was the last text brought out in the end of Gupta period (505 A.D.). It was also the last text written by Varahamihira and so his rental maturity and depth of knowledge is exhibited.

It has reflection on several subjects like science, medicine, psychology, fine arts like *vastu silpa*, sciences like Botany and astrology, etc., and it is a standard work. It is also like a *kavya* of *Mahakavi* Kalidasa and depicts the cultural life of his times. His sayings like

"Manohimulam, Hara dagdha Murtheh" (78, 14)
"Bhushanti Vanitha Ratnakantya" (74, 2)

are similar to Kalidasa's sentiments; Varahamihira was a great man who opposed people and criticised women with unkind words. He tells that women are deities of good fortune: A women should always be respected; Those faults, that are attributed to women are also found in men. Whereas men speak out, women contain silently.

Such was the impact of *Brihatasamhita*, which brought out an important phase in the cultural and scientific life of Indians, so to say.

Status of Women in his Times

All said or done, birth of a girl was not much appreciated and a woman who gave birth to girls was also looked down upon; But Varahamihira describes about a woman, well-versed in all sciences and crafts and who was known to be a *Brahmavadin* by all.

Joint family system was prevalent in his times and many cousins lived together. Varahamihira says that 'the mother commanded more respect, because she had love for all' (LXVII, 917 YY V. 38). A person's social status was judged from the family in which he/she were born and brought up. Some of his sentiments are as follows:

(a) A woman, who discarded her husband was not treated honourably!

(b) A woman, who had cordial and amicable relations with her husband, was believed to be living for the upliftment of the family.

(c) The wife and husband are not different. They are not different individuals. They are one and the same. The first step for family life is relationship of wife and husband. So, one should have 'faith' in the other and there should be identity of ideas.

Putra Means Rebirth of a Man

The very term *Putra* means rebirth of a man: Varahamihira advises man, who wants to keep up the prestige of the family to keep aloof or protect his women from "*Sanyasins*, unmarried women, *dhobis*, women who sell flowers."

Some of the qualities of a good woman are:

1. She should not sleep before the husband sleeps.
2. She should get up and complete all household work before he gets up.
3. She should be amicable to her father-in-law, mother-in-law, and brothers of her husband.
4. She should keep accounts of the family.

Varahamihira furthers says:

"The woman is the jewel created by God. So, she can attract man without any jewellery – the very thought of her creates interest in man. She is a *Grihalakshmi*. As there are many good qualities in her rather than in man, an intelligent man should treat her with respect. A man who cannot see her like that, is a bad man."

He has mentioned about several women deities especially Sapta Matrukas like, Brahmi, Vaishnavi, Roudri, Kaumari, Varuni and also Ekanamasa. Ganadevatas also were mentioned.

Patanjali's Mahabhashya – Women's Status

The great Mahabhashyakara Patanjali described woman by several names like Kumari, Kishori, Yuvathi, Vadhuti, Jarathi. Keeping in view the relationship of man and woman perhaps, he has mentioned about *Kanya Bharya*, *Patni*, *Bhagini*, *Matamahi*, *Pitamahi*, etc.

Prabhudayal Agnihotri says the word *Jaya* was used as a synonym for *Bharya* or *Patni*. The word *Panigrahana* was used as the alternative word for *Upanayana*.

Women Separated from Society

Patanjali's time was a period when women were treated with total indifference.

"A women should not attend a *sabha*. It was not considered to be respectable." Here *sabha* may mean *Yagnasabha*, where men only had access.

Even if *Sabha* is taken as *Sala* or *Nagarasabha*, participation of women was not considered to be honourable. Women of royal palaces had access to fine arts and some women of upper strata were educated and were even propagators of religious sentiments, though legal and political status was not given to them.

Patni Dharma

Patni Dharma was to serve her husband and to keep him cheerful. *Gamya*, *Agamya* are the two words used by him. There was polygamy and there are descriptions in *Mahabhashya*, where one had Astabharyas and there is mention of *Sapathis* and also of *Veerapatni*, *Dasapatni*, depicting the status of a women. The respect that a man commanded belonged to his wife also. Of course, man had to maintain his wife. She is *Bharya* because she is protected. Didishu is one who marries before her elder sister is married. Damayanthi is a vadhu, to whom father gives gifts called *Haranam*. She was a *Sahabhagini* in all her husbands deeds and also in his respectable status. There is mention in his text of Dasis and Ganikas (*Sarva bhogyas*).

But a women who was a mother, had an honourable place in society, and her children were given her status and they enjoyed all the benefits, which she enjoyed.

Women in Upanishads

Upa-Ni-Shad (sitting near means learning sacred things of life, sitting near the *Guru*. *Upanishads* are highly respected in *Hindu* society. Even *Charakas*, who opposed *Vedas*, respected these *Upanishads*.

There is a saying that upanishads are 150 in number. But out of them thirteen are more famous. We cannot decide their time and we cannot even judge the nature of society, which prevailed in those times. There are no references to women in many. But, the story of discussion of Gargi with Yagnavalkya and the conversation between him and Maitreyi, of *Brahadaranyako Upanishad* are worth mentioning. The story goes like this.

One day, Gargi as a *Sanyasin* enters the *Sabha* of Janaka and requests for permission to question Yagnavalkya. She wants to know about the matter, which is prevalent in between the earth and the sky and about that which is all pervasive and which is leading the Sun and the Moon and on account of whose power the whole universe is running in order; and days, months and years are formed and rivers are flowing towards the seas.

Yagnvalkya shuns her telling that she is a woman and she is asking for something which she should not ask. The next day, she again comes to the *Sabha* and enters into dialogue with him. One question leads to other. Finally she gets her reply and description of

Atma-Padardha, on account of which everything in this World seems to be very dear. With her perseverance and uncommon erudition and depth of knowledge, she could indulge in metaphysical discourse and obtain an answer. This was possible only because of her good background and education. There might have been some more women like her in society who could make such remarkable contribution.

Yagnavalkya preaches to Maitreyi, his wife, how to know about *Brahmapadardha*. This *Padardha* can see everything but is not visible by itself. So also, this *Mahasakti* can listen to all but by herself cannot listen. It knows everything on the face of the earth.

Maitreyi asks him whether she can attain *Amartwa*. Yagnavalkya replies even if she obtains all the wealth on this earth, she cannot get it. Maitreyi asks for that which can be attained even after death. Then he tells her to come and sit close to him and tells the path for attaining *Amaratwa*. Maitreyi had the tenacity and intellectual stamina to know about subtle things of life and the universe and the philosophy behind.

Chandogyopanishad (3rd part) tells about the meaning of marriage.

"*Yadetad hridayam tava Tad Astu hridayam mama Yadidam hridayam mama Tat Astu hridayam Tava*".

Here, the policy of 'give and take' was preached. The woman was not considered to be lesser in status of spirit. *Aitarayopanishad* (2nd Adhaya - 1, 2, 3) says, "*Tat Streeyat Ata Bhuyam Gachchati Yadhaswamangam Tadhah*". Man enters into the woman and takes rebirth in her, in his own mould. That is why the woman becomes a *Jaya*.

Women in Puranas

Dharma Sastrakaras have made 'woman' a 'Persona-non-grata' and she was viewed without any individuality. By the time, it came to the age of *Puranas*. Whatever little importance she had, was also lost, not only in the affairs of the society but in her own family. The great ideology and the philosophy depicted in the ancient texts was not understood by the common people. So, the *Puranas* were written in simple language with interwoven stories. *Puranas* were many. How many? We do not know. Even we cannot define what is a *Purana*? Our people believe that they are many in number. There are several *Upa-Puranas* also. All of them could win the hearts of the people.

Some are secular but most are religious. There are several traditions, ancestral customs, religious discussions, moral values, principles of philosophy, well discussed in all these texts.

Historians believe that all of them were written in between 300-600 B.C. Comparing Vedas with *Puranas*, several foreigners studied them in detail but differed in many respects. Keith said that "we cannot fix up the time of the traditional values in *Puranas*. So, we cannot consider them with due weight. But Purgitor said "the historical facts in *Puranas* are more truthful than the Vedas. Vedas speak of Brahmanical tradition, whereas *Puranas* speak of the 'Kstriya-dharma' (justice of the rulers). When we critically analyse both we find that the writers of all these texts were *Brahmins*. But they made their observations, keeping in view their contemporary society, and one tradition was not contemporary to another in society, and one tradition was not contradictory to another. Moreover, they were written at a time when influence of *Buddhism* was declining and *Hinduism* made revival again. So, they were honoured and respected by common people.

Prakriti was made the dearest companion of *Bhagavan*, Almighty in almost all the Puranas. Dedication of oneself to God was considered to be the only path of salvation. For instance, Dhruva's mother tells him about "Goodness", "Sacredness", and "Fraternity" readiness to do good deeds" are the desirable traits. *Vishnu Purana* says "If 'self' only forms the basis of man-woman relationship and wealth only gave status of a man, and internal virtues disappear before external things, then such society status would soon perish".

During the period, society was cemented on the basis of castes and creeds and so much of gap emerged between the different sections of society. But there is no sufficient evidence to show how women were living and what was their role or status. It became customary to get a girl married and that too at the age of five or six. *Brahma Purana* clearly says that "a girl should be married between 4-10 years." So getting married and leading a family life became the main purpose of the life of a woman. Child marriages became a common practice. "Education" in the wider sense was also denied to a girl. A girl had no right to choose her own husband. Only parents selected a partner for her. On account of child marriages, several evil effects sprang up. Number of widows increased and re-marriage of widows was not allowed. So, many women had to lead a miserable life, under the care and protection of somebody or other.

The practice of *sati* also became more prevalent. Burning the wife to keep up sanctity of the family was considered a great religious act. Number of such deaths during the Puranic period were many, when compared to other ages. '*Devadasi*' system (dedicating girls to temples in the name of God) took deep roots. This was one of the evils that turned out to be a black mark on Indian culture. Indian society, in a way, became narrow, short-sighted and crippled.

Joint family system also became unmanageable and because several people tried to live under one roof, enjoying family property, indiscipline, discontent and peacelessness became the order of the day and the whole family life became topsy-turvy.

Of course, there are some descriptions of some women, here and there who were outstanding personalities. *Devahuti* of *Bhagavatapurana*, *Madalasa* of *Markandeyapurana* are some of them. Hiuen-Tsang visited India and wrote about *Devadasis* and the Hindu society prevalent at that time. A society, which could give once some universal dictums to the whole world, forgot its elasticity and bid good-bye to its greatness, by the time of these Puranas!

Women in Ramayana and Mahabharata

Ramayan and *Mahabharat* are the two epics that remained the symbols of Indian tradition, till today. They are taken as the guiding principles for human behaviour and conduct. The whole Indian life is inter-woven with the sentiments expressed in these two wonderful epics. All the ancient texts are on a different para and these two epics are on yet another plane depicting the ideals for human existence. There is no village where there is no temple for "Rama". *Sita* is considered as the ideal for womanhood by Indians. It is due to her chastity, sacrificing spirit and dedication. Mahabharat depicts a society, which is the melting pot of morals. It was, perhaps, at an assimilation stage of *Asuras* and *Aryans*. Ramayana gives the picture of society wherein certain well established values of life were respected. We cannot also have a clear view of society prevailing at that time, as the material available is scanty.

We come across women like *Sarama*, (wife of Vibhushana) *Trijata* (daughter of Vibhishana) and *Mandodari* (wife of Ravana) and *Mekhala* (wife of Indrajit) who stand as replicas of virtue, though belonging to *Anaryan* community. *Surpanakha* is an evil force, on account of whom, the whole story of kidnapping of *Sita* happens.

There are women like *Tara*, *Ahalya*, *Voormila*, *Sabari* with intrinsic worth and talent in their own way.

Marriages were not a sacred tie among *Asuras*. Abducting the wife of an enemy was also common. Marrying the wife of a brother (Tara's story) also considered as per law. Of course *Swayamvara* (selecting one's husband) was an honoured tradition (Sita's story). But we do not know whether this custom was prevalent among the commoners also or whether it was confined only to the ruling class or the kings.

Look at this *sloka* by Lakshmana.

Nahamanami Keyure
Nahamanami Kundale
Nupurevava Janani
Nityam Padabhi Vandanat,

(When Lakshmana had to identify the jewellery of Sita he says he can identify only the ornaments she wore for her legs, as he was accosting her feet every day).

Though there was no *Purdah* among the ordinary people, it was prevalent among the women of royal palaces. There were joint families and the responsibilities of the 'head' were many.

The story of *Mahabharata* tells about the responsibilities of *Dharma* and in fact *Mahabharat* is considered to be *Panchamaveda* (5th veda). There were practices like '*Neoga*', '*Polyandry*', '*Polygamy*', '*Anlma*', '*Pratiloma*' marriages. Above all these, putting a women to indignity in the public (story of Draupadi *Vastraharana*) is found odd. Each and every sections in the society followed a different system of values and so it was very difficult to bring about a common code of conduct. So, the war of *Mahabharat* itself was fought for justice.

Though the story is well known to us, the character of Draupadi is worth mentioning. She fights for justice and asserts herself, in spite of odd situations confronting her. She is described as *Panditha* on several occasions. We find several prominent woman like Ganhari, Kunti, Prameela, Amba and Sulabha who are very capable and vocal. They play a major role in their families and speak of several *Dharma* and keep up their individuality.

From the scanty material available, we cannot think of the society prevalent in those days. There was desire to lead a duty bound life but there were several transgressions also. There were practices like *Swayamvara* and *Sati*. *Swayamvara* was there but among the royal palaces and not among commoners. *Sati* was done by the wife of Yasodara (mother of Krishna), but the wives of Krishna, after his death, did not take to *Sati*, though belonged to the same family. Satyavathi, Ambika, Ambalika (her daughter-in-law) live even after the death of all in the war. So also Kunti does not commit *Sati*, whereas *Madri* the other wife does so. So, nobody found fault with another and every one followed one's own custom. Bhishnma, speaks of woman in *Anusasana parva* as follows: "A man while practicing *dharma* depends on woman, all comforts and pleasures depend on her. So, man should conduct themselves under the control of woman." Vyasa says, "Women are embodiments of wealth. If a man wants to live in comfort, he should know how to respect woman."

Bhisma preaching dharma says

"*Kumaro Nasti Yeshancha Kanyasa Tatra Bibhochayat*" (Santi parva 32).

(If a king dies in war and if he has no male children, his daughter should be crowned and given the care of Kingdom).

To a question by Dharmaraja, Bhisma says "A woman by nature should depend on man and so man has the control over her." To another question as to how woman should be protected, Bhisma gives the story of 'Vipula' (son of Devasarma). To get another question whether a great man should marry or not, Bhisma does not give a reply in clear terms. "If he marries, it is good but if he does not marry it is all the more good." He narrates the story of Astavakra. We find several men remaining unmarried. But, nowhere, there is mention of women remaining unmarried in *Mahabharata* and it was also considered to be a necessary *samskara*. Vyasa says "a woman is equivalent to ten Gurus". Draupadi argues several times with Yudhisthira on ideologies!

References

1. *Hindu Law* – N.R. Rraghava Chariorya.
2. *Fundamentals of Indian Culture* – K.M. Munshi.
3. *Hindu Civilisation* Vol. I & II – Sri Radha Kund Mukherjee.
4. *Our Social Laws* – Prof. J.H. Dave.
5. *Freedom and Culture* – John Derey.
6. *Way of Life* – Emerson.
7. *Ethical and Spiritual Values as the Basis of National Integration* – S. Radhakrishan.

8. *Hindu Law* – N.R. Raghava Chariorya.
9. *Fundamentals of Indian Culture* – K.M. Munshi.
10. *Hindu Civilisation* Vol. I & II – Sri Radha Kund Mukherjee.
11. *Our Social Laws* – Prof. J.H. Dave.
12. *Freedom and Culture* – John Derey.
13. *Way of Life* – Emerson.
14. *Ethical and Spiritual Values as the Basis of National Integration* – S. Radhakrishan.

CHAPTER 5

Woman in Secular Texts

Chanakya's Ardhasastra

Ardhasastra is one of the few secular texts that we have. Chanakya is believed to belong to the last half of the 4th Century B.C. and is also known as Kautilya. His family background and parentage is not clearly known. But, he enunciated certain progressive ideas to run the great Mouryan Empire, as he was a great scholar, philosopher, as well as a great statesman. His intellectual acumen was so sharp as to foresee the coming generations and he made some practicable propositions applicable to all times. *Ardhasastra* resembles mostly '*Sukraneetisara*' and grants two unusual rights to women-to remarry and to inherit property. Judged from certain standards *Ardhasastra* is a better treatise than the *Smrithis* of Manu. Chanakya bases his proposals keeping in view the vedic society to greater extent. For instance Manu says that 'if a girl after attaining puberty selects her own husband, she loses here right in her father's property". (Manu IX.90, 91, II 27-30, 36, 40 IX 93). *Yagnanalkya* also supports this point of view (Yagu, su, I. 64, II, 287). But Kautila vehemently says "*Sarvesham preetyaropanam Apratishtitam*". Any marriage should be appreciated by one and all, once it is performed or over.

Inter-Caste Marriages Allowed

Mouryan society seems to have had great respect for tradition and religion. But it is evident from *Ardhasastra* that *Brahmins* (the upper strata of society) also joined the army and the State services, some also took to drinking. It was a time when caste system was observed strictly but, *Kautilya* allowed marriages between two different sects.

Manu and *Yagnanalkya* disallowed the marriages between a *sudra* woman and higher caste man (Y.S. 1.57; Manu iii 14-19). But, Chanakya allowed such *Anuloma* marriage and also granted property rights to the sons born to such marriages. This goes to show his broad vision and perspective.

Women in State Craft

Chanakya utilised women's talent for such services as Hindu women never did in any age. *Amazonian* women were made to keep watch over the *Sayanagara* (Bed room) of the king. They were made to test the bed, clothing, perfumery and jewellery, of the king. They were made to form major part of C.I.D. system in the Empire, they were also made to decorate the *zenana*. State craft in the opinion of Chanakya was an art par excellence, superior than all the rest of the arts and sciences. He arranged a sound system of Government and utilised women's intellectual capacities for keeping watch over the functioning of the entire system and to gather information from time to time from various sources.

Women were the main escort, whenever the king went out on hunt, making way with ropes on both the sides thus restricting the rush of visitors on roads.

Women Talented In Dance and Music

Another type of women also caught recognition of Chanakya. They were the courtesans. Women endowed with the gift of dance, not only pleased the king with their talent in the royal gathering (*Darshan*) but were also useful in detecting the mental set up of foreign visitors with the twinkle of an eye. Thus, they were helpful to the king in carrying news from all corners of the country. It is wonderful to note that Chanakya, thus gave status to courtesans in society and in the running of administration.

Rajay Nartaki, the royal dancer, was the first woman and she was assisted by a battalion of other women. Their income, their attitudes and movements were watched by separate establishment from time to time. Such superintendent and his deputies were paid lavishly from the State revenue.

Indica-Magasthanes

Megasthanes was a Greek traveller and he toured over the length and breadth of the large Mauryan Empire and gave an eye witness account of what all he saw and heard. But unfortunately, his book (*Indica*) is not available now, in its original form. Some of the excerpts only are available and from these writings, we can have a clear picture of the Mouryan society. But, he has got his own limitations - language might have been a problem as he was a foreigner. Dr. Smith the famous indologist opines, though his writings are based mainly on what he gathered from others, he is an eye witness to many things". So, his *Indica* is supposed to be an authority on Mouryan Emprie, especially the reign of Chandra Gupta and the times of Chanakya. Megasthenes mentions that women were the main body guards to the king, either at home or on hunt or an any other expedition.

He tells us about polygamy and describes how an ordinary citizen also had many wives and how the houses were filled with a number of children. Look at one of his queer observations that some married for the sake of mundane happiness and some for company sake. He tells us that people were fond of beautiful things, and they wore fine *Muslin*, embroidered with gold.

Women Trained from Childhood

'A woman, who could kill the king, became the wife of the coming king' - says Megasthenes. Such was the knack, with which women served the king and such was the impending danger also from women. So, some talented women were brought in early childhood from their parents and were well-trained in all the arts and crafts and were made to protect the very life of the Emperor as well as his kingdom. Thus, we can see that women were made to play a very important role in running the State. This goes to prove the intellect of Chanakya in running the contemporary society, with consummate skill and erudition.

Vatsyana - *Kama Sutras*

Main aim of our *Dharma sastras* was to teach men to achieve *Dharma, Ardha, Kama* and finally *Moksha*. Vatsayana seems to have concentrated an Worldly pleasures, leaving aside the rest. It is thus he, who imported the idea of mundane happiness, whereas all our other texts have preached about attainment of *Moksha* and implementation of *Dharma*. Vatsayana deviated from this path and had written *Kamasutras*, wherein he described the life of a *Nagarika*, a civilised man.

Nothing is known about the parentage or nativity of Vatsayana, but it is believed that he lived in between the Mourya and Gupta As he made long and elaborate description about the leisurely and luxurious life of the elite and the wealthy citizens, some believe that he lived in between 1st and 2nd century.

Zenana Women and the *Vilasinis*

Vatsayana's *Nagarika* (civilised man) is not bothered about philosophical discussions and so, wanted to enjoy all the pleasures of life. A woman was made a to or tag in man's hands. His house was in the end of the town and was full with niceties and decorations in different ways and was divided into two different protions. One was the *Zenana*, wherein his wife or 'wives' lived and their children and the servants also lived there. This consisted of the kitchen also.

The second portion was intended for the house owner entirely, wherein he entertained his honourable guests. Among his guests, there were at times women. These women were well versed in sixty four fine arts. It was a custom that respectable women of the *Zenana*, should not enter into the second portion, which is intended for the pleasures of Nagarika. It appears that it was Vatsayana who coined the Word of *Vilasini* for the first time, and strangely, the partner of life to a man was not the *Dharmapatni* but the *Vilasini*. *Dharmapatni* is supposed to keep the house and to keep up the family customs and traditions. Thus differentiation is made between two differents sects of women and two different standards are set towards these two sects definitely. This has contributed much towards lowering the status of women. The set-up of society in those days also approved this behaviour of *Nagarika*.

The Ideal Wife

Vatsayana had enunciated the good qualities of an ideal wife. Self-restraint, a sense of service and dedication are supposed to be important traits of a woman. She should serve food to the husband. Before husband takes food, she should not eat. With his permission only, she should attend the religious festivals or social gatherings. She should not talk to women of lesser status. She should not linger near the entrance door. She should not stay alone in place without informing the husband, she should not give any gifts to others. She should honour her husband's friends. She should serve husband's parents with respect, should abide by their orders and should not give a reply to them. She should lead the life of a Sanyasini when husband is away and should not decorate herself'.

Over and above all these rules, Vatsayana has enjoined on her, another rule that, "She should be amicable with the husband on all issues". (This is not found even in *Rigveda*).

He mentioned about four kinds of women:

(1) *Padmini*

(2) *Sankhini*

(3) *Chitrini*

(4) *Hastini*

Among them, *Padmini* is the best and *Hastini* is the "*Kamuki*" or entertainer. Thus two points of view were expressed - one code for women and another system of moral values for man. The main aim and purpose of a woman is to appear beautiful and to be dutiful and to attract man.

He also says that a woman should not:

(1) be a senseless woman;

(2) should not have too much greed for money; and

(3) should have interest in fine arts.

Vatsayana narrated all the sixty four arts like singing, dancing, painting and laid down the rule that a woman should be an expert in all the arts, atleast in principle. But he did give recognition to an "intelligent woman".

Sudraka's *Mrichchakatika*

The story of Charudatta, the Brahmin priest and Vasantasena, the courtesan, is well known. Sudraka, the writer had depicted the, story in a dramatic way and nicely pointed out the sentiments of people of his times.

Vasantasena was rich, beautiful and also humane. She was a dancer, no doubt, and had a prominent status in society. Charudatta was a family man, married within his caste and was having a son. He was leading the life of a simple, common man with no higher means of living. The story revolves round so many incidents like loss of the jewellery of Vasantasena, theft in Charudatta's house and finally, Vasantasena coming to his house and she being taken as a wife to him.

The simple story throws light on contemporary society wherein, the marriage between two different castes was also allowed under necessary circumstances. Because it happened so, on the principle of *Fait Accompli*, it was accepted. This is something to be noted. The law givers and the elders of society allowed certain things, when they were inevitable. This goes to show their big heart and also their elasticity in thinking. They viewed matters with a broad vision, not definitely with a rigid mind, as some believe it to be. Another important point to be noted is that women were allowed to accomplish themselves in fine arts and that they were honoured and respected by society. It appears to me that, not only during this particular period of Sudraka, but during all ancient periods, our ancestors allowed women to shine in fine arts without any reservation. They allowed freedom for women in a subtle way, within a framework of certain rules and within the family fold.

But as times went on and life became hard, perhaps, woman could not concentrate more and more on their individual achievements and merely contended themselves with leading a family life. Giving education or training in fine arts might have been a costly affair to the common man and to send a girl to a school or to the city was not possible within the means of an ordinary family. There were no facilities also. So, women were mainly restricted to the confines of the four walls of the house and led the life of a house-wife simply.

REFERENCES

1. Vatsyana-*Kamasutras*
2. Rajasedharas *Karpura manjari, Mrichchakatika, Raghuvamsa, Harshacharita.*
3. Sakuntalam Malavikagnimitram, Vikramorvaseeyam. *Indian costume.*
4. G.S. Charye PHD (contab) *Indian costume, coiffure, and ornament.*
5. Sachidanand Sahay *Indian jewellery.*
6. Mrs. Janila Brijabhushan.
7. Reports of Sri John Marshall on Indus Valley civilisation.
8. M. Rama Rao, *Satvahana Sanchika.*
9 G. Varama Murthy, *Amaravati Silpala.*

CHAPTER 6

Status of Women during the Reign of Rajputs

Rajputs ruled India, after the death of Harshavardhana, till Muslims invaded and occupied the country. It is not known wherefrom they came to India. Todd, the famous historian says that "Rajputs, Sakas, Huns, Kushans and Gharjanas sects they came to India and got absorbed in Hindu society."

They married Indian women and considered India, as their motherland. Hindus also absorbed them. This theory of Todd was accepted by the foreign scholars also.

From the *Sasanas* of ninth and tenth centuries, it is evident that some of them belonged to *Surya Vansa* and some to the *Chandra Vansa*. According to Todd "Rajputs were great patriots, full of energy, were having good qualities like patience, respect for the guest etc." Even when they achieved success, they never ill-treated their enemy. They considered that to honour women is a matter of pride. They were willing even to sacrifice their lives for the sake of piety and self-respect. They got their daughters married to people of high families.

The life of a Rajput was dedicated to war. It was their custom to teach the stories of *Ramayan* and *Mahabharat* and in a festival called "Kargu Bandayi" to present a child with a weapon. Their ideal is Rama. Vidyadhar Mahajan says, "It is the quality of Rajputs to spent time in hunting and in the company of female dancers, when there is no war."

They had no purdah. Their women had freedom to select their husbands. Gandharva form of marriage was prevalent among Rajputs. So, it can be concluded that their girls married only after attaining puberty.

Alberuni says that, "Rajput women were well-read. They were participating in social life. They were good in Sanskrit. They read and wrote well. They knew the arts of music, painting and dancing. Daughters of Kings and Samantas were good learners of Horse riding also."

Avanti, wife of Raja Sekhara, an eminent poet, was good in *Tarka Sastra* (Logic) and she could defeat anybody in it. Indulekha, Marula, Sheela, Subhadra, Lakshmi, Vijjika, Morika, Padma Sri, Madalasa are worth-mentioning poetess among Rajput women. They were great scholars in Sanskrit.

Akka Mahadevi

She was the sister of Vikramaditya. She was not only a great soldier but also a great administrator. She worked as representative of administration for four states. She was bold enough to capture the fortess of Belgaum.

Widow remarriage was banned among Rajput women. So, they remained without remarrying for their entire life.

Polygamy was prevalent. Birth of a girl was not much appreciated. Generally woman was dependent on her husband or some nearest relative. Inter-caste marriages were totally prohibited. But in 861 AD, according to a Silasasana, Harischandra, a Brahmin married a girl by name "Bhadra" belonging to Kshatriya Caste. So also Bana describes that Parsava was born to a Brahmin and a Sudra woman by an inter-caste marriage. Thus the system of castes became very rigid by the time of these Rajputs.

Most of the people were living in ignorance. When the rich were enjoying all the pleasures of life, living in palaces, ordinary man was living on agriculture. Some were living as slaves or servants. Men and women were fond of wearing colourful dresses and costly jewelleries.

Literature and fine arts flourished under the patronage of Rajputs. Raja Sekhara wrote his *Karpoora Manjari* in Prakrit. Jaya Deve wrote *Geeta Govindam*, depicting the love of Krishna with *Gopikas*. Kalhana wrote *Raja Tarangini* during the time of Rajputs. Somadeva wrote *Katha Sarit Sagara*. Magha wrote *Sisupalavadha* and Bhatti wrote *Ravana Vadha*. Dandi wrote *Dasakumara Charita*. Bilhana wrote *Vikramanka Deva Charita*, Bhartruhari wrote a good commentary on *Mahabhashya of Patanjali*; Vignaneswara wrote on *Mitakshara Nyaya*. (There is an argument that this *Nyaya sutra* was written by a Hindu woman – Excerpts from the speech delivered by Gurudass Banerjee retired High Court judge, *Calcutta Jenana Patrika*, January 1967).

Stories about the beauty and sacrifice of Padmini in the Rajput Days are popular even today. She was the wife of Bheem Singh, Raja of Chittaud. Allauddin Khiljee invaded Chittaud and heard about her beauty. He arrested Bheem Singh and bargained that unless Padmini is handed to him, he will not be released. In the place of Padmini, 100 soldiers went in *palanquins* and fought. Allauddin went back to his country. But he invades a second time and capture Chittaud. Then all the Rajput women including Padmini commited 'Johar'.

Rani Samyukta

Rani Samyukta's story is also very popular. She was the daughter of Jayachand the last king of Rajputs. She wanted to marry Prithiviraj but her father did not like this idea because Prithviraj was his enemy. At the time of *Swayamvara*, she puts the garland in the neck of Prithviraj's idol on the entrance and Prithviraj takes her on the horse, standing ready near the gate.

Women in the Golden Age of Gupta Kings in India

Gupta's rule in India, is historically considered as the Golden Age. After the decline of Buddhism, Hinduism again made its mark. Pushyamitra is the first king belonging to the *Sunga* dynasty and he performed Aswamedha yagya. It is during his time that Patanjali wrote his *Mahabhashya*.

Agni Mitra was his son and he is the hero in *Malavikagni Mitra* of Kalidasa. Official royal language was *Sanskrit*, in those days.

Chandra Gupta I ruled his empire with Patna as the capital. It is during his time that Fa-hein, a Chineese traveller visited India (396-414-Kho-Kho-Ki record of the Buddhist Kingdoms) and wrote his famous book.

Chandra Gupta's son, Samudra Gupta, was a very efficient man. He was a musician, poet and ruled for nearly 50 years. He was endowed with extraordinary skill and tact. He performed *Aswamedhayagya* and distributed golden coins to all.

His son was Chandra Gupta II. He is also known as Vikramaditya, the renowned king of Ujjain.

Gupta's Literature

It is during this period that all arts flourished. It was Vikramaditya who encouraged poets and scholars and there was overall renaissance in the country. Temples were built and sculpture got its lift in an unprecedented manner.

It was during this time that Kalidasa wrote his world famous *Kavyas* – namely *Abhignana Sakuntalam, Raghuvamsam, Vikramorva Seeyam, Ritu Samharam, Malavikagni Mitram, Kumara Sambhavam, Meghasandesam.*

Bhasa wrote his *Pratima Natakam, Pratigna Yongandharayanam, Swapna Vasava Datta, Charu Datta, Goru Bhanga, Panchatantra.*

Sudraka wrote *Mrichchakatika*. Visakha Datta wrote *Mudra Rakshasa*, Bharavi wrote *Kiratarjuneeya* and Vishnu Sarma wrote *Panchatantra*. This Panchatantra got translated into English, German, Italian, Spanish, and Latin. There were more than 200 commentaries, in fifty languages on this great work.

Yagnavalakya, Narada, Katyayana, Brihaspati, all *Smrithikaras* wrote their *Dharma Sastras* in these days. Kamandaka wrote *Neeti-sara* and Vatsayana wrote his *Kamasutras* and also a commentary on justice, under the patronage of Gupta Kings.

Aryabhata wrote *Surya Siddhanta*, a great work depicting the eclipses of the Sun and the Moon. He is the first man who formulated the principle that "earth" moves round its own. Varaha Mihira wrote his *Brihat Samhita* and Brahma Gupta discovered about the centre of gravity even before Newton.

Conditions of Society

Varnasrama dharmas were respected and put into practice by everyone. Brahmins could win the respect of one and all. The four stages of man like Brahmacharya, Grihastha, Vanaprastha and Sanyasa were formulated and they were implemented by all, with discipline.

Agriculture, industries and business went on very well and educational institutions had their patronage, as per the available Silasasanas, muslin, Silk, Calico, Linen and woollen cloth were prepared during the Gupta's time, as per some descriptions of *Amarakosa*.

Women's Status

Before Guptas' period, there was a ban that women should not read religious texts, and should not take up *Vedadhyayna* [study of Vedas]. But during their period, it appears that women of high families had ample opportunities to read and write.

Vatsayana mentioned sixty-four arts and there were women who were experts in all of them. Scholarly exercises like *Samasya Puranam* (filling verses) and filling up the blanks were taken up by women, as per some historical evidences.

Literature produced in Gupta's period and also the historical evidences say that, in addition to the upper caste women, even the children of Ashramavasis (residents of Aramas) learnt ancient history and were experts in not only reciting *slokas* but in writing them also.

Women living in royal palaces were experts in dance and music. Rajyassi learnt such fine arts and Sakuntala wrote her love letter on a leaf. From the historical evidences available, it can be presumed that there were institutions to teach such fine arts, and women, in addition to men, learnt these arts and crafts. For example, Mahasweta and Kadambari were very good experts in dance and music.

Amarakosa, a treatise written in Gupta's time tells us about 'Upadhyayi'. From this, we can conclude that women could learn Vedas and there were women who worked as *Acharyas* (Professors) also.

Institution of Gandharva Marriages

On a critical study of literature produced during this period, it is evident that the type of Gandharva marriages were more prevalent. Kings and men belonging to higher communities, could respect this form of marriage. In *Malathi Madhavam*, a sanyasin by name Kamandaki gives a sermon like this, "Generally, fathers should decide the future of girls. But Sakuntala selected Dushyanta, Orvasi selected Pururava, so also Vasavadatta selected Udayana. There are all examples worth mentioning."

Institution of Marriage

The institution of marriage was respected by all, as enunciated in *Smrithis*. According to the writings of Huyan-Sang, it is evident that marriages were performed within the race and even within the *Jati*. Vatsayana says, "If marriage is performed with a pious, efficient Kanya, one can get, good *Santana*, good name and prajadarana" (people's appreciation). One should not marry a girl belonging to "a high caste" and a woman who was "already married", he prohibited.

So also, a man should not marry a girl belonging to a lower caste than himself.

He laid down a rule that either the parents or the guardians should decide marriages. He advised man "to select a girl who is good to his eye and to his heart". Out of *Brahma, Praja Patya, Arsha* or *Daiva* form of marriages, "receiving a decorated girl as *Kanyadaan* by *Brahma Paddhati* is better" he further says. Vatsayana also tells how one should select a girl to his liking and how he should bring her round to his way.

So also, Vatsayana says, "under what circumstances, a girl should select her husband by herself."

"For a girl it is better to select a man in "whom she has confidence, She would make her happy." "Even if he is poor, if she feels that he will be dedicated to her, she can select him" he says.

"Even if one is good and wealthy, if there are many wives whom he likes, such a man should not be selected" he further advises.

"A woman should never marry a person who is much older to her, a gambler or person having wife and children under any circumstances."

In the form of *Gandharva Vivaha*, if the girls likes him, her lover should walk three times around the fire brought from a pious family and then it becomes a legal marriage even if there are no eye-witnesses. Nobody can question or deny such marriage. But, the couple should inform their parents about the marriage.

In the form of "Paisacha" or "Rakshasa" marriages, Vatsayana says that there is no necessity of *Mantras* (recitation of slokas) or celestial fire; But, the relations and friends should be informed about such marriage. "Because once happened", it is over. So others should accept such marriage.

But he mentioned specifically that Gandharva form of marriage is respectable out of the three.

Stridhana

Stridhana was recognised in those days also. A women can do with it, in what manner she likes. She may gift it away to anybody.

Sati Sahagamana (Burning oneself on the celestial fire along with the dead body of husband) was also prevalent. But, it was not a common practice applicable to all. There was evidence of Goparaju's wife (a *Senanayaka* in the Raja *durbar*) committing *sati*.

Age of Marraige

Vishnu Purana, prescribes that the bridegroom should be three times older the bride. But Angirasa proposes to lower this age restriction. *Vatsayana*, depending on *Apastambha Grihyasutra*, says that marriage should be performed before the girl attains puberty. In another place, he says that man should marry a *Kanya*, who is younger by 3-4 years to him.

Writings of Huyan Sang

Huyan Sang was a Chinese traveller who visited India in the 7th century. He was a Buddhist monk, who studied in the university of Nalanda.

He wrote "out of the income of Harshavardhana, one fourth was spent on the maintenance of Nalanda University."

He says, "Indians of Harshavardhana's time take anything as wrong. They maintain a low profile than what is required. They believe that they have to suffer the curse of *papa* (sin) committed in the last *Janma* (birth) and so, they are afraid of sin. They do not know what a "sin" is. They keep up their word."

Huyan Sang, after witnessing the pomp and luxury of those times, says, "people lived with great prosperity. Gold and silver coins, pearls, shells were used by them." Because the lands were very fertile, there were enough crops. People were using in their food, "in addition to cereals, sugar, ghee, milk as main items." On some occasions, they were eating "fish and mutton" also.

Describing the city of Kanauj, he says "it was full of high walls, beautiful gardens, tanks and people were wearing nice silk clothes and they were much interested in literature and fine arts."

"There were people of four *varnas*. A person belonging to one Varna should not marry a person belonging to another *varna*. Such marriage was prohibited. There were several restrictions in the matter of taking food also among the different sects of *varnas*. But there was no restrictions to live together and the above restrictions never came in the way."

Widow marriages were not there. There was no *purdah* even among people of high castes. Huyan Sang mentions that Rajyasru, sister of Harshavardhana spoke to him without wearing a veil.

Sati was there. Rani Yasomathi committed sati, when here husband

Prabhakara Vardhana passed away. But Rajyasree was saved when she wanted to commit sati and she becomes a Boudha Sanyasin later on.

Women of high castes, were good experts in dance and music. Sanskrit was the medium of instructions. Generally age of nine years to thirty years was the stage of studentship. After completion of the stage, the students were entering the other Asrama namely the *Grihastha Asrama*, after bidding good by to their *gurus*.

But, there are no evidences to show whether women also could wait till 30 years before entering married life or were learning education as students till 30 years.

Huyan Sang says in his writings that there were people in India, who were students throughout their life. But we cannot definitely say that women, like in Vedic times, remained unmarried.

Harsha's *Priyadarsika* and *Nagaveli*, were full of sarcasm about the events in Law Courts, and about the theory of love. In *Naganandrin*, the greatness and generosity of Harsha was depicted.

So, in those days, it was art for sake of art. It never reached or depicted the common people. There are no clear evidences to show about the status of women.

But, it can be presumed that in a prosperous country, people lived happily, there was good administration, social obligations were agreeable to all and there was no discontent of any sort among people.

Gupta Period: Position of Women

From the epigraphic records of Guptas, we do not get much information regarding the position of women. But some information is available from contemporary literature.

The laws about women, under Guptas, show clearly that their status in society had been considerably raised. That may be due to the influence of Buddhism. For the first time in history, the right of inheritance was granted by Yagnavalkya in his *smrithi*. The same is the case of *Neoga*. The prerogative of a widow to get a son through her diseased husband's brother was recognised. Yagnavalkya seems to have recognised the necessity of the changed social conditions in the Gupta period. Though he does not actually recommend *Neoga*, he does not at least condemn it. A similar attitude was taken towards widow's remarriage also.

In the family of the Gupta Emperors, Chandra Gupta II,

married Dhruvadevi, the widow of his elder brother Ram Gupta. Yagnavalkya also suggests that a girl may select her husband after puberty. The plays of Kalidasa tell us that post-puberty marriages were not uncommon in the days of Guptas. Most of the heroines in the play were adults only.

In the age of Guptas, the custom of *sati*, seems to have been almost unknown to the common people. But stray instances were there among the aristocratic circles.

In a stone-pillar inscription of Iran dated 510 A.D., Goparaja, a Chieftain, had gone to the place in the company of Bhanu Gupta and fought a battle. He was killed and his wife, who had accompanied him burnt herself on his funeral pyre. In the contemporary literature, we come across such stray incidents.

In *Kumara Sambhava*, Rati desires to burn herself after the death of her husband Madana. In the *Mrichchakatika*, Dhuta, the wife of Charudatta, prepares herself to commit *sati*, in the belief that her husband is already executed. Bana did not approve of *sati*.

Of course, some information about the status of women is available from the sculptures and paintings of Gupta's period. The Ajanta paintings show women without veils and mixing freely with men in public life.

There are instances of the mother taking up the administration if necessary. During the minority of her son Pravarasena II, Prabhavati Gupta, the daughter of Chandra Gupta II, carried on the administration of the Vakataka kingdom.

We learn from coins that Kumaradevi, the Lichchavi princess, who was married to Chandra Gupta I, was a capable woman and she played an important role in the formation of Gupta Empire. The coins with the joint figures of Chandragupta and Kumaradevi, issued by the founder of the Gupta Empire bear testimony to the help and cooperation received by him from his wife.

Girls in royal families were given the necessary training to shoulder responsibilities, in times of necessity. Vedic education was denied to women. Vedic *mantras* were not recited at the time of rituals intended for them. They were considered ineligible for *upanayana*.

Of course, literary and cultural education was given to them. Some women were poets and some others wrote treatises. Women were trained in dance and music. Wife was supposed to honour her husband as a deity. When her husband was abroad, she had to lead an ascetic life. She had to give up all ornaments except the marks of marriage.

She could engage herself in religious rites and fasts. She had to look to the worship of the God in the household. She did spinning and weaving. She looked after agriculture and the cattle. She had to prepare budget and adjust expenditure, in accordance with their income.

The view of Katyayana appears to be that the wife should never live apart from her husband. She must serve him during life time and lead a life of chastity after his death. She must join her husband in religious duties. The husband had complete authority over her.

Rich men and rulers had many wives. A man could remarry if his first wife was stupid or barren or she repeatedly gave birth to daughters only.

A woman, who becomes pregnant through a man of other caste becomes impure till her delivery and she regains her purity after next menstrual period. Widows had to lead a simple and ascetic life. They wore no ornaments and used no ointments. They should not decorate their hair. According to Brihaspati, the widow had to burn herself on the funeral pyre of her husband. This was not the view of other *Smrithikaras*. Narada and Parasara permitted remarriage of widows. Her status was placed midway between a virgin and a harlot. She never enjoyed the social status of a married wife.

Courtesans had high respect in society. They were notorious for their greed and cunningness and famous for their beauty, wit and other accomplishments Girls were maintained as *Devadasis* in temples for the worship of Gods. They were kept at *Mahakaleswar* temple at Ujjain in the time of Kalidasa and at the temple of *Sun God* in a city east of Sind in the time of Hiun-Sang.

Sculptures and paintings of Gupta period show that women could move about freely in society and were not confined. Dr. R.C. Majumdar is of the view that the Gupta Empire rose and fell but left a deep impression upon posterity, by the standards it set in all the walks of life and culture. Its greatness was such that even after fifteen hundred years, the Gupta Age is regarded as the Golden or the Classical Age of India.

The important religions of that period were *Buddhism*, *Jainism*, *Vaishnavism* and *Saivism*. They changed the whole religious outlook of India. The Vedic Gods and the sacrificial form of worship went into the background and some of them were transformed beyond recognition. The religious movement moved forward from the abstract to the concrete in the form of images. The spirit of religion was generally ignored and undue emphasis was put on formal details. In the matter of religion and philosophy, an attitude of blind acceptance was created among the people.

Hinduism and Buddhism were more or less evenly balanced during the Gupta period and philosophical conflicts took place very frequently. There are some references to these religious debates here and there in the inscriptions. Among the followers of Puranic deities also, there was complete harmony. Families changed their principal deity of devotion, according to individual inclinations.

It was made possible by the imperial suzerainty of the Guptas, the sense of security and affluence engendered among people during this period and the strong creative life among them. The inscription of the Gupta period show that the people were staunch adherents to Hinduism and followed the religious practices both of orthodox Brahminism and also popular Hinduism. While they called themselves Padmabhagavathas, they themselves helped others to perform various Vedic sacrifices.

The Vedic religion was represented in its sacrifices. *Asvamedha* was revived by Samudra Gupta and Kumra Gupta I. The Poona copter inscription of Prabhavati Gupta described Samudra Gupta I, who set up a sacrificial pillar. Maharaja Vishnu Vardhana, erected Yupa after performing Pundarika sacrifice. This sacrifice was undertaken to obtain objectives *Sri Yagna – dharma – Sreya*.

The cult of Rama had not been popular in the Gupta period. The name of Rama does not appear in *Amarakosa* as a deity. His temples were also very rare during Gupta period. But Kalidasa refers to Rama as an incarnation of Vishnu and there is a temple dedicated to Rama in Ramtek near Nagpur.

Worship of Sakti

Sakti was worshipped under different names as *Bhagwati, Bhavani, Devi, Gauri, Katyayani* and *Parvati*. A minister of a local king named Viswavarma, constructed a temple, for the worship of the divine mothers (Matries) "a very terrible abode, full of *Dakinis* or Ghosts who make loud and tremendous shouts in joy and stir up the very oceans with the nighty winds rising from the performance of *tantrika* rites."

Along with images of Sapta Matrukas (seven mothers) the temple also has a image of *Sakti* or Mahishasura Mardini. The Bihar stone pillar inscription of Skandagupta refers to the construction of a group of temples dedicated to the divine mothers including Goddess Bhadarya, also named ad Bhadraryaka, who may be taken as Parvati.

Some of the Gupta coins show Goddess Durga as *Simhavahana*, seated on a lion. The coins of Samudra Gupta introduce Goddess Durga as *Simhavahna*, Goddess Ganga as *Makara Vahana* and Goddess Saraswati as Goddess of music, having a *veena;* several other goddesses are also mentioned in the inscription such as Devaki, Janati, Jambavati, Lakshmi, Vaishnavi, Saraswati, Sachi and Paulami.

Worship in public places like temples became fairly common during the Gupta period. Temples became centres of Hindu religion and culture. Their construction and decoration encouraged sculptors, architects and painters. Their service in public worship required the musician and the dancer. That way, temples were contributing to the cause of culture in the name of religion.

Temple authorities spent most of their income on relief to the poor. They started free feeding houses. The ritual of worship was almost similar to what is today. *Puranas* were composed and revised during the Gupta period. Public recital of these *Puranas* in temples became a regular feature of Hindu religion. *Puranas* helped in popularising Hinduism by simplifying its message and carrying it to even to the lowest strata of society. Hinduism was thus simplified the ancient religious practices. A large number of *vratas* and fasts were mentioned in the *Puranas*. The difficult path of *Sruthies* was replaced by popular and easily accessible path of the *smrithis*.

The practice of giving *dana* (gifts) became popular. A large number of inscriptions of Gupta Period record the grants of land and of entire villages to Brahmanas. The establishment of free boarding houses also was common. These charities were freely endowed not only by the Kings but also by the common people. There are references to pilgrimages to holy places in the Gupta inscriptions and contemporary literature. The sacredness of the Ganges was recognised.

We learn from the inscriptions of Gupta Period that the Kings were imbued with the true spirit of Hinduism, which implies tolerance for other religions. This aspect is clear when we see their attitude towards Buddhism and Jainism. Hinduism assumed a positive and assertive role and movements of Hinduisation of foreign tribes and the spread of Hinduism in foreign lands were actively promoted in the Gupta Period. A significant advance was made in every aspect of philosophical speculation.

The general view that Buddhism was on the decline during the Guptas is not correct. The Gupta Age was the Golden Age for Buddhist Art also. Saranath, Paharpur, Ajanta, Nagarjankonda, Kapilavastu, Ramagrama, Sravasti, and Vaisali were places connected with the life of Buddha, when Fahien visited them. It is very clear that Kashmir, Afghanistan and Punjab were under stronghold of Buddhism during the Gupta period. Fahien saw thousands of monasteries and monks in those areas. In the upper Gangetic plain, Hinduism and Buddhism were equally popular and the same was the case in Bihar and Bengal.

Buddhist men were admitted into the Buddhist faith in the early Buddhist period. There was a nunnery in Junnar in Western India. The practice of admitting nuns into the *Sangha* was getting unpopular.

The caves of Ajanta and Ellora show that they were centres of Buddhism. Andhra country was studded with Buddhist *stupas* and *viharas*.

Dress and Ornaments

Dress consisting of an upper garment and a lower *dhoti*, neither of which required stitching were the dress of majority of the males. The Scythians have introduced coats, overcoats and trousers and they were worn by Indian kings. Gupta Emperors hunted lions and tigers with dhotis and sashes. Head dress was worn on auspicious occasions. Shoes were not common. Most of the people walked barefooted.

Women in Gupta Period wore a petticoat below and a saree over it. A bodice was used below the sari to cover the breast. Its two ends were tied. Jackets, blouses and frocks were used by Scythian women. Cotton garments were used for daily purpose. The fashion of dressing the hair was also common. Women as also men were fond of ornaments.

Rule of Pandyas

The capital of Pandyas was Madurai, the abode of deity Meenakshi; it is living monument, a great symbol of Pandya's greatness.

Marcopolo, a citizen of Venice, visited India during Pandya's time and wrote his experiences.

He says that "in a part North of India, they prepared such fine muslin cloth like 'the threads of weaver's web.' He also tells about the rule of a Telugu queen by name Rani Rudrama. She was the queen of Kakatiyas, ruling Warangal as their capital. The great Ramappa temple and the thousand pillared temple of Warangal, are symbols of the greatness of Kakatiyas.

She was the only daughter of Ganapati Deva; "she was an expert in all arts and crafts. She could take over administration of Kakatiya empire and could rule for forty years very efficiently" says Marcopolo, praising her to a great extent.

Nritta Ratnavali, is a great work on dance by Jayappa, an employee of her.

Kakatiyas were *Saivites* (Hindus) but also showed patronage towards Buddhism.

The great "Kakatiya Dwaram" is popular sculpture of Kakatiyas, and the famous women 'images' of Ramappa temple are great pieces of art and sculpture.

Megasthanees, who travelled to India in the 4th century, says sarcastically that "women were ruling this empire."

Satavahana Rule

The Nanaghat inscription mentions the statues of Simukha, Krishna and Satakarni and of queen Naganika. It seems that the Satavahana conquest of the Maratha country was consolidated by Satakarni's marriage with Naganika, a Maratha lady. He is said to have performed two horse-sacrifices indicative of his imperial position. Paithan (Aurangabad, district – Nizam State) on the Godavari was his capital.

Gautami putra Satakarni was the greatest of the Satavahanas and his splendid achievement is enshrined in the Nasik Prasasthi of his mother, Gauthami Balasri, published in the 19th regional year (AD 149) of her grandson, Puramayi. She refers to herself "as the mother of a Maharaja and grandmother of a Maharaja" and describes Gautamiputra as the "destroyer of Sakas, Yavanas and Pahlavas, the restorer of the glory of Satavahana family, the elevator of his family to high fortune, the unique Brahmana who crushed the pride and concept of the Kshatriyas."

Satavahanas (30 of them) ruled for 460 years "for the entire southern India." Their rule was between 234 to 250 BC.

It is not clear where from they came. But it is evident from the Puranic stories that Simukha, their first king came to power after killing Susarma, a Raja of Kanvas. He ruled for 23 years. He constructed several chaityas and Jain temples.

Their rule is historically and culturally a landmark. They were Brahmins. But they respected all others of different castes. It is during their time that cave temples were built in Nasik, Kanheri, Karle and Ajanta.

Satavahana king 'Hala' was a great patron of literature. A Pandya Kavya by name *Gadha Sapta Sathi*, written in Prakrit language was his creation.

Capital of Satavahanas was Srikakulam, on the banks of Krishna river, in Krishna district. It was during these days that they built the Boudha Arama at Amaravathi. They constructed pillars at Bhattiprolu, Ghantasala and Gummadidurru also.

Gauthami *putra* Satakarni is known by his mother. It is not known who his father was. He administered justice as per *Dharma Sastras*. There was polygamy in those days. But, there is no evidence to show, that there were disputes, about division of property or for inheritance.

Vidyadhar Mahajan in his *From Hand to Mouth,* (p. 241), says that Satavahanas being rulers "never travelled in golden palanquins. They never wore jewellery studded with diamonds and pearls. They never led a luxurious life exhibiting their wealth and grandeur. They led a simple common life." They never believed that the rulers were God sent. The king was himself the *Senadhipathi* and he led the army during war.

Satakarni's wife was Naganika. She was very generous and offered many gifts. Another interesting aspect of the rule of Satavahanas is, Sanas, Yavanas, Pahlavas and Akharas – all foreigners – accepted Buddhism are settled in India.

Dr. B.R. Ambedkar, telling about Satavahanas tells "that there is mention of them in Aitareya Brahmana. Andhras are belonging to Viswamitra and they lived before 500 BC. Dr. Smith also agrees with this argument that Andhras ruled for 460 years as narrated in the Puranas".

"Small waists, good bodily built-up, beautiful clothes hanging loose and playing on delicate instruments of music, very attractively and with aesthetic sense, several idols of women were found." B.C. Sen says that they belong to Satavahana period. The credit of constructing the world famous *Arama* of Amaravati also goes to Satavahanas. The grandeur of Ajanta caves goes to them. Buddha's statue in the 10th cave is very attractive. Buddha sits on a carpet dressed in saffron nobes and some *Bhikshus* and a *Grihasthu* stand by him. Buddha of Amravati caves is 'Bhagwan' receiving worship.

Pulamavi IV was the last king of Satavahanas and with him, their dynasty disappeared.

King Asoka

Asoka was a great king not only in the history of India but also of the whole world. He took up the title of "Devarampriya" or beloved of the Gods. The name Asoka is found in literature and also in the Maski Edict of Asoka and the Junagadh inscription of Rudraman I. The name Dharmasoka is found in the Sarnath inscription of Kumara Devi.

Asoka had been compared to many great men of the world by many writers. He had been compared to the Roman Emperor, Constantine, The Great.

From the Buddhist writings, it is evident that an emperor called Asoka ruled "Vidisa" as capital and got married to one "Devi" and he had a son by name Mahendra and a daughter called Sanghamitra.

Kalinga war was a great event and a turning point in the life of Asoka. He was greatly moved after seeing the bloodshed. There was none like him, either before or after, in the history of India, who got moved like this. Instead of feeling proud about his victory, he changed his heart and decided not to resort to such violence or warfare.

His rock edicts and pillars are nearly 30 in number, available here and there in his vast empire. His empire was spread from Shahabajgarh to Sourastra and upto Mysore in the South. His original name is found only on one pillar and all the rest carry 'Devanampriya', (Beloved of the Gods).

Queens of Ashoka

Tishya Rakshita

Even today, when you go to Taxila, as a travellor, they will show you a pillar of seventh century and tell a story about "Kunala", a prince and son of Asoka.

Asoka marries a woman called Tishya Rakshita after the death of Asandhi Mitra in his old age. But she develops love for Kunala, her step son. But Kunala never responds, treating her as a mother perhaps. Her love turns out to be prejudice. She orders that Kunala should be sent to Taxila. Respecting the word of his father, Kunala goes to Taxila. When Asoka was sleeping, Tishya Rakshita, using the stamps of Asoka had issued orders to send Kunala to Taxila and take out the eyes of Kunala, taking him into mountains. The orders were carried out. Blind Kunala, comes to Pataliputra with hunger. Moved by the injustice done to Kunala, Asoka, orders that Tishya Rakshita should be burnt alive.

But with the grace of "Gosha", a Buddhist Monk of Mahabodhi, Kunala gets back his eyesight.

Vedisa Devi

She was the first wife of Asoka. She was the mother of Sangamitra and a disciple of Buddha. But the credit of making Asoka a Buddhist, does not go to her. Another woman Asandhi Mitra was very near and dear to Asoka. She could convert Asoka. She was issueless. She joined the cadre of Buddha as a *Sanyasin*.

Padmavathi

Padmavathi was the mother of Kunala. A pillar in Allahabad mentions that she was the second wife of Asoka. She gifted many on occasion to the Buddha *Sanghas*.

Karnbakee

She is from a very high family and was very good looking. She was the first woman in Kalinga Deva to become a Buddhist from a great origin. When Asoka wanted to marry her, she says that if Asoka takes to Buddhism, she would marry him. Asoka agrees to her condition and marries her. There is a story that Asoka killed her first husband to marry her. But there's no evidence to show how far this story is correct. But, it is a fact that Asoka married her.

Culture and Civilization During the Mauryan Age

The basis of the Mauryan social organisation was 'varna', the four traditional *varnas* might have generated some tensions. The Vedic way of life is extolled and the Vedic sacraments like *Chauta Karma, Upanayana, Godana* and the like are prescribed for the prince also. These tendencies say that there was continuation of the traditional society. Kautilya refers to the traditional four castes, while Megasthenes refers to seven classes like, philosophers, farmers, soldiers, hardsmen, artisans, magistrates and councillors evidently confusing the caste with their occupation.

Mixed Castes

In addition to four castes, Kautilya refers to 15 mixed came into being as castes by the general name *Antya Vasayin* (living at the end) that came into being as a the result of mixed marriages. They were required to live outside the main settlement, near the cremation ground.

Joint family system was a feature of the Mauryan society. Emphasis was laid on conjugal fidelity. "The wives prostitute themselves, unless they are compelled to be chaste". Again "A woman who kills the king when drunk, becomes the wife of his successor."

Marriage between the members of the same caste were preferred though inter-marriage between different castes was prevalent."

Rules about remarriage in the *Ardhasastra*, follow the rules laid down in the Dharmasastras. Kautilya is liberal towards women in the matters of marriage, contract and divorce.

He said "a woman can remarry, if her husband was abroad for a long time, if he suffered from any incurable disease, or was sterile, if he had become an outcaste, if he was of bad character, or was guilty of high treason or was dangerous to her life."

So also, a husband could divorce his wife, on account of her infidelity or if she fails to give birth to a son.

Divorce on the ground of ill feeling was also possible by mutual consent, but not at the will of one party alone. Thus Kautilya places husband and wife on an equal footing.

Status of Women

Women were well-educated. They were allowed to participate in social and religious function. They were employed as spies and bodyguards. However, there privileges were restricted to only upper strata of society.

In general, many restrictions were imposed on the liberty of women. They were not allowed to move freely. The system of *Sati* was practised at a few places in north-west India. But, it was considered to be a general practice.

Monogamy was the general rule but men belonging to rich and ruling classes had many wives. Among Hindus, the murder of a woman was regarded as equal to the murder of a Brahmin.

Buddhism offered a better status to women. So a large number of women became nuns. *Ganikas* or courtesans enjoyed a good social standing. They were appointed as spies by the state. They carried a license by paying two days' earning every month to the state.

We come to know from the *Ardhasastra*, that a prostitute known for her beauty, youth, and accomplishment was appointed as superintendent on a salary of 1,000 panas.

Dress

Both men and women put on good clothes. While the common people used cotton garments, the rich wore garments of silk, linen, decorated with embroidery, precious stones and even jewels. Woollen clothes were also used during the winter season. Both men and women used all sorts of ornaments and cosmetics to beautify themselves.

The sources of entertainment of the people included bouts between men and animals, chariot races, chess, gambling, drama, music and dance. Social and religious festivals also provided occasions for merriment.

Slavery: Whether there existed slavery or not is controversial. Megasthenes tells us there were no slaves in India, but the Arthasastra of Kautilya contains detailed laws about slavery.

Slaves were mostly *Sudras* and they supplied the bulk of labourers. In special circumstances, the members of higher *varnas* also could be mortgaged. Kautilya refers to them as "Ahitakas". He laid down certain rules to regulate the treatment of slaves. They were not outcastes and were employed in households. Forcible production from slaves was non-existent. They could buy their freedom and become honourable members of society. A slave girl bearing a son to her master automatically became free. In his edicts, Asoka exhorted people to be "humane" and "considerate" to their slaves. Slaves were employed in agriculture for clearing goods, tilling fields, sowing, harvesting, tending cattle etc. They worked in royal estates as well as private firms. Slave labours were also employed inmonastery lands. The wide use of slave labour for house-keeping was a typical feature of ancient Indian slave ownership. They were sent out to work for money sometimes.

Post-Gupta Period

In the post-Gupta period, the caste system prevailed, in which the Brahmans occupied the highest position in society. They had some special privileges over others. The punishments awarded to them were very light when compared with others.

Medatidhi (825-900 AD) forbids not only corporal punishment but even a money fine to be inflicted upon a guilty Brahmin.

Brahmanas were granted villages free from taxes. All the taxes which the king previously collected were now transferred to Brahmanas. They also got the right to govern the people living in the donated villages. The officials of the king and royal retainers were not allowed to enter the gifted villages. Brahmins not only collected taxes from the peasants and artisans but also maintained law and order in the villages granted to them. Villages were granted to Brahmanas for ever and that undermined the position of the king.

The Brahmanas laid great stress on the purity of blood and made the rules regarding the marriages, food and choice of professions, more rigid than before. Many Brahmanas became warriors and adopted the profession of Kshatriyas. Some adopted trade and became Vaisyas. Many foreigners such as the *Hunas* and indigenous tribes such as the *Gonds* were regarded as Kshatriyas. In the Vaisya caste were included many Kshatriyas, who had adopted the profession of traders. There was a serious crises in the social order. The society based on the activities of the peasants who were called Vaisyas and labourers who were called Sudras took shape. The taxes collected by the royal officers enabled the kings to pay salaries to their officials.

From the seventh century onwards, a large number of new castes came into existence, rather created. Thousands of mixed castes were created on account of the connection of women with men of lower castes. The Sudras and the untouchables were divided into countless sub-castes.

Many tribal people were admitted into Hindu society on account of the land grants granted to them. Most of those people were enrolled as Sudras and mixed castes. Every tribe was given the status of a separate caste in Hindu society.

During this period, the institution of slavery existed. Vignaneswara refers to 15 kinds of slaves. Female slaves helped their mistresses in the household work. Some of them were used by their masters in sex matters also.

The feudal lords were very often at war with their neighbours and the persons taken as prisoners were used as slaves. The Muslim invasions also resulted in more prisoners, who were made slaves. During famines, many persons sold themselves as slaves.

As a general rule, girls were arranged in marriage by their guardian but love marriages were also known. The *Gandharva* form of marriage was censured by the Medhatidhi. A woman was allowed to take a second husband in the event of five calamities (1) when her husband was lost or unheard of, or (2) was dead or (3) had adopted the life of a recluse, or (4) was impotent or (5) had become an outcaste.

There was great emphasis on the purity of sexual life. Heavy punishments were inflicted on those who were found guilty of the offence of adultery. In some cases, both the man and woman were put to death. In other cases, lesser punishments were inflicted.

Married women were required to be devoted to their husbands; and also obey them. They were required to serve them. This was so if the husband followed the righteous path. It was the duty of the husband to maintain her under all circumstances. The faithful wife was not to be abandoned even if she was not good looking or harsh in her speech etc.

The widow was required to live in strict celibacy and self-restraint.

The rite of *Sati* enjoined by some authorities but condemned by others. However the wives of kings sometimes burnt themselves on the funeral pyre of their husbands but it was for them to exercise their option in the matter.

The custom of dedicating maidens for service in the temples (*Devdasi*) was prevalent. The class of prostitutes known as *Ganikas* existed as a distinct social unit during this period. A *Ganika* was expected to have high qualifications both of body and mind.

People had a high standard of living. This is proved by a number of professions mentioned by Medhatidhi.

The variety of garments and ornaments current in those times were remarkable. There are references to woollen blankets, petticoats, armlets, neck ornaments, finger rings, waist-bands, and women leg ornaments. Woman's golden as well as jewelled girdles and large ear ornaments are mentioned by Rajasekhara. Ladies of high families were habitually delighted in display of ornaments. There is a reference to a woman adorned with ear-rings, rows of bracelets, a ruby-encrusted girdle and emarald anklets. The same lady at night time appeared in a robe of Chinese silk, with a pearl necklace around her neck, camphor powder on her bosom and sandal paste thickly applied to her limbs and she looked like a goddess descended from the moon.

As regards popular amusements, it was the fashion for high born girl, to play with balls. On the occasion of swing festival, they enjoyed the swing from trees in a garden.

There are references to dancing for recreation by ladies and dramatic representations in honour of deities. Reference is made to the Goshto of persons in high life of a queen and other women. There are referneces of young pleasure-seekers with their mistresses, excursions to gardens, excursions for drinking and water sports.

REFERENCES

1. Agarwal, V.S : *Gupta Art* 1947.
2. S.K.Ayyangar : *Ancient India.*
3. A.S. Altekar – *Position of Women in Hindu Civilization*, Benares 1938.
4. J.N. Banerjee : *Development of Hindu Iconography.*
5. Jha, D.N. : *Ancient India – An introductory Outline,* New Delhi, 1983.
6. R.N. Dandekar : *Some Aspects of the History of Hinduism,* 1967.
7. A.K. Kumaraswamy : *History of Indian and Indonesian Art.*
8. R.D. Banerjee : *The Age of the Imperial Guptas.*
9. V.R.R. Dikshitar : *The Gupta Polity*, 1952.
10. Thapar, Romila : *A History of India,* Vol. I. 1963.
11. Yazdani G. : *Ajanta.*
12. Yagnavalkya Smrithi : Bombay 1918.
13. H.C. Roy Choudhuri : *Political History of Ancient India.*
14. Majumdar A.K. : *Concise History of Ancient India,* Vol. I, New Delhi.

15. R.C. Majumdar : *The Classical Age*, Vol. I, Bombay, 1970.
16. Mookerji, R.K. : *The Gupta Empire*, 5th edition, 1973.
17. Mookerji, R.K. : *Ancient India.*
18. B. Upadhaya : *India in Kalidasa.* 1968.
19. Winternitz M. : *History of Indian Literature,* Vol.I, Calcutta, 1933.
20. Smith V.A. : *History of Fine Art in Indian and Ceylon.*
21. A.S. Altekar : *State and Government in Ancient India*, Delhi, 1977.
22. N.C. Bandopadhyay : *Kaultilya*, Calcutta, 1927.
23. D.R. Bhandarkar : *Some Aspects of Ancient Indian Policy.*
24. K.P. Jaiswal : *Hindu Polity*, Benaras, 1929; Calcutta, 1924.
25. Thapar R. : *Asoka and the Decline of Mauryas*, Delhi, 1983.
26. B.M. Barma : *Inscriptions of Asoka*, Calcutta, 1934 .
27. S. Bhattacharya : *Selected Asokan Epigraphs.*
28. R.C. Majumdar : *The Age of Imperial Unity.*
29. R.K. Mukherjee : *Asoka.*
30. H.C. Raychoudhuri : *Political History of Ancient India.*
31. K.A. Nilakanta Sastri : *A Comprehensive History of India.*
32. V.A. Smith : *Early History of India.*
33. R.Thapar : *Asoka and the Decline of the Mauryas.*
34. H.S. Bhatia : *Political Legal and Military History of India* Vol. I and II Edited by H.S. Bhatia.
35. A.K. Majumdar : *Early Hindu India: A Dynasty Study.*

CHAPTER 7

Woman and Buddhism

Buddhism came into existence, in 6th century A.D. at a time when caste system became very rigid and certain religious norms became very complicated. Only certain castes had the right to perform *Yagnas* and *homas* and birth in a particular community was considered to be a privilege and a birth right and all the rest of the communities were debarred from performing such religious acts.

Especially, *Sudras* and women were considered to be unfit for *Moksha* and there was so much of discontent among some lower castes. Then what was the path of salvation for such people? In fact it was this that caught the imagination of Buddha and he tried to evolve a code of conduct, for attaining *moksha*.

Siddardha, by himself being the son of a Maharaja had ample opportunities of leading a highly luxurious life. But, after seeing the misery and discontent of some, he left the palace, his riches, his beloved wife and his son and went out into the wide world, in search of a path for salvation.

Finally, he enunciated four principles of religious conduct. In the language of Buddhists, they call them 'Bhavanas'. They are:–

(1) *Sarvam Dukham Dukham*
(2) *Sarvam Kshanikam Kshanikam.*
(3) *Sarvam Swalakshanam Swalakshanam*; and
(4) *Sarvam Sunyam Sunyam*

He also preached three ways for *Nirvana*:

(1) *Parisuddha Alochana*
(2) *Parisuddha Vakku*
(3) *Parisuddha Acharanam*

Buddha felt that all souls cannot be of the same order. While some are nearer to *Niravana*, some are far away. Therefore, a single path or code of conduct will not be applicable for one and all. That is why, some, those who are on the low edge, should have married life.

Buddha, of course, preaches that worldly pleasures should be discarded but nowhere has he said that *Sanyasa* is the only way of *Saranya* for all.

He spoke on several occasions on family life, especially on the duties of women in several contexts. All these ideas are recorded and kept safe even till today.

In *Angadattara Nikaya*, a famous Buddhist text, Buddha addressed girls of marriageable age as follows:

(1) If parents get a girl married to a person, they do so wishing for the welfare of the girl.

(2) A *Gribini* should get up early, before all others get up and should go to bed after every one in the house slept.

(3) Women should learn to speak pleasantly and with affection. In the Kingdom of the house, there will be servants, workers, guests etc., *Gribini* should keep watch over smooth functioning of all of them. She must supervise why a person is not able to do his work properly and what are the reasons for his negligence. She must take care of their food arrangements. She must pay special attention to the sick and the infirm or the weak.

She must take care of the wealth and the corn brought by her husband and store them properly. She must respect all those whom her husband respects. May be his father, mother or *Sanyasi*, she must give them proper status and respect them. One, who can possess, all the above good qualities will attain *moksha* or *Sidhi* after death, says Buddha. In a nutshell, he made a women, guardian of all in the house.

In the same text, in another context, Buddha says that "Buddhist *Sanyasis*, should respect their parents because mother and father give birth and sacrifice their happiness for the sake of the children. So, a house, where there is respect for the parents, is equivalent to *Brahmaloka* he preaches.

In another text entitled 'Ayilayadhyarna Sutram', Buddha says, 'more respect should be given to the mother rather than to father." One Ajatasatru wants to kill his father and makes him starve. Orders his people not to serve him with any food. But, his mother, who goes to see her husband applies honey every day to her body which the father licks and lives. Ajatasatru comes to know of this at a later stage and gets angry. But, his advisers and council of Ministers tell him that "some thousands of people have killed their fathers. But there was no son who killed his mother." There is an interesting story that Ajatasatru gave up the idea of killing his father finally.

In the same text, Buddha says "If a son cannot give protection to his parents in their old age, he will have the same pitiable status, in his old age also." Buddha's preaching for housewives are many.

For an ideal wife, "obedience, respect for elders, efficiency, love for peace are like jewels." Like this, in several contexts, Buddha spoke of women. But, nowhere, he talked of the word 'Pativratya'.

It appears that during Buddha's time, there were several disputes. There are instances, where the daughters-in-law sought admission into Buddha *Sangha* unable to bear the sufferings by the mothers-in-law. So also, there were several instances, where, mothers-in-law, left houses wearing robes of *Sanyasa*, unable to bear the indifferent attitude of the daughters-in-law.

There is a wonderful story in 'Dharma Patha'. Four daughters-in-law neck out their father-in-law. They throw out their mother-in-law in a tank where there were mossallu. Buddha tells a son, who does not want to have such a wife who cannot have respect for his parents should never marry. Buddha interferes in family disputes and suggests solutions. One day Buddha goes to *Anarta pindake*, a friend, asking for alms. A big quarrel is going on in the house. Loud cries are there. Annadatha comes out of the house and tells Buddha that his daughter-in-law, Sujatha was responsible for all the trouble. Sujatha is the daughter of a famous businessmen and so, she looks down upon the people belonging to her husband, out of her pride. She refuses even to accost Buddha. Buddha calls her to come out and questions her "There are seven kinds of wives. Do you know who they are?"

Sujatha tells she does not know. Buddha further questions "one is a murderer, one is a thief, one is a mother, one is a sister, one is a friend, one is a servant. Out of them, what are you!"

Sujatha tells "I cannot understand the meaning of your words, tell me in detail." The Buddha tells about the good qualities of a woman, a *Grihini*.

Sujatha's heart melts! She folds her arms and bows down to Buddha and promises him to be a good servant and a good '*grihini*' thereafter.

By the above stories, it is clear that Buddha made the women, the guardian of the family in a way and also made her to lead a life of dedication and as an amicable woman, not only to her husband but to one and all in the family-fold.

He gave recognition to the fallen women also. From the story of Ambapali, Buddha's ideas on prostitution are evident. At the age of 80, Buddha comes to the city of Vaisali. Ambapali was a famous prostitute of that city and she invites Buddha to her house. Buddha accepts. This news spreads throughout the city like wild fire. The rulers come to him and try to convince him that Ambapali has no place of honour, to give him Atidhya. Buddha never accepts their plea. They finally try to prevail upon Ambapali, not to take the risk of inviting Buddha. But, she does not yield to their arguments. Finally, Buddha goes to her house and accepts her donation, a mango grove. Buddha never mentions about her profession. During their dialogue, Ambapali also never mentions that she is committing a sin.

But, Buddha deprecates the profession of prostitution. "Abhor the sin, not the sinner" may be his policy. As per *Karma siddhanta,* to attain perfection, man has to take several births. Buddha himself had 500 births. "Before putting a foot foreword, take care to see that it is a proper step" was his main preaching. If not in this birth, you may attain 'Atma Suddhi' in your next birth – was his preaching.

Ambapali, surprisingly gives up her profession and becomes a Sanyasini, under the influence of Lord Buddha. Nobody criticised her or blamed her.

In *Jataka* stories also, there are several descriptions of prostitutes and they had patronage of the rulers and the nobles of those times.

Buddhist Cannons of Literature: *Theri Gadhas*

We have seen in an earlier chapter that women, during Vedic period, made several writings and they were known to be very popular. So also, some women, who took to Buddhism, wrote some interesting episodes and they are known as 'Theri gadhas'. Most of them are full of descriptions as to how they took to Buddhism and why they developed aversion for worldly pleasures. Nearly seventy three *sanyasins* wrote these gadhas.

Some of them are drawn from palaces; some were from huts and some were from the class of courtesans. Their writings are full of 'depth of knowledge', 'sense of dedication' and 'real longing of *Nirvana*'. Apart from all these, there are the hidden feelings of a tormented soul.

The longest story written by 'Sumedha' is very popular. She was the daughter of Kronche Desa's ruler. Right from her childhood, she developed longing for a pious life. The King of Varana, named Anikanta, wanted to marry her. But she refused the offer and with the permission of her parents, became a *Sanyasini* and led the life of a Buddhist nun."

The story of 'Ishidasi' is also an interesting one. She was the only daughter of a rich businessman belonging to the city of Ujjain. So, she was brought up with so much love and affection by her parents. She was married and sent to Suketapura to live with her husband's family. She describes the life she spent there in detail. Ishidasti wrote that she woke up early in the morning and rendered service to her in-laws, cousins and father-in-law and mother-in-law; cooked food with her own hands, and fed them; but in spite of all this, she was not liked by her husband. His parents tried to convince him that she is faultless and is a cultured woman. But, her husband could not even tolerate her presence in the house. "If the parents insisted" about her staying in their house, he told them that 'he would leave the house'. Under those circumstances she came back to her parent's house.

After some time, her parents gave her in marriage to another youngman. After living together for some time, he also developed aversion for her. So, again Ishidasi came back to her parent's house. Because money played a major role in breaking both the marriages her father gave her in marriage, a third time, to a common man walking in the street and after a fortnight, he also left Ishidasi and also the riches, and walked away. So, finally, Ishidasi, out of disgust became a *Sanyasin* and her parents also permitted her to do so.

Another story is that of 'Utpalavara'. She was beautiful and intelligent. She was the daughter of a rich man. After puberty, she was married to another rich man. She gave birth to a girl child. Suddenly, her husband left the house and went away. She came back to her parents' house and live with them. After some time, her daughter was married to her husband; surprisingly when she came to know that her daughter became a wife to her husband, she got disgusted and became a *Sanyasini*.

The story of 'Buddha Kundalal Kesi' is still more pathetic. Like Ishidasi, she was the daughter of a rich man. She loved 'Sardhaka', son of their family priest. Sardhaka commited theft and was caught. The crime was proved. He was sentenced to death. At that time, she told her father about her love for him and after paying some big amount, she got him freed. She later on marries him and tries to reform him. But, she came to know that it is highly impossible. One day Sardhake took her to a hill on the pretext of worshipping God, but after taking her to a secluded point he tried to murder her. She entreats him to leave her safe, after taking "all the jewellery". But he argues that if she is alive, she would speak out about his crime and would see that he is sentenced. Then she begins to hate him. Pretending extraordinary love towards him, she takes him to the topmost point of the hill and throws him down. Removing all her jewellery, out of sheer disgust towards life, she joins the Buddha *Sangha*.

Apart from these people, several other rich women joined Buddhistic order. The daughter of Emperor Ashoka becomes a sanyasin; 'Sanghanodhra' the sister of Harshavardhan becomes the first ambassador in the world history; goes to Srilanka and propagates Buddhism and dies there only.

Courtisans like Ambapali, Padmavati of Ujjain, Ardhakari of Benares also depicted how they could attain mental peace in the presence of Buddha.

Each and every 'Theri Gadha' is thus very interesting and thought-provoking.

Buddhist era in Indian history is a 'Mahayanga'. Buddha invented and propagated a new idea and philosophy of life. So, scholars, ordinary men, rich and low, women and men adopted '*Buddha Dharma*', without any distinction of caste or creed. So, all had place in 'Buddha *Sangha*'.

Inspired by his new ideology, several women left their houses and joined these '*Bhikshuni Sanghas*'. This sort of formation of 'Sanghas' was first of its kind in the world history. These Bhikhunis roamed about as *Sanyasin* and preached Buddhism.

Yasodhara was the first woman among them. Thathagata left her when she was asleep. Knowing about his exit, she never regrets. She also discards luxurious life.

After Siddhardha becomes Buddha and comes to Kapilavastu as a traveller on foot, Yasodhara sends her son 'Rahul' to see him. She herself sees him as a Sanyasin.

Gautami is the youngest sister of Mayadevi, the mother of Siddhardha. She leads a *Sangha* of 500 women. She requests Buddha for the first time to form a *Bhikhshuni Sangha* but he does not accept. She requests Ananda a second time walking all the way to Kapilavastu, then Ananda convinces Buddha to form a *Sangha* for women. From then onwards, a separate *Sangha* for women was formed. Kisa Gantami is another women, who joined Bhikshuni Sangha, after suffering from her mother-in-law.

Supriya was the daughter of 'Anadhapindaka' a rich man of Sravasthi. Her intelligence was far excellent and she had knowledge of her previous *janma* in childhood. At the time of famine in Sravasthi, Supriya moved from house to house and collected alms after begging. Sanghamitra's work in Ceylon is still alive even after some thousands of years and she carried the message of love and peace to women of distant Indians say that she is the daughter of Ashoka lands. But foreigners say that she is his sister.

'Soma' attained higher status out of her wisdom and crudotion and she was made a *Sanyasin* by Buddha himself. She was the daughter of a man, who was close to Bimtisara. 'Anupama' cut her beautiful hair; gave-up lovely life; toed all the four corners of the country and preached Buddhism. 'Sujatha' was the wife of a rich man. She leaves luxurious life and joins Bhikhshuni Sangha. 'Chapa' herself becomes a Sanyasin and makes her husband also a Sanyasi. 'Patachara' lost her child and so, overwhelmed by grief, she became a Sanyasin. 'W. Sakha' was the head of Bhikhshuni sangha in Vaisali. Like these several women left family life and joined Buddhistic 'Sangha'. Buddha himself praises thirteen of them as outstanding. 'Dhamma dinna' is the topmost among them. She could answer several questions as though she cut the flowers. Her wealth of knowledge was her real wealth. She attained knowledge out of meditation and principled life.

Women Mentioned in Jain Texts

There is a story that there were 3,600 women, at the time of Mahaveera, who discarded family life and adopted Jainism as a way of life. Mahaveera's paternal aunt was the President of this *Parivrajaka sangha*. Upper strata women like Payabai were members of this 'Sangha'. Very well to do, who joined this order, were commanding much respect and had their high place in society.

'Marudevi' was the mother of Rishavhanadha, who was the first Tirthankara. 'Mallinadha' a princess was the 19th Tirthankari. According to Swetambaras, she was the daughter of Pridhiladhers. She was a beautiful woman and also a great scholar. All this, many came forward to marry her. But her father did not accept them. So, all of them got angry and invaded Mithila. When the father was about to be defeated, she invited all the princes to the Raja's darbar and she herself enters the durbar from another gate, dressed as a Sanyasin.

'Arya Chandana' was a contemporary to Mahaveera and she was the first disciple to him.

Jain Sanyasins

Jain sanyasins were shown great respect by Jains. These *sanyasin* travelled in groups throughout the country just like men. It appears they were making 'Mantropadesam' instead of men.

Their daily routine also (preaching of *mantra*) was like that of men. They were going out once in a day for alms and were taking food only once in a day. They were sleeping only for a few hours in the day. They were doing meditation twice in the day. Whereas a healthy sanyasin could tour the country, a weak and fragile woman spent her life confined in a particular place.

When a *Sanyasin* died, her funeral was performed in a grand manner. Those, who had no children, used to take pieces of her cloth from the dead body, thinking, by wearing such pious cloth, they would have children. Dead body was carried in a palanquin and it was considered to be a sacred duty. Students of Jain schools kept watch as soldiers. They used to announce about the death of a Sanyasin to the elders in the vicinity. 'Logassa' was read and prayers were offered for the salvation of her soul. Jain schools were closed on the day of her death and people never grounded their corn, at the time of her death, as a mark of respect.

Out of 14,000 Jain sanyasis, 3,600 were women. Chandana was the head of them. Some say that she was the niece to Mahaveera and some other say that she was a paternal aunt. Whatever it may be, here is a very interesting story. One day, when she was roaming about in the garden, one Vidyadhara kidnapped her, out of love for her beauty. But he was afraid to take her home. So, out of fear for his wife, he left her on the way, in a jungle. A tribal took care of her and sold her to 'Vrishabhasena', a businessman of Kousambi. His wife, out of jealousy, puts her to trouble and ill-treated her. When Mahaveera comes to Kousambi, Chandana, with an agonised mind and a broken heart, joined his sect of disciples. Another story is that she was a captive in a war and a soldier sold her to a businessman. Whatever may be the truth behind such stories, Chandana became the head of all Jain *sanyasins* and turned out to be an exceptional disciple to Mahaveer.

Apart from these *Sanyasins*, who discarded family life and joined Jain order, there were three hundred thousand women, who were in the family life and were following their preachings and observing '*Sanyasa*' to a limited extent. Well noted among them was 'Sulasa' and 'Revathi'. Even now, women of Gujarat sing songs about her as one among the 16 *Pativratas*. Revathi made several gifts, with generosity. When Mahaveer fell ill once, and came to her house, she treated him with much respect and served him.

Jains considered the 'mother' as the 'most respected person'. 'Trisala', mother of Mahaveer was given the highest place in Jain literature. So also, all Jain Tirthankaras gave utmost respect to their mothers.

Even courtesans had their due place in Jain society. In a text called *Naya dharma Kaha* there is mention about a courtesan by name 'Champa'. She was well versed in all the 64 fine arts. She was a good scholar and a singer. She learnt several languages and used to travel in a chariot, under 'Chatram' (umbrella) 'Chamaram' (fan), with the patronage of the king. She was rich enough to maintain a thousand servants.

There was the system of *Purdah*, in royal palaces. Their women were not seen by ordinary people. It was only the middle class and the lower working class, that were roaming about in the streets.

In a text by name *Vaga Surya*, a king called Mahasena had a hundred wives and Simhasena had five hundred wives. So, polygamy was very much in vogue in those times.

But one point is to be noted, that Hindus gave only a limited interest when the husband died to a widow. She was only given a small amount by way of maintenance. But, Jains gave widows absolute rights over the entire property of the husband. This is really a very progressive step. She was able to take away her property if she wanted. Such a thing was not allowed in Hindu society.

REFERENCES

1. *Ancient India as described* by *Megasthanes* J.W. Mecrimdle.
2. *Glimpses of world history* by Jawaharlal Nehru.
3. *Kautilya's Ardhasastra* Trans. R. Shamasastry (Kegan Paul).
4. Same as above (Telugu) by Mamidipudi Venkatarangayya.
5. *Vatsyana Kama Sutra The Hindu ritual of love* Castle Books-New York.

6. *The Hindu art of love* Sir Richard Burton.
7. Mahabharata Bhavan's Book University By Sri C. Rajagopalachari.
8. "The Ramayana and Mahabharata" (Everyman's Library) Sri Ramesh C. Dutt.
9. *Studies in the epics and Puranas* by P. Pusalke.
10. *Old issues of Bharati* (Telugu Monthly Bharati).
11. *Ramayana Myth or Reality* by H.D. Sankalia.
12. *Ramacharitamanasa: A Study in Perspective* by K.P.B. Chadur.
13. *Mahabharata Myth and Reality* – Differing Views Editor S.P. Gupta and K.S. Ramachandran.
14. Sanskrit-texts of Ramayana and Mahabharata.
15. *A History of Indian Political Ideas.*
16. *Mahapurushulu*-by Sri D. Krishna Murthy (1958).
17. *The Story of the Buddha* by Edith Holland.
18. A guide of sculptures in the Indian Museum.
19. *Rulers of India – Asoka* Vincent A. Smith.
20. "Bharathi" – (Nandana Sravananm).
21. "From hand to Mouth" Vidyadhar Mahajan.
22. Political and Cultural History of ancient India.
23. *Buddhist records of the western world* by Hiuen Tsang
24. *Women in Buddhist Literature Ceylon* (1927) by Bimala Charan.
25. *History of Buddhist Thought* (London-1933) by Thomas E J.
26. *Life of Buddha* 3rd Edition (London-1949).
27. *Religions of Ancient India* – (London 1953) Renon (Louis).
28. *Hinduism and Buddhist-A Historical Sketch Eliot* (Charles).
29. *Women under Primitive Buddhism* (London 1930) Horner (I B).
30. Vinayapitaka.
31. Dighani Vaya.
32. Jatakas.
33. Dhammapada.
34. Spools and Seets in Jaina Literature (Calcutta-1931) Sen Amdlya Chandra.
35. *Elements of Jainism* (1953) (S.A. Chandra).
36. *Some Jaina Canonical Sutras*-Bombay Manct Royal Asiatic Society Publication, Bimala Charan.
37. *Lectures on Jainism*-Banaras Dass.
38. *History and Literature of Jainism*-Bardia V.D.
39. On the Indian Sect of Jains (1903) Bnhler.
40. The Religions of India Barth A.

PART – II

Medieval Times

CHAPTER 8

Our Smrithis—*Dharmasastras*

Aitaraya Brahmana says that "a son is like a ray of hope. But a girl is the cause for mental agony."

Weber, a foreign scholar, referring to a *sloka* in *Yajurveda* says that "girls were thrown out as soon as they were born. But Indian *pandits* have opposed this giving a different interpretation of that sloka. Anyhow, by 11th century, some strange ideas about girl's birth became very popular and a wide gulf was formed between a 'Putra' and 'Putrika'.

The major crimes visualised by the Dharmasutrakaras were three – causing harm to others, clandestine relations and theft. A king was not considered to be an authority, on dharma. He was there only to implement the 'dharma' laid down by Veda, Vedangas and Puranas. He must protect all castes.

Gautama, Boudhayana and Vasistha were the three important writers of *Dharmasastras*. There is no similarity among them on any issue. Foreigners believe that there were 46 *dharmasastras*. But they are not available now. Later on, *Smrithis* like Manu Smrithi, Yagnavalkya Smrithi, Narada Smrithi and Parasara Smrithi were written and they became interntionally famous.

What is *Dharma*?

From an angle *dharma* is nothing but a 'code' that dictates duty. Its meaning had been changing from age to age. It was religious custom in *Rigveda*, religious eligibility obtained through practice of 'Kratus', and in Brahmanas, it was simply implementing of religious duties. *Upanishads* have laid down different *dharmas*, for a student, for a sanyasi and for a *grihayajamani* differently. Several commentaries gave wide meaning to this word and said it is of six kinds like Varna-dharma, Asramadharma, Varnasrama dharma, Naimithika dharma and Guna dharma.

Jaimini said it is the *Sarvato Mukha Vikasa* that man achieves through Vedas and by practising it, one attains moksha.

But anyway, they felt, that the main purpose of life is to implement *dharma* enjoined on man. A code of conduct was prescribed and they were called *Dharmasastras*. The commentary of Medhatidhi on Manudharma *Sastra* and the commentary called *Mitakshara* written by Vignaneswara on Yagavalkya Smrithi are very popular. Anyhow, there is a saying that this *Mitakhara Nyaya* was written by a woman. But, these two were the texts that were useful in fixing up justice before the Britishers came.

Though Vedic ideology was given a different interpretation, as times passed on, and became narrow in approach, Hindu dharma, respected by all, had its own basic values, duly carried on.

Bharat Ratna Sri P.V. Kane, a retired Judge of the High Court of Nagpur, wrote history of Dharmasastras in seven volumes. He could cull out 40 rules of *dharma* from *Vedas* and defined that dharma as 'the duty that a man had to perform depending on his *Varnasrama*.

The general saying is *Vedo-dharma Moolam*. But Nelson, a foreigner opines that *dharma* is a strange word.

When we critically view Vedas, they are full of music, literature and prayers. *Rishis* have not spoken of *dharma* anywhere nor preached any dharma.

Why Practice of Dharma is Required?

Without dharma, can a man live? From the story of Padmavarna, which is found in *Puranas*, the definition of dharma is given. Padmavarna leads a life of sanctity after a career of lust and greed and propagates *dharma* during the rest of his life. He says "dharma is king of kings. Very powerful. It enables the weak and helpless also to win over the strong ones."

Narada telling the importance of dharma says: "The dead body is left by friends. But only his dharma goes along with him."

So, dharma had its due place, in the lives of men and women. Kalhana in Raja Tarangini says:- "Brahma, wanting to keep goodness in women, kept it in Susruthas and made the rearing of children as the main aim."

There are several texts and treatises and we cannot say which is the first and which is the next. Some say that we had a hundred *smrithis*. They were all written in different ages to suit the then existing social conditions. Some are in prose and some in mixed prose and poetry.

Gauthama DharmaSastra

This is supposed to be the first among all *Dharmasastras* and it was Gautama who said '*Vedo Dharma Moolam*', Haridatta, the commentator said that there were 28 chapters in this, where there is mention of 21 kinds of sinners and about *Mahapatakas* (major sins) and *upa pathakas* (minor sins). *Prayaschitta* is also was suggested to all patakas. Scholars have decided that this treatise was written in 7th century B.C. The rules laid down by Gautama are as follows:

Social set-up According to Gautama

Marriage: In his view, it was social agreement. Any two, not belonging to the same *Pravara* can enter into this tie and they must count upto six generations on the fathers' side and four generations on the mothers' side for fixing up the relationship. The girl should be unmarried and should be younger in age than the boy.

Gauthama mentions these forms of marriage – *Brahma, Daiva, Prajapatya, Arsha, Gandharva, Asura, Rakashasa* and tells that the first four are according to dharma.

Every girl, who attains the age of puberty, should necessarily be married and if it is not done, it is a 'sin'. But he has not mentioned the age of marriage anywhere. If the father cannot get her married, the girl can select her own husband. Such a girl should lose her right over the property of her father. When a elder sister remains unmarried, the younger one should not marry.

Neoga: To increase the clan and to give place to 'Pitru Devatas' he said, 'a son is required' and so, he has given recognition to all kinds of son. If a woman loses her husband, she can bring forth a son, with the 'husband's brother or a 'Sagotra' or a 'Sapinda'. But, he should be of the same caste to which she belongs. It appears that this custom was prevalent at the time of Gautama. He gives permission to give birth to only two children. Later on, she should lead a life of celibacy and as per *dharma*. Later Sastrakaras said that she should wait for some time after the death of her husband.

Children

It appears that in order to protect morality, he gave maximum protection to children. 'Kanina' (born to a girl pregnant at the time of marriage) 'Pounarbhavan, (born to a woman who re-married)

'Ourasa', Kshetraja, 'Datta' and Gudhaja (born secretly) are also given recognition by Goutama and he provided right of property belonging to their father.

Right of the Inheritance

Gautama gave 'right of inheritance' to a girl, as in the age of *Rigveda*, when there were no sons. Because such a girl cannot go to another family, Gautama said, she is unfit for marriage. When there was no girl even, such a man's property belongs to his wife, who shares it with his *Sapindas* or *Sagotras*.

Streedhana

Gautama made provision for 'Stree Dhana'. A woman can own her own property separately. This, she can acquire from her mother. Though the girl is married, she gets this if she is poor.

Inter-caste Marriages

Gautama made marriages between different castes lawful. Children were not made 'Outcastes' but provided due status in society. Children born to the first three varnas, were known as 'Savaras', 'Anubasthas', 'Ugras', 'Nishadas', 'Parasavas', if wives were of upper castes their children were known as 'Sutas', 'Magadhas', 'Ayognas', 'Khatris', 'Vaidehikas'.

The children born to a higher caste woman and a lower caste man had to remain aloof from the performance of pious duties of dharma but were given due recognition in the matters of property.

Status of Women

According to Gautama, women had no freedom in the discharge of their duties. Without the permission of her husband, she could not do *Pavitra Karmas* even.

The duties enjoined on her are-

'She should be loyal to her husband'.
'She should not forget her duty towards her husband.'
'She should keep her tongue, eyes, and acts under control'.
'She should lead a righteous life after the death of her husband.
'If he suddenly disappears, she should wait for six years. If he

does not turn up, she can re-marry. If he returns, she should live with him' says Gautama'.

Boudhayana Dharmasastra

His writing is not carried on in its original form to the later generations. Burnell, a foreigner says that one 'Bhanaswamy' has written a commentary on this *Dharmasastra* and he belongs to the eighth century. But the one written by Govindaswamy appears to be more meritorious.

The first three parts seem to be written by Boudhayana but the fourth was written by somebody else, according to scholars. Maharnava says that Boudhayana is from the south of the country but from which part is not known.

In his *Dharmasutra*, the influence of Gautama is evident. He mentioned about woman in the first chapter itself.

Dharmasutras according to Boudhayana

Marriage

Like Gouthama, he also recognised eight forms of marriages. He mentions that the first four apply to upper classes, whereas the last four are sinful, one over the other. But some say that at the time of Boudhayana, *Gandharva* form of marriage applied to all classes.

Highlighting a Vedic line, that children born depend on the form of marriage, Boudhayana says secret marriages are not to be allowed.

He criticized vehemently, *Kanya Sulka* saying a wife bought for money, has no right to participate in *Pitru-Tarpanas*. The parents, who accept such *sulka* are to be punished, he said

Tasmat Striyo, Nirindriya Ada Ada
Api Papat Poovisat Upasthitat

is Vedic dictum. Boudhayana, depending on this, says that women are to be protected. They have to live under the control of somebody or other. But Celebrooke has not accepted this. Because some words are confusing, it cannot be definitely said that this is the real meaning of those words.

Boudhayana says—

"if a woman tries to live amicably with her
husband, she would attain *moksha*".

He allowed a man to discard his wife under some circumstances.

"If a woman is a burden, she can be discarded after 10 years. If she gives birth to all girls, in her 12th year; if all the children born die, after 15 years and if she is quarrelsome, she can be discarded immediately" he said. He can remarry.

But Boudhayana nowhere mentions what happens if wife discards her husband:

"A girl should be married compulsorily. If one dies without marriage, offering of *pindas* for her is not required."

Further Boudhayana said that there should not "be any access for women to pious texts". The aim of the life of a woman is to become a mother. "A woman, who is pregnant should be honoured" Boudhayana said. It is not known, whether it is his opinion or was added later on by somebody else.

So, the girl is given no importance, when compared to a boy.

Widow Marriage

Boudhayana was not unkind to a widow. For one year after the death of her husband, the wife should not touch honey, mutton, or salt. She should sleep on floor. But after the prescribed time limit, she can re-marry or can give birth to children through *Neoga.* Children born to her are made inheritors of father's property.

Inter-caste Marriages

Boudhayana approved of even inter-caste marriages. Children born through such marriages were made to inherit the property of their father.

"If the children belong to different wives of different castes, father should divide his property into 10 parts and divide it as per the caste of their mother" he said.

"If the father had two or three different wives, if the first wife is bad and the second one is good, even though the first wife belongs to higher caste, her son is not entitled to Agra bhaga (higher part).

Sons

All kinds of sons get recognition of Boudhayana. They were

not penalised for the fault of their parents. Thirteen kinds of sons were recognised. Some were given membership in father's family.

Inheritance Right to Women

Women were totally denied right of inheritance. Boudhayana debarred them from such right.

"Even if there was only one daughter, she was not entitled for her father's property." But because her son is *Dauhitra* to her father, the grandson is entitled for grandfather's property. It was for the first time that this 'Putrika-Putra' slogan came into existence and Boudhayana enunciated it.

But he gave a woman a right on the 'jewellery of her mother'.

Apasthamba Sutra

He is supposed to be next to Boudhayana. But Mahadeva, a commentator, mentions that one Bhavacharya was there in between and somebody else also wrote *Dharmasastras*. But those writings are not be found.

Apastambha's whereabouts are not known. He differed in several respects, from the other Dharmasutrakaras. For instance, he disallowed 'Neoga' system. He disapproved *Paisacha* and *Praja Patya* form of marriages.

'Haradattas' commentary on this text is the only one.

No doubt he made some sensitive suggestions. These indicate the changes that came in the society. There appears to be some influence of Buddhism on his *Dharmasastra* and on account of this, some new trend was introduced in the thinking of Hindus.

Dharmasastras of Apastambha

Marriage

Apasthambha allowed women a status on par with men in religious matters.

Without sufficient reason, man could not discard his wife and take to another women. He laid down that one cannot remarry, when the wife is willing to live with him and is able to give him sons. Only when she could not fulfil the above conditions, one can marry a second time, said Apasthambha. He vehemently opposed a second marriage for man, because 'discarding a wife is injustice.' A man who discards his wife should cover with the skin of a donkey and beg in seven houses and lead such life for six months. That is the only punishment for him."

He compares 'wife' with a 'ship'. She is the ship for crossing the *samsara sagara* (ocean of life). She is an instrument for '*moksha prapti*' (reaching Heaven). So, she should not be made impure. She and her children should be pious, to do pious religious deeds."

"The promises made at the time of marriage are very pious. Neither the wife nor the husband should forget them. In such a case, they go to hell."

By the above sayings, it is clear that Apasthambha wanted to make marriage tie a pious one and wanted to protect it to the maximum extent.

Neoga

Opposing Neoga custom, he says "It is better to go to hell, rather than giving birth to children through *neoga* system."

He said a married woman should be treated with respect. Depending on the age of their husbands, their wives should be given more respect.

Apasthamba was more sympathetic towards women who committed a mistake. Such a woman should perform 'Kruncha Prayaschitta' and then she becomes pure as she was before such mistake, because the relationship between wife and husband is formed legally." He has also, laid down, like other *sutrakaras* that 'if a man belonging to a lower caste, commits mistake with an upper caste women, he must be put to death."

He laid down rules for the proper conduct of males also. "If a youth enters the place or abode of a married woman or a *kanya* (unmarried damsel) he commits an objectionable mistake. "To be friendly with another's a wife is a crime. A man who commits such mistake is like a body without a head. He must be burnt with burning iron and should be sent away from the country."

Right of Inheritance

Apasthambha never allowed women to have property rights. A 'Putrika' of a father, was not entitled for the father's property. Firstly sons, if born, or sapindas or religions Guru or Sishya are eligible for taking his property. But, jewellery or presents received at the time of marriage by friends or relatives belonged to a girl. That is *Stridhana*, he called.

He did not give legal status to sons not legally born. But they were treated to be respectable citizens.

"A 'Kshetaya' was not a son; only on durasa born is the real heir of the father" Apasthambha said.

"Belonging to the name caste, and born to a *Kanya* and not belonging to another man, out of lawful wedlock, if a son is born, only he is an 'Ourasa' he defined.

If a man approaches a woman of his caste, already married, though there is no marriage legally performed, both are committing sin. So how can a son born to them became an 'Ourasa' he questions.

"A woman is not eligible to receive *pindas*" Apasthambha clearly tells.

Inter-Caste Marriages

He prohibited inter-caste marriages. Taking food with *sudras* and marriage with them is not allowed. A marriage is an important event in *Grihastha Asrama*. So, also *Upanayana* in social life as man takes another birth becomes a 'Dwija'. He attains 'gnana' only through *Upanayana*. During student days, one cannot look at a woman; recite pious *mantras* before a *sudra* woman, because they are sins."

Vasistha's Dharma Sutra

Some foreigners say that he is not the *Maharshi* mentioned in *Rigveda*. Vasistha, while adopting some of the ideas prevalent in 'Arya Varta Dasa', laid down his rules, similar to those expressed by previous *Dharma sastrakaras* like Goutama, Boudhayana, Yama, Hareetha etc.

Vasistha allowed a Brahmin to marry three wives. A *Dwija* can marry a *Sudra* woman. For such a marriage, Veda *Mantras* are not required.

Status of Women

As regards women, it was he who described that women are not pious on certain days. He bases his argument on a *sloka* in Vedas. But, nowhere in any veda, such an idea is mentioned:

He also says "women cannot live independently, only men are the masters."

Status of Children

Like Gouthama and Boudhayana, he recognised twelve kinds of sons.

He gave 'legal status' to a son born to a *kanya* and made him legal heir to the grandfather also. He spoke of three crimes, namely, killing the husband, killing a Brahmin scholar and a 'Foetus in the womb of a woman."

So, if we go on analysing the *Dharma Sutras*, we find that various opinions were expressed to work as guidelines for society. Some, times, they are contradictory also. But, we have no proof of how society received them. History was written only after 18th century in a chronological order.

Smrithis

Several Smrithis were written later on based on these *Dharma Sastras*. Max Muller and Bhuler, the two famous foreigners who have studied them very critically and expressed some valuable opinions. Bhuler has translated all the above four *Dharma sutras* into English.

There are several smrithis like Manu Smrithi, Yagnanvalkya Smrithi, Parasara Smrithi and Narada Smrithi. But Manusmrithi is famous and formed the basis for Hindu law.

But Jaiswal differs with this idea in 1924 and said for Hindu Law, Kautilya's *Arthasastra* had also great influence in addition to *Manudharma sastras*. Certain social value enunciated by Kautilya are important than the *Dharma sutras* of Manu.

Manu Dharma Sastra

This is the text which gave rise to much criticism as per the principles in it. It is not clear who wrote this. There were several Manus like Prachatasa Manu, Swayambhara Manu, Vainaswata Manu, Bhrugu Manu etc. Some say that 'Manu' was not a person but a position.

Vinobha Bhave, a great Sanskrit scholar also, told me that 'Manu' was a post like a 'Commissioner', in charge of the implementation of Dharma. (I spent a few days in Povnar Ashram and had personal discussions with Vinobhaji, in 1976).

This was not written in one day. Several additions and alterations were made and several Manus contributed their ideas for the writing of this text. What we call now *Manudharma Sastra* is a hotch potch of some controversial ideas.

But this formed the basis mainly during the Britishers time for the customary law of Hindus and was practised in the Courts started by Britishers. So, it led to some confusion and misery.

Mainly his saying:

"Na Stru Swatantrya Marhati"

led to much controversy and affected the status of women in Hindu society.

There are several opinions expressed by several scholars as regards the time of writing of this text.

Dr. P.V. Kane says it is of 2,000 years and dates back in between 200 B.C. to 200 A.D. But Jaiswal syas it is of Pushyamitra Surashin's time. No doubt, it is a standard work, not only on Dharma, but on politics, justice, economics, religion and social duties. The definition of dharma was different in those days and was not used in the sense that we are using now. 'Dharma' meant for them 'a duty' which a man had to observe in various stages of life.

This Manu's code has dictated the lines on which a man had to lead his life. Privy Council took this text, as the standard, in implementing the Hindu law.

I would now, briefly, mention the norms that *Manudharma sastra* preached.

1. Women were born to be mothers. Men were born to become fathers. Therefore, to perform Vedic religious acts, man had to take help of woman and 'do along with her.'

2. A man is getting his wife through the 'Devatas'. He is not marrying according to his will or volition. He is doing acts which are dear to *Devatas*. So, man has to maintain her until she is loyal to him.

3. The highest ideas is that man and woman should have faith, one against the other.

4. Discarding, or selling a wife, on the ground that there is no liking, is unlawful because tie of the wife and the husband is indivisible. The wife should not be far from her husband.

5. A man who considers himself, his wife and his son, as one unit; is a 'Sampurna Purusha', according to Vedas. Intellectuals among

Brahmins have enunciated this principle. So, the wife and the husband are not separate.

6. For happiness in this world, children are the cause. They are also instrumental in attaining 'moksha' in the other world.

7. A woman should be protected as a girl by her father, by her husband in her youth and by her son in her old age. She is not fit to live independently in any stage.

8. She should not feel like to be separate from her father, or husband or son. By discarding them, she is doing harm to both the families.

9. A woman should always be cheerful. In domestic affairs, she should be efficient, careful in keeping the household articles and should be economical in spending.

10. To whomever she is given by her father, or with his consent, her brother, she should be obedient to him throughout her life. Even after his death, she should not commit any act which brings disgrace to his 'Smrithi' (Memory).

11. Where the woman are adored, there Gods rejoice, where they are not respected, there even a pious act cannot yield good results.

12. Further, brothers or husbands or brothers-in-laws, who wish for their welfare should respect their woman and should also decorate her with jewellery.

13. A *putra* (son) is equivalent to oneself. A *putrika* is equivalent to a son. So, when a *putrika* is alive how can any one else inherit property, he questions.

14. *A rakshita Gruha – Ruddhah*
Purushai rantha karibhih
Atmana Matmanayasthu Rakshayusthah
Surakshitah.

(Really women protected by their men and kept in the houses are not safe. Those women, who can protect themselves are safe).

Moderners mostly criticise this *Dharma Sastra* very vehemently. Some of the ideas expressed were put to a lot of criticism and controversy on several occasions. But, the very fact that it is still living even after some thousands of years, shows that there is some strength in some of his arguments for the welfare of society at large.

Manudharma sastra, first published in 1813, had several editions, with the commentary written by Kulluka, Madhatidhi and Govindaraju. It was translated into English; the preface written by Dr. Bhuler is worth mentioning.

Narada Smrithi

Narada, in his 'Samithi' said that there were 10,000 slokas, 1080 chapters and 24 prakarnas. Now let us study some salient features of this *Dharma Sastra* in detail.

Marriage

According to this *Dharma Sastra*, marriage was considered to be the most pious tie, which cannot be broken. (Kautilya said it is an agreement entered into by a man and woman).

Manu felt that getting married and begetting children, is for attainment of 'moksha' in the other world. So, men-women, relationship is 'a Sadhana', an instrument for 'moksha prapti'. So a man, along with his wife and son is one.

A wife is an 'Ardhangi'. So, she has no separate individuality, Manu said.

Neoga System

Manu vehemently opposed the system of neoga. In the sacred texts, nowhere it is mentioned (Manu ix – 65), he felt. Madhatidhi, the commentator, struggled hard to write on this argument.

In Rigveda (x – 40 – 2), it is clearly written. "The foolish Vanaraja descending himself as Rajarshi, has transgressed *Varnasrama Dharmas* and has brought this Neoga system into existence and some others followed him and gave publicity to some stories on *Neoga*. But, good people never supported this" (K.P. Jaiswal) said Manu, supporting his argument.

After his first Prakarana, Manu has totally changed all the laws in existence, as per Kautilya's *Arthasastra*. Manu made several amendments and changed the very shape of those laws.

Widow Re-marriage

For example Kautilya gave permission for a women to remarry a man of her choice if the husband died or went away to another place, or is childless. But Manu said:

1. A woman should not marry any one else than the youngest brother of her dead husband.
2. Their relationship also should be within limits.
3. If she has children through the dead husband, she should never remarry.
4. If the husband made provision for her maintenance and went away, she should wait for his arrival leading a pious life. If maintenance is not provided, she should live on her earnings, through a work, which is not to be criticised.
5. Like that, she should wait for 8 years, 6 years, or 3 years, depending on the nature of the trade for which her husband went away.

But Manu was silent on what she should do, if the husband does not turn up after waiting; Commentators gave different opinions in their own way. Nandana said "she should remarry. It can be presumed that Manu argued for remarriage. Some commentators said that 'after waiting for some time, if the husband does not turn up, she should go out in search of him." This is nearly equivalent to the law of Mauryan times.

Mauryan law is as follows:

1. If there are children, if the husband goes out, wife should wait for him for 1-8 years. If she is not a mother, she has to wait for 4 years and then remarry, as per law, with the permission of the court of justice."

2. If the husband goes away before she joins him, the wife, after attaining puberty, should wait for some months and can remarry a man of her choice, with permission of court. But if the husband makes provision for her maintenance and goes away, she is not independent to remarry.

Manu also said the same thing but made some slight changes. (M.Dh.S.ix 72, 73).

3. If the husband wants, he can 'sacrifice' his wife (Here, the word 'sacrifice' means living aloof). Though they live separately without any relationship after marriage, when once it is performed, he should live as a wife to him." When once she is given as a gift to

him, she belongs to him.

Kautilya gave right to the wife to file a defamation suit, if she is ill-treated by her husband, barring some small scoldings or beatings. So also a man can go to Court if the wife ill-treats him.

Manu similarly gave permission, but suggested some more changes.

1. A wife is a gift of God. So, nobody should think that one selected one's wife. (M.Dh.S. ix – 95)

2. Relationship with her is divine and pious. (M.Dh.S.96)

3. If 'Sulka' is received at the time of marriages, it lowers down the prestige and sanctity of marriage. (M.Dh.S. ix 98).

4. The crux of the marriage *dharma* is mutual respect and confidence. It should not perish.

It appears that Manu never gave recognition to individual but to *dharma* and its implementation. He wanted to keep up the marriage tie a sacred one and wanted to take precautions to keep it up.

Inheritance

Manu said a *Putrika* is equivalent to a 'Putra' but he denied right of inheritance. He said 'She is worthy of love and affection. (M.Dh. S. 185).

"A *putrika* is a replica of her father." (M.Dh. S.135).

"He lives in her. A *putrika* is his 'prati rupa' says Manu (M.Dh.S.130). This sort of sentiment is not expressed in any other *Dharma sastra*. But he has not made 'her' (the girl) equivalent to her brother.

He made the daughter eligible to take the 'Yotaka' of her brother. But he has not clearly mentioned what this 'Yotaka' is (M.Dh.S.131). He also mentioned that the brothers have no right on this property. This is not part of *Stridhan* mentioned by him. (M.Dh.S. ix. 194).

Manu has given a right to the 'daughter's daughter from the grand father's property. As a symbol of love, she has to receive something, he said, but he has not made such provision fot the 'son's daughter.

It is the duty of the father to get a girl married, so he must bear all the expenditure. But *Stridhana* belongs to her entirely, Manu said.

Yagnavalkya Smrithi: (AD 100-300)

It contains 1010 *slokas*. Apararkas Anandasrama edition has only 1006 whereas, Trinandram edition with Viswarupas commentary contains only 1003 *slokas*.

Yagnavalkya made some changes in all the laws of Manu. The most important of Yagnavalkya's doctrine is giving "right to choose" a husband for a girl after attaining puberty. This right was prevalent during Rigvedic times, but later *Dharmasastra karas* did not give permission to choose one's own husband.

Manu said that, after attaining puberty, a girl should wait for three years and if her father or brother or other relatives, do not find a husband, then only she is allowed to make her own choice. But Yagnavalkya gave freedom to a girl to choose by herself a suitable husband.

"When once a promise is made, she is deemed to be married" he further said He allowed even neoga system. But he laid the principle that "a woman should be confident of her husband."

"If the husband suddenly disappears, she has to lead a life of a *sanyasin* and her relatives should protect her." After this he never went a step further. "If the wife dies, a man should not remain without another marriage." he said. "If the woman is at fault, she can be discarded after giving maintenance and another woman can be taken in marriage."

But, woman should be thankful to Yagnavalkya because he gave right of inheritance to them. He clearly stated if "a man dies childless, his wife and his daughter are the chief inheritors to his property." Manu never included women as inheritors. But Yagnavalkya, basing his argument on Kautilya included "Wives" also for the first time, on par with daughters." (Kautilya allowed daughters but not wives).

Yagnavalkya feels that wife is half of man, and marriage tie is sacred and unbreakable. So, when such a woman is living, how can others claim such a man's property?

Kautilya allowed a 'right' over the streedhana acquired by a woman but not any other kind of property. But Yagnavalkya never mentioned about this streedhana. He made 'wife' also eligible to share her husband's property, along with her 'sons'. But on this, commentators differed. Whether it is "full right" or "only right to maintenance", they could not decide. Sreekara before Vignaneswar said he meant only "right to maintenance". But, Vignaneswar vehemently gave the opinion that Yagnavalkya clearly meant 'right to property' and 'not maintenance'. Lakshmi Devi, a commentator on *Mitakshara Nyayasutra* said that a woman was entitled to 'right of maintenance' according to Yagnavalkya. But Mirta Missra, another intelligent lawyer defended saying that there is no question of division among the wife and the husband and so, when the man dies, he has to leave his property to his wife as a token of love. Later law givers like Brihaspati and Vyasa followed him.

Yagnavalkya recognised nine kinds of sons like 'Kshatraja', 'Gudhaja', 'Avitha', 'Kaneena', 'Dattaka', 'Sahoda', 'Pounarbhava', 'Kreetaka', 'Parikrita'.

Parasara Smrithi

In the first chapter, it is mentioned why Parasara father of Vyasa spoke about 'Kali dharma'. By that time, the sentiments about 'suchi', 'asuchi' were much propagated.

Some rules enunciated by him are as follows:

1. If a woman defames her husband as a sick man, as a poor man or a dullard, she takes birth after death as a dog or a pig, several times.

2. If a 'Ritusnata' does not fulfil the wish of her husband, she will go to hell and will become a widow in several births.

3. If a woman neglects doing service to her husband but spends time in *vratas* and fasts, she goes to hell and takes the life of her husband.

4. If a woman performs *vratas* without the permission of her husband, they will not please the *devatas*, they belong to *asuras*.

5. If a woman poisons any of her relatives or resorts to evil deeds, she is '*Pataki*' (sinner) and so, nobody should talk to her.

6. If a woman leads a life of celibacy after the death of her husband, she goes to heaven.

7. If a woman does *Sati* with her husband, such a pious woman, would go to heaven and would live there along with her husband for three crores and fifty lakhs of years happily.

Another important rule that he enunciated is on the re-marriage of a woman.

"Naste, Krite", preprajitha kleebecha Patitanpatan
Pancha swapatsu Nareenam, Patiranya Vidheeyata".

If the husband dies, leaves the country or becomes a Enuch, becomes a *sanyasi* or a sinner, a woman can remarry and have another husband.

(Madhavacharya, later on, condemned this).

In the seventh chapter, Parasara speaks about the age of marriage for a girl.

CHAPTER 9

Woman in Medieval India

Medieval India (1206-1761 AD) by and large remained under Muslim rulers. Advent of Europeans started when Vasco-da-Gama, a Portuguese reached the famous port of Calicut in 1638 AD. Dutch docked Goa in 1639. Captain Hawkins, an Englishman made first definite attempt to establish a factory in India. The French appeared later on the Indian coast in 1667 AD, an expedition was sent under Francis Caron, a Frenchman, who established a factory at Surat. Later period saw many wars among these foreigners in which the final victory went to English people.

The conservation of medieval period added to various problems. In the absence of any superior methodology or technical excellence, Hindu India, became a prey to successive invaders. Some of them were assimilated into Hindu culture, but the Muslims, adhering to their rigidity could not interact with Hindus and so remained as a separate entity. No one could influence the other. Muslims started recording the historical events in an orderly manner. So, we can know more facts about society during their times.

Though they tried to keep their women in *purdah* and in isolated *harems*, we find many women rulers, administrators, writers, dancers and poetesses, who could shine as outstanding personalities. Muslims influence on Indian society started in the 11th century with the invasions of Ghajni Mohammed. It was the first stage. In 1525, Babur established Moghal's rule in India which is the second stage.

We find, in addition to Babur, very capable rulers like Akbar, Jehangir, Shajahan, Aurangzeb and during their rule, it is said, by and large, that life of the people was peaceful. Fine Arts were improved. Though they were mainly fighters and warriors, they had affection towards their sisters, their wives and also their dancers and encouraged them, wherever extraordinary talent was found.

Thus we find many outstanding women during the Muslim rule also, who could have great influence on the rulers. Some of them managed statecraft with consummate skill and sagacity. They could suppress rebellions and intrigues very successfully. Aurangzeb, in spite of his sternness, had a loving and warm heart. He held his, sisters particularly Jehanara in high esteem. In his later year, he was very kind and affectionate to his second daughter, Zinat-Unnissa Begum, whose wishes, he respected.

The sister of Azam Shah, Zebunnissa Begam was honoured with the title of Badhshah Begum and her allowance was doubled. Other ladies were also treated gracefully and generously. Tara Bai was set up by the Moghuls to divide Marathas. She espoused the cause of Shivaji, the son of her husband Rajaram who according to her opinion, was the builder of the second Maratha dominion. She was supported by such leaders as Senapati Dhanaji Jadava and Parasuvam Pant Partinidhi. The treachery of Dhanaji weakened the cause of Tara Bai and brought progressive support to one Sahu, who marched on the Satara, which had been evacuated by Tara Bai. Encouraged by Sahu's Chief Minister Balaji, Rajasbai, a younger widow of Rajaram, succeeded in imprisoning Tara Bai and her son and placed her own son on the thorne of Kolhapur.

Bahadur Shah's two senior wives, Mihar Parwar (Mihar-un-Nissa Begum) and Amat-ul-Habib (Azia-un-Nissa Begum) used their instinctive wisdom to keep the *harem* on an even keel. Their minds and the capacity to hide realities behind their perfumed dresses ensured for the aging Emperor a pleasant place of retreat from the raging conflicts all around. Her much quoted saying that "we cannot command a royal husband except by obeying him" is perhaps a good indicator of her inner mind. Like Nur Jahan Begum she wanted to rule by being ruled by one man. Aziz-un-Nissa Begum was more strong willed than Mihar Parwar. Bahadur Shah adored her and loved her.

It is an irony of fate that neither Parwar nor Aziz bore a child.

Of the other four wives of Bahadur Shah, the most distinguished was Nur-un-Nissa daughter of Shujat Khan and Zeenat-e-Alam a grand niece of Mumtaz Mahal Begum. She exercised much influence over Shah Alam, when he was Viceroy in the Deccan. Aurangzeb liked her, not for her noble heritage but because of her readyness. Once she did the rare act of rallying a defeated Moghal division. This gallant act, in the words of Bhimsen, was in the high tradition of Rajput queens and princesses, who kept themselves in readiness to take the field in an emergency. The emperor applauded her bravery and gave her rich gifts of money and jewellery. "We are proud of our Nur", he recorded in the official history of the war against Maharattas.

Her wisdom and faithfulness endeared her to Shah Alam to a point of complete surrender to her will. He took no decision and mounted no single action, without ascertaining her wishes. When she died in Kabul in 1701, after a short illness, the prince lamented, "Allah has snatched away from me, my best friend and counsellor. The vacuum frightens me. Her virtues were not her looks, but her irrepressible loyalty". News of her death was not conveyed to Aurangzeb for nearly a year. When he came to know in 1702, he sent an urgent message to Shah Alam to build a tomb "worthy of her virtues".

Rani Chatter Bai was a dazzling damsel of eighteen, when Shah Alam inducted her into her seraglio. Besides looks, she possessed intelligence. Her colour and health faded away quickly, so also the infatuation of Shah Alam. Aurangzeb frowned on this marriage. Shah Alam's marriage with Amrita Bai, daughter of Raja Roop Singh Rathod was simply a political alliance. Amrita was a simple woman, honest to God and to herself. Her alertness and her sense of humor aroused in Shah Alam a secret admiration for her. She remained the centre of prince's affection for nearly two decades. Her two children daughter, Daulat Afza and son Mohammed Azim, were the target of envy of other ladies of the *harem*.

Nizam Bai (controversy about her identify. A British traveller, Jack Hogg, described her as dancing girl in the house of a Nawab in Hyderabad) was married to Shah Alam at the age of seventeen and she belonged to the noblest house in Hyderabad. Her father Fatehywar Jang did great service to Aurangzeb in wars against sultanates. This matrimonial allowance was in recognition of his "devotion, loyalty and courage". The writer of *Bahadurnama* records that "though at one stage, she exercised a great influence over the prince, she never abused it". She never meddled with public affairs so she limited her interests to religion, arts and charity. A large part of her privy purse was spent on providing dowries for the marriages of poor girls.

The story of Jahandar Shah is the story of Lal Kanwar; the daughter of Khadsayat Khan, a musician of great repute in northern India in the last decade of the 17th century. She was a descendant of Rupmati, from the mother's side. The prince met her in a function where she sang Thumri. She entered the palace after two days. His first wife was the daughter of Mirza Mohd., a high ranking nobleman of the court of Aurangzeb. He again married in A.D. 1684 one Syeed-Unnissa Begum, a spiritual conversationalist.

Anup Bai, a Rajput princess was the only other legally wedded wife who "for a while became a partner in the princes, pleasures". A princess by birth and a princess by marriage, she was always busy with buying diamonds, pearls and rubies of finest quality from Gujarat and Kashmir. Rabi Begum, daughter of a concubine, was a child gifted with good looks, intelligence, and sensitivities of a poet. At 12, she read not only Persian and Arabic Khusran, Kabir and Surdas. In 1710, at the age of 15, she was betrothed to one Badardil. She died after an attack of high fever. Her tutor bemoaning her death says that "it is an irreparable loss to the realm of letters. He likened her to a "bird of paradise who would fly as high as the sky and then return to earth without an iota of ego in her shapely head".

Social Conditions in Early Medieval India

Indian society was divided into two divisions of people – Hindus and Muslims. Alberuni explains the general attitude of the Hindus towards the Muslims "all their fanaticism is directed against those who do not belong to them – against all foreigners". It is time that even before coming of the Muslims, India had been attacked by Iranians, Greeks, Parthians, Sakas, Kushans and Huns. In their case, the invaders were absorbed into Hindu society and religion but that did not happen in the case of Muslims. The reason given by Alberuni is that Hindus had lost their quality of catholicity and adaptability, which had enabled their ancestors to win over foreign conquerors through a process of assimilation. However, Hindus at the time of Muslim invasion suffered from a superiority complex. They believed that "there is no country which is like theirs, no king like theirs and no science like theirs" in the words of Alberuni, political developments outside India forced the Hindus to develop an attitude of isolationism and that crippled their mental horizon. Muslims were not prepared to accept the religion or social structure of Hindus position of women. It was not as high as it used to be in ancient India. No woman was allowed to have an independent status. However, it was laid down that a husband must honour his wife. Even if he left her for some valid reason, he had to make provision for her maintenance.

Seclusion of women came in the wake of Muslim invasion. Child marriage and *purdah* brought about segregation of girls. *Sati* was common, but not compulsory. Remaining as a widow throughout her life or burning herself on the funeral pyre of her husband were two alternatives. According to a Law made by Sultan of Delhi, permission had to be obtained before burning a widow. Birth of a girl was not considered auspicious. Slavery was common. *Devadasi* system came into existence.

Razia Begum (1236-39 AD) was a wise and capable daughter of Altmash. Even during his life time, he allowed her vast powers. Whenever her father was away from Delhi, she looked after the affairs of the state. She showed great qualities of administration and organisation. She successfully suppressed the rebellions and intrigues. By her manoeuvres, she created dissentions among the various governors and maliks, won over some to her side and crushed others. She cast off her female garments and tried her best to play the king. She took an active part in campaigns against Hindus and the rebellions Muslim chiefs.

She is credited to have raised to laws and reformed the abuses of the government. But the turbulent Turki chiefs of the court could not tolerate the rule of a woman. She offended the nobles by her preference to an Abyssisnian slave. So, revolt broke out and she was taken as a prisoner by Altuma, the rebel governor of Sarhind; she captivated her captor, married him and setforth her husband to regain her lost throne.

Razia fought two bloody battles with her brother but was captured along with her husband and both of them were put to death in 1240. Her rule thus continued for three years and some months with troubles. Her downfall was due to the opposition of her brothers.

Rajput Period

The period on the eve of the Turkish invasion in India is called the Rajput period in the history of India. Their feudal system was the main cause of the political instability during this time.

Status of Women

Women suffered from several handicaps although their honour was dear to Rajputs. They were denied the right to study Vedas. However women belonging to higher families received higher education. They followed high ideals. They gladly immolated themselves along with the bodies of their husbands. This practice later on degenerated and "Satipratha" emerged. Earlier there was

'Johar' ceremony. The women folk immolated themselves 'en-masse' on a burning fire.

But there was no *'purdah'* system among Rajput women. "Swayamvar" type of marriages were prevalent in royal families. Infanticide and early marriage of girls came into practice.

Earlier Hindu society had an enormous capacity to embrace into its fold several foreign races like the *Greeks*, the *Shakas* and the *Huns* etc. But now the Rajput society did not possess this capacity to absorb foreign elements.

Slaves maintained by the Muslim rulers were very faithful to their masters and they were provided with high offices. It was a decaying society, because the caste system divided Hindu society and injected the venom of hatred, humiliation, inequality, prejudices and untouchability. In the words of V.C. Vaidya "superstition acted like a double edged sword towards the fall of Hindu India. Such a superstition demoralised and discouraged them.

Alberuni, a famous historian, gave an account of India of those times (977 AD to 1084 AD) saying that several evil practices like child marriage, prohibition of widow remarriage, *Sati*, and *Jauhar* existed in Hindu society and people had a very narrow outlook. Feeling of nationalism was almost absent.

Sultana Razia (1236-1240) daughter of Iltumish, was the first and last woman among the Muslims as well as Hindus, to occupy the throne of Delhi. According to the account given by a historian called Minhaj, her rule lasted for three years, six months and six days only. She gave up her *purdah* and started appearing in court in male attire wearing a 'Kuva' (coat) and 'Kulah' (cap). She started horse riding, hunting and commanding to army etc. She took keen interest in all the administrative activities of the state. She herself appointed several Iqutadars, commanders and other officers. She conducted affairs of the state in an open *durbar*.

But being a woman was a cause of her failure. Secondly, Razia's becoming Sultana was against the traditions of Islam. This made many Turkish chiefs to work against her as they felt that it was a humiliation to work under a woman. Her brothers considered her a usurper of their throne. So, they gathered several disgruntled forces round them.

The popular episode of Rani Padmini, the beautiful queen of Raja Ratan Singh, saving from the captivity of Ala-ud-Din though not adequately authenticated by historian records is often cited in the conquest of Chittaud by him. The Rajputs offered stiff resistance but were finally defeated. Padmini with other Rajput women performed 'Johar' (immolation) to preserve their purity and to protect themselves from captivity or pollution by enemy.

Bhakti Movement

Bhakti movement had an impact on medieval Indian society and many women seem to have participated in it. Its main features are:

1. Unity of God or one God though known by different names
2. Bhakti—intense love and devotion, the only way to salvation.
3. Condemnation of rituals, ceremonies.
4. Rejection of idol worship by many saints.
5. Open mindedness about deciding religious matters.
6. No distinction of several castes, higher or lower.
7. Need of a guru for guidance.
8. Preachings through local or regional languages and travelling from place to place for spreading the religious message.

Under the impact of Muslim rule, Hindus suffered a lot materially, morally and spiritually. The rulers wanted to enforce Islamic laws on Hindus. Some healing touch was needed. Some Sufi Muslim saints were liberal in their outlook and they emphasised the virtues of love and devotion. This helped to bring the two communities together or nearer. It also helped, to some extent, to harmonise the conflicting interests. The saints of the Bhakti movement rejected the difference of caste and '*Jati*'.

Bhakti saints were also social reformers. They condemned several social evils.

Social Impact

The most important social impact of the *Bhakti* movement was that followers of Bhakti movement rejected the caste distinction.

The evil practice of '*Sati*' received some setbacks. The status of women received more importance.

As the movement encouraged religious participation, more and more women participated freely in the religious congregations and it was not considered disrespectful.

Bhakti movement had moral influence on individuals. It encouraged the value of social service to the poor and the needy. It developed, on the whole, a humanitarian attitude.

Bhakti Mira Bai (1498-1546) was the daughter of Rana Ratan Singh of Mewar and wife of Bhoj Raj; she dedicated her life to Lord Krishna. Her songs are rich in devotional fervour, poetic expression and tuneful music.

Vijayanagara Kingdom

Vijayanagara empire, which lasted for 200 years in the Deccan had a well-organised administrative system and under its several capable rulers, the state made a remarkable progress in economic, cultural, political and social fields. Many foreign visitors like Nicolo (Italian), Abdul Razaq (Persian) Domingos Pins (Portuguese), Borbara etc have praised the prosperity of the state.

Abdul Razaq has given a vivid description of the city of Vijayanagara, the like of which was never seen in the whole world. The jewellers sold diamonds, pearls and rubies etc. in the streets.

Women occupied a high position in society. They took part in the literary, political and social life of the society. They were educated and worked at various posts in the government departments. They were trained in fine arts like music, dance and painting. They also received training in wrestling and fighting. They were also employed as bodyguards.

Women worked in different occupations. According to Nuniz, "The king of Vijayanagara has also women who wrestle and others who are astrologer, and sooth sayers, and has women who write all the accounts of expenses that are incurred inside the gates of the palace and others whose duty is to write all the affairs of the kingdom and compare their books with those of writers outside. He has women also for music, who play instruments and sing. Even the wives of the kings are well-versed in music... He has judges as well as watchmen, who every night guard the palace and these are women."

Of course, social evils like child marriages, polygamy, dowry system and practice of sati were prevalent.

Social and Economic Conditions

Princesses of the royal family received very good education and so they were well-versed in literature and fine arts. The Chalukyan princess, Akka Mahadevi carried on administration of a province and personally and actively engaged in fights and sieges. Hoysala Ballalas I's queens were highly accomplished in music and dancing. Sovaladevi, the queen of Sovideva used to display her accomplishments in fine arts in large assemblies comprising of nobles, scholars and artists from different countries. The Portuguese chronicler Paes (1520-22) and other foreign writers often described the costly establishments of the Vijayanagar queens, as well as the large number of women attendants, the lavishness of their clothing and jewellery.

In the provincial court of Raghunatha Nayaka of Tanjore, there were many learned women poets, who were capable of expounding works written in various languages. So, we learn that the role of women in high society was varied, important and pleasant also. *Sati* was not unknown among the upper classes, but by no means was common.

The Italian traveller Pietro Della Valle (1623) had left a vivid account of village schools and the method of instruction they followed and the process of learning using the fine sand spread on the floor for writing. Ibn Batuta (1334-45) records "I saw in Hanaur thirteen schools for the instruction of girls and twenty-three for boys, a thing, I have not seen anywhere else. Robert De Nobili, in a letter of 1610, says that in Madura, there were 10,000 students who went to the professor in Theology and philosophy. Education was provided throughout the country by endowments in temples for recitation and exposition of epics and *puranas*.

Information is not available whether there were separate schools for girls. But besides 'Mathas', 'Jain Pathis', Buddhist Viharas, played a role in educating people and there were many libraries of books of all branches of learning. Fairs and festivals were many and women were allowed to participate in them. All the Hindu festivals like Mahanavmi, Dussehra, Sankranti and Ugadi were celebrated with pomp and luxury.

Barbosa's account of Vijayanagara empire is interesting. He says that villages in the empire were inhabited by Hindus and some Muslims. Polygamy was practised by them and their women observed 'Sati'. Brahmins were priests in charge of temple worship.

According to Nuniz, a large number of women were employed in royal palaces as dancers, domestic servants and palanquin bearers. There were also wrestlers among them. Some women were also appointed as accountants, judges, bailiffs, and watchwomen.

Custom of Devadasis

The practices of dancing girls attached to temples was also in vogue. From the account of Paes, we learn that *Devadasis* held a highly respectable position in society and were given land grants, maid servants, jewellery etc.

Women were having honours as writers and poetesses. Ganga Devi, wife of Kampara, wrote *Madhura Vijayam*. Hannamma was a prominent scholar in the court of Pronda Deva. Tirumalamma was a distinguished poetess in Sanskrit in the reign of Achutaraya. Thus, under the rule of Krishnadeva Raya, the Hindu Empire of Vijayanagara, was at its height politically, economically and culturally also. Foreign travellers and diplomats were dazzled by its wealth, prosperity and power.

Social life in the Bahami Kingdom was greatly influenced by Arabic, Persian and Indian practices. Upper classes of Muslims were divided into two classes – one comprising the original inhabitants and the other coming from countries like Africa, Arab, Persia and Turkey etc. Mutual rivalry always existed between there two groups.

The life of the upper classes was very luxurious. They generally lived in beautiful palaces. They kept horses and wore lavish clothes and ornaments. The shoes of several officials belonging to upper classes were decorated with rubies and diamonds.

Polygamy was the order generally among the upper classes.

Among the Muslims, 'purdah' was common and easy divorce practices were prevalent in society.

Advent of Mughals

Babur captured the throne of Delhi and thus won the fame of founding the Mughal empire. He was a conquerer but not a ruler according to Brooke Williams. Babur's *Memoirs* is one of the precious gifts for all times. This has been accepted as meritorious. It is a historical document. Babur has written about the climate, the people, their economic and social conditions and about the kings and political events in India. The following are some interesting extracts.

"Hindustan is a country of few charms. Its people have no good looks, no good manners, no genius or capacity."

Dress: males wear only 'languta' and females cover their body only with one cloth.

"Pleasant things of Hindustan are that it is a large country and has masses of gold and silver.

Political conditions: "When I conquered the country there were five Muslim and two Hindu rulers".

Babur wrote this book, whenever he had leisure. It was written in Turkish. It was twice translated into Persian. It was also translated into English in 1826 and in French in 1871. He gave his impressions very frankly and so, his work is an authority on the history of his age. The only unfortunate thing is that it is not complete. There are gaps at certain places. He says: "peasants and people of low standing go about naked. They tie on a thing called languta....women also tie on a cloth, ('Lang') one of which goes round the waist. The other is thrown over the head".

It is contended that Babur's description of Hindustan is coloured by his prejudices. Babur was not very much impressed by the social life and manners of people of India. His view was that Indians were not dressed properly and were not cultured.

Though he was a great General and a writer, he was not a good administrator. He gave away to his followers all that was captured by him. In spite of some shortcomings, he laid foundation for a mighty structure on which Akbar built up later on. Anyhow, Babur is one of the most interesting figures in the history of medieval India.

Akbar

Akbar was a national ruler. He extended hands of friendship towards Rajputs. He married the daughter of Raja Bisarimal of Amber (modern Jaipur). He got his son Jehangir married to the daughter of Raja Bhagwan Das. His marriage in the family of Jaipur is considered to be of great significance. In the words of Dr. Beni Prasad, "It symbolised the dawn of a new era in Indian politics. It gave the country a line of remarkable sovereigns, it provided to the four generations of Mughal emperors the services of some of the greatest captains and diplomats that medieval India produced."

Culturally, the Hindus and Muslims came together and closer. Akbar's interest in the Hindu society, led to some awakening regarding the evils of *sati* practice. Widow remarriage was encouraged.

With all his genius for practical achievement Akbar was an idealist and a dreamer. According to Abul Fazl, he wanted to bring about reformation among people. He forbade infanticide, *Sati*, excessive drinking, Cow-slaughter etc. He encouraged widow remarriage and tried to cement the differences between Hindus and Muslims by setting an example of inter-communal wedding, making no distinction of caste or creed.

He passed orders that "Hindu girl, whose husband died before the marriage was consummated, should not be burnt. If a Hindu woman wished to immolate hersekf along with her husband, they should not prevent her; but she should not be forced."

It was also forbidden to marry one's cousins or near relations, because such marriages are destructive of mutual love. Boys were not to be married before 16, nor girls before 14, because the offspring of early marriages were weaklings. No one was to have more than one wife – except in cases of barrenness. But in all other cases the rule was 'one man and one wife'. If a widow liked to marry, she might do so though this was against the ideas of Hindus.

The reform described above were not brought in overnight.. They were product of gradual evolution because Akbar lived in an age of spiritual awakening in India.

Nurjahan emerged as the most powerful woman figure in medieval history, on account of her personality and influence on Jehangir, son of Akbar. She was the only queen, in the entire history of medieval India, who exercised such a tremendous influence on the emperor husband and consequently on the affairs of the state. In Jehangir's own words "I have sold my kingdom to my beloved queen for a cup of wine and a dish of soup." Nurjahan was a cultured, educated, intelligent and dominating lady. She was fond of music, painting and poetry. She composed verses in Persian. She designed new varieties of cotton and silk fabrics. She suggested models of jewellery. Thus she set the fashions of the age. About Nurjahan's influence on Jehangir, Dr. Beni Prasad has observed "Nurjahan ruled him for 14 years and during the last five years of his reign, Nurjahan alone controlled him."

Nurjahan got her name stuck upon the coins of the 'Firmans'. She also appeared in the Jharoka along with the emperor. She listened to the complaints of her subjects. She and her 'Junta' exercised full control over the state and the highest nobles and dignitaries of the state presented themselves before her and listened to her dictates. All important appointments, promotions, postings, transfers, and dismissals were done at her behest and consent. "She was", as Dr. V.A. Smith says, "a power behind the throne."

Sir Thomas Roe, ambassador of the King of England who stayed in the Moghul Court (1615-1618) has remarked. "All power vested in the Junta of Nurjahan at that time. It was impossible to get any work done without the help of her brother Asaf Khan and his son-in-law prince Khurram. Jehangir himself was in pleasure, day and night, resigning the entire administration to her."

Sher Shah Suri (1540-56)

According to Dr. Tripathi, "Sher Shah is one of those great men of history, who blossomed out of dust into glory and rose to the highest pinnacle of distinction by dint of their courage, ability and resourcefulness as also by their strength of sword. He was neither born in purple nor could he boast of his origin from any high family of religious or military leaders".

According to Dr. K.R. Qanungo, Sher Shah was a greater constructive genius than Akbar himself. Had he lived longer, he might have taken the wind out of Akbar's sails. He was undoubtedly one of the greatest statesmen among the Sultans of Delhi.

Social and Economic Conditions in Moghul India

Contemporary witers, especially Mohammedan historians tell us about practically nothing about the common man. As V.S. Smith points out, Mohammedan writers confine themselves to maintaining a record of the events of courts, conquests, kings etc. rather than on social or national evolution.

Society in Moghul times was organised on a feudal basis. The king enjoyed an unparrallel status. Moghul rulers were notorious for their large *harems*. It is stated that Akbar maintained as many as 5,000 wives. There was a separate staff of women officers to look after them. A big kitchen was run by the king. Feasts and festivities were common. There are references to music concerts, dancing, Jashans and elephant-fights. Hunting was also a fashion but in course of time, it became expensive. Mughal nobles lived a life of extravagance. They had a large establishments. They maintained large number of mistresses and dancing girls. The middle class consisted of wealthy merchants, professional men and petty *mansabdars*. The lower class consisted of cultivators, artisans, small traders, shop keepers, household servants, slaves etc. *Sati* was common among the Hindus. Child marriages were also prevalent. Both the Hindus and

Muslims spent a lot of money on ornaments. Use of Liquor, Opium etc. was common. There was no scheme of popular education for the people.

Some foreign travellers, who visited India, made certain references to the social conditions of India.

Babur Namah

It ranks very high in the historical literature of Moghal India. It is considered to be an authority on the history of Moghul India and is considered as most enthrilling and romantic works in the history of all times. Its Persian translation was completed in 1589-90 by Abdul Rehman. It gives an account of 18 years of Babur's life.

Humayun-Namah was written by Gulbadan Begum. She was the daughter of Babur. She was born in 1523 and died in 1603. She was held in high esteem. It is stated that Akbar carried her bier a little distance and distributed money for the benefit of her soul. Gulbadan tells that she received a command from Akbar to write about Babur and Humanyun. She wrote what she knew about them. Her account of Babur is brief. Most of her work is on the life of Humayun. She tells us about the victories, defeats, hardships of him. She has omitted some very important matters about her times. In spite of that, we get a glimpse of social customs of her times. We get an interesting picture of the loves of the people of her times.

The reign of Shah Jehan is considered the Golden Age of the Mughal period. There was peace and prosperity in the country. He built a large number of buildings, which are masterpieces of Moghul architecture.

Many foreign travellers visited India and recorded their views about it. According to Travernier, Shah Jehan "ruled as a father over his family and children." According to Edwards and Garrett "Modern India owes much more than a superficially apparent to the administrative genius of the Great Moghul".

There is also criticism that the economic and social results of Moghul rule were disastrous to the prosperity and happiness of the people of India."

Taj Mahal was built in memory of the beloved queen of Shah Jehan, who died in 1630. Prominent artisans of the world were invited in designing and constructing Taj. A French traveller, who visited Taj in 1660 wrote thus, "This superb monument is sufficient to show that Indians are not ignorant of architecture and though the style may appear to be curious to Europeans, it is of good taste and one could only say that it is fine." It took 22 years to complete construction of this great monument. It is estimated to have cost 3 crores. It is a "dream in marble" and the "finest monument of conjugal love and fidelity in the world".

Chand Bibi and Ahmednagar

Chand Bibi was the sister of Burhan Nizam Shah who died in 1595. She was the widow of the former ruler of Bijapur. She was a remarkable woman who virtually ruled the state of Bijapur for 10 years. She went to Ahmednagar and took up the cause of her nephew. To fight the Moghuls Miyan Manjhu entrusted the regency to Chand Bibi. Chand Bibi decided to fight the Moghals. She shut herself in the fort with the boy King Bahadur and played a heroic role for four months. Glittering with armour, a veil on her face and a naked sword in her hand, Chand Bibi came out riding an elephant to lead her soldiers. That raised their morale. Chand Bibi was left alone and was captured and murdered; though she was in favour of a treaty.

The decay of the Moghul society, helped the rise of the Marathas. The Moghul empire which earned the admiration for its extensive territories, military might and cultural accomplishments, disintegrated after the death of Aurangzeb. Within a short span of 50 years, nine emperors occupied the throne in quick succession and were not able to provide any effective government. Taking advantage of their weakness, many adventurers carved out independent principalities of their own and for feed themselves from the central rule.

Social Life in 18th Century

Social life in the Eighteenth century was marked by stagnation and dependence on the past. There was no uniformity of culture and social pattern all over the country. People were rather divided by religion, region, tribe, language and caste. Social life of upper classes was different from that of lower classes. Higher classes were conscious of their superiority. Entire wealth of the country was concentrated in their hands.

Every caste and group was isolated within its own customs and social traditions. Any deviation from established laws and conventions resulted in excommunication. People were so absorbed in the celebration of marriages, feasts, festivals and other family ceremonies that they had no specific urge to create any new social values.

Family system was primarily patriarchal. It was dominated by the senior male member. Inheritance was through him only. Women were expected to live as mothers and wives only. They had little individuality of their own. However queen Ahalya Bai administered Indore with great success from 1766 to 1796. Many other Hindu and Muslim women played an important role in the politics of that time as we have observed in the previous pages. Status of woman depended on her capacity to bringforth sons and so, they were prepared to make any sacrifice for that sake. But a mother had tremendous influence on the affairs of the family practically though she had no legal rights.

The custom of 'female infanticide' was very much prevalent in society. Child marriage was more for social security. There was great anxiety among the parents about the honour of their daughters and hence, they were married at a very early age. Women were excluded and *purdah* became an established custom both among the Hindus and Muslims. Insecurity and lawlessness prevailing in society made exclusion of women more tight and that deprived women of any opportunity for education. Their physical and mental health also suffered. The custom of *Sati* prevailed more in Bengal, Central India and Rajputana. It was uncommon in the South. The *Peshwas* discouraged *Sati* in their dominion with limited success. Polygamy prevailed among the rich families of Bengal and Uttar Pradesh.

Remarriage of widows was looked down upon though it prevailed in some places. So, the lot of Hindu widows was very pitiable. There were many restrictions on their diet, dress and movements. They were expected to serve selflessly, the family members of the husband or brothers family and give up all worldly pleasures of the earth for their sake. There was untouchability. The untouchables were denied even basic privileges of living. They could not use tanks, wells, inns or schools which were only meant for upper classes. Hindus resorted to human sacrifices on some occasions. The family was a close-knit unit. Elders were conducting its affairs. Sometimes, for economic convenience, brothers had separate establishments. But they were considered as one unit by the village. They were getting together at religious functions and ceremonial offerings. Polygamy was permitted by the *Sastras* and social convention, though this practice was not common.

Muslims were also observing polygamy. Bahmani Sultans, as a rule, took more than one wife. The well-stocked *harem* of Firoz Shah Bahmani is a notable example.

Furishta states that among the Hindus, child marriage was common (and girl's father and mother as is the custom of the Hindus wanted to marry her at a tender age ... Fer. 1,600 if: M. Somasakhara Sarma, *op.cit.* 328).

Marriages were performed spread over many days and certain conventions about bridal procession were observed by different castes. The practice of *sati* was prevalent. Rama Deva Yadavas' queen Kamaisa was forced by her step-son Singhana to immolate herself as a *sati* in spite of her entreaties (Smrithisthala 50, 123 cf. Jananesmari XVI, 187, 440).

But such cases were rare and *Sati* does not seem to be common. Gurucharithna (XXXII) enjoins the practice only on women who had the courage and who could face the ordeal. It clearly lays down that woman with child must not undergo this supreme sacrifice. Among some castes of lower social status, widow remarriage also was permitted.

Many Sultans took Hindu wives and some members of the ruling class married Hindu women. But this was only a one way traffic. Religious life of the people of Bahmanis centered around the Temples, Mosques and various Shrines. Every village had its patron deity and some towns and cities boasted of their deity belonging to Hindu Pantheon.

Most of the people were Hindus and the rulers were Muslims. So, a new set of cultural values came into existence. There was considerable influence of one set of values on the other but both remained as different entities.

Marriage, according to Muslim Law is not a sacrament or a sacred tie. It is a contract and so divorce also was easy. By simply announcing *Talaq* three times, a man could divorce his wife. This right is also given to woman. But, because of the *purdah* and lack of education, Muslim women could not take bold decisions.

There are couples even among Muslims who remained very loyal to each other throughout life. The two stories of Shah Jahan and Mumtaz as well as that of Jahangir and Nur Jahan are well-known.

Evolution of Indo-Islamic Culture

Establishment of the Delhi Sultanate marked a new phase in the cultural development of India. When the Turks entered India, they had well-defined faith in Islam and also had definite ideas about government, arts, architecture etc. Interaction of Turks with Indians, who had strong religious beliefs, resulted in a rich development. But the process was a long one with many pitfalls.

Generally a Muslim girl's marriage was performed only after attaining puberty. It was performed with the consent of the girl. As per Muslim Law, a man can marry four times but Khurram enjoins on him the rule that he "should do justice to all the wives".

A Muslim women was barred from marrying a non-Muslim. But a man was free to marry a non-Muslim, rather a Hindu. A Muslim woman has as much right on the property of the father as her brother has. Even after her marriage, she does not lose this right. In this aspect, a Muslim woman is better placed than her Hindu counterpart. If she wants, she can give this property, to any one she likes. Even her husband does not possess any right on her property. Such rights are denied to a Hindu woman, as we can evidently see. If minors are married, with the consent of their parents, after attaining legal majority, any one of the spouses can dissolve such marriage, if they do not like each other. This right is not prevalent among Hindus. So, child marriage was a curse on a Hindu girl.

May be on account of the *purdah* system among Muslim women, Hindu women also began to observe *purdah*. So, Hindu kings and nobles also wanted to have *harems* or *Jenanas* on the lines of Muslims. Because of the *purdah* system, the system of prostitution developed.

Hindu women began to spend an isolated life, confined to four walls of the house. Her only duty was to do all the household work, remain loyal to her husband throughout her life. Education was thus denied to her and so, she had to live depending on her husband.

Though they were no opportunities for education, some women were contributing their talent to Goddess Saraswati and writing. 'Indravati', was the wife of Prananath and she wrote 'Dohas' in the 16th century.

During the time of Akbar, Hindu women by name, Ganga, Jamuna, Kalamasthee Devi, Raminar dhari, Nahlala Devi were known poetesses. But more details are not available about them. In the 12th century, a Muslim woman by name "Taj" wrote several songs on Krishna in "Vraja Bhasha". Praveen Roy Pahter, Rupmathi Teen

Tarang, Rangarajan wrote romantic *kavyas*. Ratnavati, Khaganuya, Padmacharini, wrote on several topics. Priyamvada wrote Syama Rahasya.

Influence of religion appears to be quite high on women mostly in medieval culture, may be a Hindu or Muslim. Hindu women visited temples occasionally. Bibi Fatima Saiman, Bibi Julkha led a life of nunnery and spent life reading religious texts.

REFERENCES

1. Sircar, J.N., *Fall of the Moghul Empire.*
2. Owen, S.J., *India on the Eve of British Conquest,* London, 1805.
3. Raghuvansi V.P.S., *Indian Society in 18th century.*
4. Suri, Pushpa, *Social Conditions in the 18th century.*
5. Williams, Monier, *Religious Though and Life in India* Vol. I Government of India, New Delhi, 1961
6. Wilson, John, *History of the Suppression of Infanticide in Western India,* Bombay 1899.
7. Ives, Edward, *Voyage From England to India,* London, 1773
8. Hodges, William, *Travels in India,* London, 1793
9. Uranfurd, I, Sketches Chiefly related to the History, religion, learning and manner of Hindus, London, 1790.
10. Irvine, William, *The Army of Indian Moghuls*, London, 1903.
11. Grme, R, *Historical Fragments of the Moghul Empire,* London, 1805.
12. Beveridge, A.S., *Memoirs of Babur.*

CHAPTER 10

Muslim Woman in Medieval India

Muslim period started in the 11th century with the onslaughts of Ghajani Mohammed. There are more evidences now to know about the age of the Muslim rulers, than before. In fact Muslim rulers had started writing down history in a systematic way. Rulers like Akbar, Jehangir, Shahjahan and Aurangzeb ruled for nearly 200 years, and life of the people was happy. Fine arts flourished and there was a stable government. Strangely there developed a new 'culture', many of the subjects were Hindus and the rulers were Muslims. Both had their own distinct culture. So they maintained their own individuality and one did not change the other. But both definitely influenced each other in some way or the other.

As per Muslim Law, marriage is a contract entered into by individuals. If necessary, one could get separated from the other. But Muslims also respected their marriage and the story of Shahjahan and Mumtaz and the construction of Taj Mahal is too well-known. So also the love story of Jehangir and Noorjahan.

Rights of Woman in Islam

Muslim women have a right of inheritance on par with men. A girl has an equal right over the property of her father, just like her brother and even after her marriage, she does not lose this right. Her husband does not have any right over such property, which she acquires through her father and if she wanted, she can bequeath that property, even without the consent of her husband, to anybody whom she liked. It is easy for taking a 'Divorce' also; she need not to go to a Court of Law. But, on account of *Purdah* and lack of education, Muslim women could not utilise the opportunities given by Prophet Mohammed. A Muslim woman could not marry a non-Muslim. But a Muslim man was allowed to marry others. As per Muslim law, a man could marry four women. But he should do justice to all, as per *Quran*. Usually a Muslim marriage is possible only between two adults, because it is an agreement. If they are minors, only when father or guardian gives consent, such marriage can be valid. Marriage contract is by giving some money and so, if this is returned, such marriage can be revoked. But, normally, no Muslim resists to divorce. The 'dower' is of two types:

1. That which is prescribed by elders at the time of marriage.
2. At the time of divorce, that which is to be given by the husband. This will be generally a huge amount. This may be perhaps thought of by elders to prevent frequent divorces.

Duties of a Wife/Husband As Per Muslim Law

Duties of wife:

1. She should live in the husband's house.
2. She should obey his orders.
3. She should be able to command his respect.
4. Unnecessarily, she should not have acquaintance with many.
5. Unnecessarily, she should not go amidst several persons.

Duties of husband:

1. One should maintain his wife/wives as per his status.
2. If there are more wives, he should arrange for their separate dwellings.
3. Nobody should be harassed. All should be treated equally. His company should be given to them equally.
4. He should allow his wife to visit her parents atleast once in a year.
5. If she incurs debts, he can control her.
6. A woman cannot leave the husband on the plea that he is having connection with another woman.

An overall view of all these sayings, shows that Muslim law is also male-dominated like in any other society.

Purdah System

Purdah was encouraged among Muslim women generally for two reasons:

(a) To protect women from evil forces.

(b) To keep aloof women from manouvrings of all sorts. This spread to even middle class woman of Hindus during the rule of Muslims.

When and how did this Purdah Start?

Purdah started with the Arabs and for the first time with Islam.

Niece of Prophet Mohammad by name 'Ayesha' did not accept this *Purdah* system. "God has given me beauty. If others appreciate it, I feel so happy. I thank God. But I would not cover my face. Because in any Gods act, there cannot be a fault." There might not have been many women who spoke like her. That too, the resistance was found only in the early stage of Islam. It might have not been very difficult for men to introduce this Purdah system. So, it spread to one and all in course of time. In the early stages of Islam, women also used to go to *Masjids* and offer prayers. But by the 13th century, this custom was discontinued.

By the introduction of this *Purdah* system, prostitution took its deep roots. Allauddin Khilji had to bring about a special law to control prostitution. The following simple story would reveal how Muslims viewed *Purdah*.

Shahabji was the wife of one Ameer Khan, who was an employee in the *Durbar* of Shahjahan. One day, she travelled in a palanquin through the main streets of Delhi. The elephant of the rulers, escaped and moved about freely causing alarm. So, the bearers of the palanquin left her and ran away frightened. Shahabji, so as to protect herself, jumped from the palanquin and took shelter in a nearby shop. This was the simple fault committed by her. Because she broke the custom and showed her beauty to all, Ameer Khan discarded her and sent her to her parents.

Writings of Bermier and Mausukhi

Bermier, a French traveller met several women in *Purdah*, saying that he was an eligible bridegroom and recorded some of his experiences and observations. Mausukhi was an Italian; his writings are mostly allegatory whereas Bermier opinions are trustworthy.

Bermier says Moghul princesses remained unmarried because, the rulers were damn afraid of the son-in-law, who may think of toppling down their throne. Jahanara, Roshnara, both daughters of Shahjahan remained unmarried. Bermier says that 'Jananas' were the places where many evil conspiracie were bewed. As he knew medicine, he was taken inside the Janana several times for treatment of the women inside. He was escorted with eunuchs in the *Janana*.

There are several stories about the love affairs of Jahanara who killed her lover in a tank of water. But Aurangzeb was lenient towards the lovers of Roshanara (he acquired power by killing his father, with the help of Roshnara).

The most interesting thing for the *Janana* women was the 'Mela', which was arranged in the garden next to the *Janana*, once in a year. Any woman could open any shop and the purchasers were all *Janana* women only. Bermier writes that 'Gold jewellery, embroidery material, fine sarees with zari" were sold in this festival. Padusha with his wives used to attend and buy all things. He used to bargain and shop owners used to take liberty and hackle him that 'he cannot buy as he had no money'.

Padushas spent their leisure time in the company of famous dancers. (Shahjahan used to stay with them till late in the night) and dance performances was arranged every week in the *Durbar.* They used to go on excursions and visiting different places was a favourite pastime. Bermier describes the palanquin in which Roshanara travelled and several graceful women decorated nicely who used to follow, escorted by Eunuchs and men holding sticks. Their grandeur was stunning and excellent.

Writers and Rulers Among Muslim Women

Razia Sultana is one of the three queens of 13th century. His father recognised the good qualities in her and made her his legal heir, instead of sons, who were leading an easy life. She ruled for three and a half years, dressed like a man and led the army. An Arabian prophet said "a woman well qualified is very valuable in the world, but the same gentleman said "For a nation, which made a woman a ruler, has no salvation." Her capacities and talents created jealousy among others. They could not see her on the throne. Finally, her own subject caught and killed her in the forest.

Gulbadan Begum daughter of Babar, wrote *Humayunnama* which is historically an excellent work. The sociological conditions prevalent in the times of Babar, the mighty maker of Moghul dynasty are incorporated in this treatise.

Jahanara, Shahjahan's daughter wrote the life history of a Muslim Prophet known as 'Kwaja Mohinuddin Chistie'. Jebunniesa was the daughter of Aurangzeb who wrote poetry giving place to the culture and finesse of her contemporary society.

Noorjehan, Jahangir's wife was not only a great ruler but also a good poetess. Sir Thomas Ro, an English traveller visited her *durbar* and wrote the following:

"Jahangir's wife has an upper hand, Jahangir respected and loved her so much. She is Persian born in India. After the death of her first husband, who was the captain in the Moghul Durbar, she married Saleem, she sent away all the women of *Jenana* through marriages and by other ways intelligently. So also she replaced all captains and Officers of the *durbar* and filled with her men tactfully and most of them are of her blood."

Md. Hathee, who wrote "memoirs" of Jahangir says "Noorjahan is the crownless king. Saleem is only for name sake the ruler. He is a tool in her hands."

Jehangir used to say "Noorjahan is very intelligent. She is selected for setting right the royal problems. She will look to every thing." Saleem only needed some mutton and drinks. Noorjahan used to give him what he wanted and run the affairs of the kingdom, all by herself. Whoever approached her for help, she did justice. For people who suffered, she was like a 'Saranalaya'. For helpless girls, she used to perform marriages with her own money. Nearly 500 such marriages were performed. For some thousands, she gave gifts and donations with a large heart and generosity. This Persian princess was so influential that Jahangir published her photo also along with him on the coins he brought out. Her style of functioning was unique and no other Muslim ruler adopted her methods. Her style is unprecedented in history.

There is a story that she was appointed as finance minister for one day and on that day she got the coins printed with her photo. Whatever may be the truth behind this story, she was adored by Jehangir and she was not only beautiful but intelligent, capable of handling things with tact and skill.

Chand Bibi ruled Ahmad Nagar. She had to face many internal squabbles and many onslaughts by foreigners. Syed Ahmadulla Kadri, the famous historian of Hyderabad wrote her life story, after so much of research. The reforms she introduced, the love and affection shown towards her by the people are exemplary. She is an example by herself. When Mohalana invaded Ahmed Fort, the valour shown by her is beyond all comprehension. Finally, she had committed suicide by jumping in an acid well.

REFERENCES

1. *Medieval India under Mohammedan Rule (AD 712-1794)* Stanley Lane Poole M.A. Litt; D.
2. *Memories of Chand Bibi* by Sayyid Ahmad Ullah-Qadri.
3. *The Imperial Treasury of Indian Moghals* by Abdul Aziz.
4. *Woman in Islam* by Late Al-Hajj Kwaja Kamal-ud-din.
5. *Akbar, the Great Moghal* by Vincent Smith.
6. *Memoirs of Babur* – L Ving (1926).
7. *Travels in the Moghal Empire* Fracis Bernier Ad 1658-1668.
8. *Memoirs of Jehangir* – Tr A Rogers London 1909.
9. *Sociology of Islam* – 2 Vols Cambridge 1931 Levy R.
10. *Mohammedan Law relating to Marriage, Divorce etc.* Tagore Law lectures (1891-2, 3 vols).
11. Regions of Mohammedan Jurisprudence-Oxford 1951 Schachi (Joseph).
12. *Forgotten Empire.*

PART – III

Modern Times

CHAPTER 11

Woman During British Rule

Towards the end of 18th century, social conditions in India came to such a low level that neither the rulers nor the people's leaders could control them easily. Some unusual notions crept into the minds of people and took very deep roots. India, that could once give birth to some universal ideas with a broad vision and perspective, sank into oblivion and began to lose its identity. Society became narrow-minded.

India, which could shine as the mighty force for the whole of Asia, once upon a time socially and culturally speaking, lost its place. When countries like Sumatra, Java, Indo-China could respect the very principles, once propagated by India, our own country, unfortunately could forget those very principles and began to think in a petty minded way. By that time, the rule of Moghuls came to an end and politically the country was facing turmoil. There was disunity everywhere and one force was vying with another with vindicative spirit. There was no single rule by which people were governed. It became customary to perform child marriages even among respectable Hindus and this spread to Muslims too. *Sati* was observed in almost all parts of the country. Though their religious leaders banned this custom, Sikhs also began to observe *Sati. Purdah* which was once prevalent among Muslim women spread as a custom, to Hindus, especially among Rajputs. Education brings most evil to women, it was believed. Even upper strata women belonging to Sanatan or traditional families, felt it to be beneath their dignity, to speak out openly that they know fine arts like singing or dancing. (A.S. Altekar – *Position of Women in Hindu Civilisation*)

"To educate a woman is morally wrong. Fine Arts and education was considered necessary only for dancing girls" it was felt. Three social evils changed the very image of the society during the time of the East India Company:

1. Polygamy became very common among all sections. Men could easily take a second wife even when the first wife was alive,

without any hurdles. In fact, man got the freedom to marry any number of times and society never looked down on him. Some even felt that it was the birth right of a man. The children born to such wives, because the mothers were different, posed a big problem to the family indirectly. There were children born secretly or illegitimately. There was none to take care of them and so, they turned out to be heavy burden on society already ridden with several other problems.

2. Prostitution became rampant. To arrange *melas* or *nauch* parties with dancing girls became a symbol of status. Dancing in temples, day and night, became a common feature. Such dancers were given lands and gifts. To protect or maintain them became a fashion of the day. Society never considered the habit to be beneath the dignity. Women became mere things of luxury.

3. Child marriages became very common. Sri Tatvananda Swamy in his Telugu translation of Gandhiji's lectures in *Streedharma Pradestika* tells about the evils of child marriages. *Young India* in an article entitled *Evils of Child Marriage* dated 26th August 1926 throws more light on this aspect and the society for prevention of child marriages". In 1931 it publishrd the following details.

Age (yrs)	*Marriages (percentage)*
Below 1	0.8
1-2	1.2
2-3	2.0
3-4	4.2
4-5	6.6
5-10	19.3
10-15	38.0

So, it can be concluded from the above table that even below 1 year of age, one girl in every 100 was married. Even for girls below 15 years the same was the position. When in 1921, there were 9066 married girls before one year by 1931, there number increased to 44082.

As an offshoot of child marriages widowhood also became rampant. The number of widows was 759 in 1921 and their strength increased to 1515, within 10 years.

More Particulars About Widows

Age (Year)	*Number*
Below 1	1515
1-2	1785
2-3	3485
3-4	9076
4-5	15019
5-10	1,05,482
10-15	1,85,339

On account of child marriages, women became mothers at a very early age and many died during child birth. As a result, death rate among women went up. On an average, the number of the dead per year were 2 lakhs. To put in other words, 22 died per hour. 'Sati' was another evil that took its toll.

In 1815-1828, the number of women who died in Bengal itself is as follows:

Year	*No. of Dead*
1815	378
1816	442
1817	707
1818	839
1819	650
1820	598
1821	654
1822	583
1823	575
1824	572
1825	639
1826	518
1827	517
1828	463

Birth of Reform Movements

Britishers, who were foreigners were not prepared to tinker with the personal laws or customs of the people and the leaders, though they gave statements, could not bring about any drastic changes because they were not rulers. The alarming conditions prevailing in society, caught the imagination of some people with social consciousness and they gave a serious thought to put an end to these social evils. This is how some reform movements sprang up. Mainly, putting a woman to flames, on the pyre of her dead husband (Sati) was considered to be a ghastly affair and Rajaram Mohun Roy, moved by the burning of his own brother's wife, sent a petition to the privy council. Some religious leaders objected strongly to this, saying that it was a religious practice dictated by ancient texts. There were arguments and counter-arguments for and against *Sati*. Ram Mohun Roy opposed vehemently with firm determination and read out the texts clause by clause and exposed that an inhuman act like the *Sati* was nowhere mentioned. He personally went to England and being a lawyer, convinced the privy council, that all Indians were opposing this evil custom. Finally, as a result of his efforts, Lord Bentinck, abolished, *Sati* in Bengal by promulgating 17th regulation Act on December 1829. Such acts later came in states like Bombay and Madras in course of time. There was no opposition as expected from the side of the people and *Sati* was abolished in some parts of the country.

Widow Remarriage Act

Some prominent Indians like Ishwar Chandra Vidyasagar fought against widowhood also. He gave life to the argument that *Parasara Smrithi*, a standard work allowed remarriage of a woman. Petitions were sent to the rulers. Finally on 20th July in 1856, Sir J.P. Grant issued an ordinance depending on the people's will, exhibited in 40 petitions, signed by 60,000 people; only 5,000 people signed against the ordinance.

But, this was not much respected by the people for some time. It remained on paper only. Later movements like *Brahmo Samaj* and *Arya Samaj* also supported them. Widow Remarriage Society was established and provided information to those who wanted to marry widows. Only some child widows were married here and there, but the majority of widows remained unmarried, as their kith and kin never allowed their remarriage. By 1881, there were 2.1 millions of widows, as per an estimate. Govind Ranade, Dadabhai Naoroji, Jeranjee Malabari took special interest in this aspect and sent petitions to the British Government but no serious steps were taken by them.

Institutions that Wanted Reform

Brahmo Samaj

Under the banner of *Brahmo Samaj* and under the leadership of Maharshi Devendranath Tagore and Rajaram Mohun Roy, more than 500 middle class youth and educated boys were organised (Tagore Devendranath, Atma Jivani (Bengal) Visva Bharathi Grandhalaya – 4th ed. 1968. p.46). But this *Brahmo Samaj* could not capture the imagination of people because the main purpose of *Brahmo Samaj* was to fight the influence of western civilisation on Hindu traditions and not on reform. But a section of the organised youth, under the leadership of Akshaya Kumar Dutt, agitated for widow remarriage. *Tatwa Bodhini*, the journal of *Brahmo Samaj* published several articles on Polygamy. Ishwar Chandra Vidyasagar proposed to fight for widow remarriage but Devendranath showed disinterest. So, the members exhibited several different ideas. But, several branches of *Brahmo Samaj* (as many as 50) were established by 1860 in different states. Kesava Chandra Sen opposed the caste system. Sivanath Sastry removed the sacred thread and first widow marriage was performed by *Brahmo Samaj* in 1862. Some youth of their Samaj showed interest in women's emancipation and the spread of education. As a result of their efforts, a college was started in Calcutta in 1862. Annoyed by the act of these youngsters, some elders moved away and started *Upasana Samaj*. There were some differences also on the caste division. Under the leadership of Siva Chandra Sen, another organisation called "Bharata Varsheeya *Brahmo Samaj*" was formed.

Because the members of Adi Brahma Samaj were clinging to some Hindu ideals, there was not much impact and they could not pave a new path. But, there was lot of enlightenment and awakening among the people and they began to openly speak out there ideas. Bankim Chandra Chatterjee, supported there novel ideas. Raj Narayan Bose stated 'National traditional Sabha and Nanda Gopal Mitra started 'Chaitra Mela', which paved the way for swadeshi movement in Bengal.

There was discontent among educated youth towards the western ideas but some upper strata people vyed with each other for some clerical jobs, which were few in number.

Members of Bharat Varsheeya Samaj, concentrated more on missionary work. They performed 19 reform marriages, out of whom 9 were inter-caste marriages. They could achieve promulgations of

'Nature Marriage Act', by which such marriage were made legal. In 1820, Kesav Chandra Sen established 'Indian Reform Association', which started as one of its performances, spread of education among women.

By that time, there was no contact between the people and the educated youth, so, with a view to have this linkage, a paper called *Sulabha Samachar* was started, which cost only one paise. With this they propagated some new ideas among people.

So, as a result of this *Brahmo Samaj*, some intelligent thinking was induced among the middle class, not only in Bengal but in all the other parts of India as well.

Arya Samaj

Though Swami Dayanand Saraswati, started this initially as a religious institution, it soon took the shape of social reform movement that came in as a storm in the beginning of the 19th century.

Lala Lajpat Roy, was its pioneer in Punjab and in almost all the states, several branches started working. Efforts of *Arya Samaj* brought also out some change in the minds of Indians with regard to the position of women.

Prardhana Samaj

Eminent personalities like Mahadev Ranade, Bhandarker, Chandavarkar were members of this Samaj and so, it gained momentum. They wanted to bring about reform by the spread of education. In 1870, in Calcutta, night schools were started for workers. Primary schools were started in all parts of Bombay. In Pandarpur, an orphanage and educational institutions for women were started.

Thus on account of the above institutions, there was great awakening and some women like Sarojini Naidu, whose parents were Brahmos, came forward to work with noble ideas. Nineteenth century made a beginning for the emancipation of women and for the rise of the national spirit.

Smt. Rama Bai Ranade did wonderful work in Maharashtra and also Smt. Rajyalakshamma, wife of Sri Kandukuri Veeresalingam-pantulu in Andhra Pradesh. They had to face a lot of opposition and criticism but took up the movement with dedication, and with undaunted courage.

Gopalakrishna Gokhale

The youngest of the social reformers and nationalist leaders of the 19th century was Gopalakrishna Gokhale (1866-1915), who served not only for the cause of India's freedom but also for women's emancipation. He was one of the ablest and most talented national leaders India has produced. One finds in him a blend of rare and precious qualities of both head and heart. He was a brilliant public speaker and a skilful writer.

He began his career as a professor in Fergusson college in Poona and turned out to be an ardent political leader of the country during the first decade of the 20th century.

Indeed his Educational Reform Bills, particularly his Bill for Universal Compulsory Primary Education in India and his speeches supporting them before the Legislative Assembly are of classic significance in the history of Indian Education.

He was interested in women's education. One of the clauses in the Constitution of the Servants of India Society which he founded in Poona in the year 1905, provided for "assisting educational movements, especially those for the education of women."

His concern for women's education was brought out well in the following speech. It was a speech made by him before the Educational Section of the Victorian Era Exhibition in 1897.

"A wide diffusion of female education in all its branches is a factor of the highest value to the well-being of every nation. In India, it assumes additional importance by reason of the bondage of a caste and custom, which tries to keep us tied down to certain fixed ways of life and fixed modes of thought, and which so often cripples all efforts at the most elementary reforms. One peculiarity of the Indian life of the present day is the manner in which almost every single act of our daily life is regarded as regulated by some religious notion or another. We must eat and sleep and even stand and sit and walk only in accordance with certain religious beliefs and the slightest departure from the accepted ideas in these matters is understood to increase the difficulties in the path of our salvation."

Gokhale went on to say "And naturally, these ideas have a far stronger hold on the minds of women than of men. All who know any thing of Indian women know that the turn of their mind is intensely religious, a result due in no small measure to their being shut out of all intellectual pursuits. And this combination of enforced ignorance and overdone religion, not only makes them willing victims of customs unjust and hurting in the highest degree but also makes them the most formidable and the most effective opponents of all attempts at change or innovation."

Gokhale concluded "It is obvious that under the circumstances, a wide diffusion of education with all its solvent influences among the women of India, is the only means of emancipating their minds from this degrading thraldom of ideas inherited through a long past and that such emancipation will not only restore our women to the honoured position which they at one time occupied in India, but will also facilitate more than .... anything else our assimilation of those elements of western civilization, without which all thoughts of Indian Regeneration, are mere ideal dreams and all attempts at it are foredoomed to failure. The solution appears simple enough and yet no problem in India is surrounded with greater difficulties or requires a more delicate and patient handling.

(G.A. Natesan, Ed. *Gopala Krishna Gokhales Speeches,* p. 961)

So realising the manifold difficulties of women, he made the cause of women's education a part of his life's mission throughout his distinguished career. On a careful scrutiny of the events that passed on from time to time, it is evident that side by side with men, there were some outstanding women also, who contributed to the cause.

Among such women pioneers, Pandita Rama Bai Saraswati's name is the foremost. She was an outstanding scholar both in Sanskrit and English who devoted her entire life to the cause of women. Her life is a source of great inspiration to the younger generations.

Pandita Rama Bai

Pandita Rama Bai (1858-1922) was born in a very progressive Brahmin family and was well taught at home by her parents. Even before the age of 10, she was conversant with Sanskrit and could recite 10,000 verses. At sixteen, when her parents died, she was a scholar in Sanskrit. She learnt Marathi, Kannada and acquired knowledge of Hindustani and Bengali. She remained unmarried till the age of twenty. She travelled with her brother, addressing large gatherings in different parts of India on women's education.

(Syam Kumari Nehru Ed. *Our Cause – A Symposium*, p. 10)

Her scholarship and learning were highly appreciated by

conservative men, who opposed women's higher education before. "It must be said to the credit of the Pandita, that they received her with enthusiasm, bestowing on her titles of learning reserved for men scholars, not even thought to list her with the texts which had for so long held up the education of Indian women."

In Calcutta, the learned pundits, after long and searching examination, recognised her merit and conferred on her the distinguished title of "Saraswati".

Rama Bai bravely went out of her caste and married Bipin Bihari Medhavi, a Bengali. Although she incurred the displeasure of society later on, she set out to reform the society. Within a couple of years, she lost her husband and with her infant daughter Manorama, she set out afresh to do service of her country. She once again travelled, this time in Bombay Presidency, winning audiences for the promotion of women's education. In 1881, she gave evidence before the Education Commission presided over by Sir William Hunter, emphasising the need for urgent reforms such as the abolition of child marriage and the promotion of women's education.

In her enthusiasm and love for service and her desire to learn scientific methods, Rama Bai went to England in 1883 with her little girl and joined the ladies college at Cheltinham to study English literature. At the same time she worked as professor of Sanskrit. She embraced Christianity also, in the same year. Later on, she went to America and devoted much of her time to the study of kindergarten system in Philadelphia. To a Chicago correspondent, who questioned her about the reason for such study she replied, "I wish all the educators would understand Froebel as I do. I see in his system, the true meaning of reforming the old ideas of religious and secular education. In the first place, Froebel's system enables a child to think. All his senses are trained by it and this is just what education means to do. In the second place, an intelligent thinker will not accept or trust any belief without taking time to think whether it is profitable or whether it is true.

Truth is the spirit of Froebel's teaching and I think if the kindergarten system were introduced into India in secular and religious schools, it would give to the people not only an advanced mode of thinking, but would also dispel the illusion of many superstitious beliefs, the wrong ideas that now keep women and children in subjugation."

Rama Bai went on to say, "My idea is to reach the minds of the mothers. You know nothing will attract the mother's attention so strongly as the welfare of her children and if there are some women in our country, as I know they are to be found everywhere, who are opposed to their own progress and education, the kindergarten system when presented to them in its true light will convince them that the welfare of their children depends mostly on themselves and if they are not as intelligent and judicious in training as they are in loving, they will do more harm than good."

(E.F. Chapman – *Sketches of Some Distinguished Indian Women* – W.H. Alben & Co., Calcutta, 1891, p. 39)

When she returned to India in February 1889, she was full of ambitious plans and schemes for child education and the amelioration of the status of women.

Herself being a widow, she realised all its bitterness and hardships of Hindu widows. She succeeded in opening her first home for widows called "Sharada Sadan" (Home of Learning). This was an undertaking that she had planned when she was in America. With their generous help, a society called 'Rama Bai Association' was started in Boston mainly to collect funds for her work in India. In order to enlist public sympathy and make clear the cause for which she was working, Rama Bai wrote *The High Caste Hindu Women*, a work which created widespread interest in the United States. Americans, with their usual generosity, helped her to collect Rs. 6000 for a modest beginning.

Rama Bai's experiment of widow's education begun at Sharada Sadan in Bombay, grew rapidly, especially during the time of Great Famine in 1896; when the house was thrown open to all girls in need. They came and joined from all parts of India.

Another centre was opened at Khedgaon, near Poona, called Mukti Sadan. Then a rescue Home called Kripa sadan was opened. The number was increasing and the compassion of this great woman made her admit as many helpless woman as came to her. One of the members of her teaching staff, Mrs. Nikambe, narrates the story like this.

"In 1900 with the Gujarat Femine, came a new time of trial and test. Twenty of her helpers went out to the area. Eight of them were women who had been saved from starvation in 1896. When she had resource in 1896 for fifty girls, she had admitted three hundred. Now she had resources for five to six hundred and admitted one thousand three hundred and fifty, thus bringing the total population at Mukti Sadan upto one thousand nine hundred.

With the help of one hundred and fifty devoted young women she dealt with this situation.

A school was organised with over fifty classes and teachers. From hundred children were enrolled in the kindergarten. A training school for teachers and an industrial school with garden field, oil press, dairy, laundry, department for baking, sewing, weaving and embroidery was opened. For only those who could do coarse work, there were grain parching, tanning, culinary utensils, dyeing and so on.

It was a wonderful organisation.

Her great aim was to bring joyousness and blessedness into the lives of these girls, often untrained, sullen, coarse on their first admission. She never forgot any detail in the management of this large-scale work. Through the busy life of the place, moved the slight, serene figure with the great brow and the wide grey hair, spirit soaring above her age, sorrow, labour, till at last she was called in 1922, to the rest she always denied for herself."

(Gedge E and Choksi, M. *Women in Modern India*, Taraporewala, Bombay, 1929, p. 21)

Rama Bai Ranade

Pandit Rama Bai was the first great woman pioneer, who laid solid foundation for Indian women's freedom and education. Rama Bai Ranade (1865-1922) wife of Justice Ranade, one of the founder presidents of Seva Sadan, a well-known educational institution in India is another pioneer in the cause of women. Seva Sadan was started by G.K. Devadhar, whose endeavours in this connection may be well described in his own words.

"While engaged in famine relief in the United Provinces my conviction grew that India needed just as much an army of trained women in various fields of national advance as men. On my return to Poona, I called a dozen small meetings of friends, both ladies and gentlemen, who would feel interested in this idea and those meetings resulted in a resolve to undertake the education and training of half a dozen poor widows as social workers. (*Young India*, March 4, 1926)

Accordingly, the institution was founded with twenty members, who met at Mrs Ramde's house. It later blossomed into one of the first of the schools, particularly for married women, emphasising adult education, with a daily attendance of one thousand members. It has now many branches in India. Rama Bai Ranade remained its president till the end of her life. She was born in an orthodox Brahmin family in a small town of Satara district. When she was 11 years old, she was married to the then widowed Ranade, who was thirty two. Twenty seven years of companionship with her husband, prepared her for the useful service she was to give to the country by being the simple, unassuming leader of many unfortunate and under-privileged women.

She has been described in an intimate pen portrait by Margaret cousins as a "typical daughter of her land, Maharashtra, simple, hard-working, hard-headed, soft-hearted, practical, idealistic, patriotic, parochial, shy, brave, conservative, pioneering—a paradox of good qualities but supremely a servant of her sisters with life dedicated to their advancement. (M.A. Cousins, *Awakening of Asian Womanhood*, Ganesh & Company, Madras, 1922, p.23).

In the field of politics, she threw herself whole-heartedly into the campaign for women's suffrage. Nor did she forget the unfortunate. She visited prisons and spoke to the women there and comforted them, reading aloud Tukaram's "Abhangas" (Hymns) which she used to translate into simple Marathi.

Mrs. Ranade managed to find some time to write her reminiscences, considered as a classic in Marathi, parts of which were translated into English by Mrs. K.V.A. Gates under the title "Himself". After Mrs. Ranade's death, her work was carried on by women who were trained by her.

Some Other Outstanding Women

Another outstanding young women, who distinguished herself by the courage and conviction, with which she worked as a Physician, was Dr. Ananda Bai Joshi (1865-1887).

She was a friend and relative of Pandita Rama Bai. She was the daughter of a rich landlord in Bombay, who did not object to his daughter's learning Sanskrit and English.

She was married while very young and the death of her only child was the turning point in her life. She had started thinking about poor medical aid in India. She was determined to become a doctor. Her husband was understanding and helpful. With the help of some missionary friends, he arranged for Anand Bai go to England in 1883. After a short stay, she went to America where the Women's Medical College in Philadelphia, she took her degree of Doctor of Medicine in 1886 and returned home.

She was the first Hindu woman to have landed in New York. Her achievement, in spite of her; frail health was hailed at home and abroad. A brilliant career awaited her-unfortunately she passed away.

There were other pioneers among Indian women. Francina Sorabji (1833-1910) and her daughters, in particular her fifth daughter Cornelia who planned and organised the establishment of girl's schools in the west of India. Mrs. Sorabji established three large schools in Poona. One of them was for children, who could understand only Marathi, the second for Muslim girls who were not allowed to attend mixed schools, and the third for training teachers, the only one of its kind in the Presidency of Bombay. (Chapman, *op. cit.*, p. 126).

Miss Cornelia Sorabji, like her mother, was deeply interested in studies. She distinguished herself in school and college, and in 1887, she was declared in the university results as one of the top four in first division. Immediately afterwards she received the offer of a teaching fellowship at Gujarat College for Men at Ahmedabad. One of her friends say that she accepted the call "thinking that it would be good for Indian men to be controlled for a change by a woman". But it was a formidable undertaking, which required a great deal of courage. Her work in the college was highly appreciated. She was very popular as a lecturer and was soon made acting professor of English.

Later Miss Sorabji went to England and qualified herself in Law and was appointed as a legal advisor for women in *purdah*, to the Bengal government. Mrs. Sorabji was already there at the invitation of the Indian Female School and *Zenana* Missionary Society. Both mother and daughter gave their thought and energy to the cause of women's education, at a time when one could count the number of educated women in India on one's finger tips. The courage and perseverance of such people coupled with their pioneering work, did much to inspire others.

There was another doctor named Anne Jagannadhan who went to Edinborough in 1888 and joined the School of Medicine for Women which had just been started. She obtained the triple qualification of the Scottish College in 1892 and returned to India, to take up the post of House Surgeon, at the Cama Hospital in

Bombay. But the Indian women were not not to benefit much and this young woman doctor died in 1894.

Another worthmentioning name is that of Rukma Bai, who rebelled against tradition in order to enter a Medical College. Her case raised a storm in the country because she refused to live with her husband, who appealed to the Law to make her to do so. The High Court ordered that she should either live with him or go to prison for six months. The matter was finally brought to a compromise by which a sum of money was to be paid to her husband; but it was decreed that according to Hindu Law, she could never marry again.

She studied medicine at London university, took the degree of Doctor of Medicine in 1895 and returned to India. Until her retirement in 1929, she was incharge of a hospital for women in Rajkot and worked for the cause of women.

These outstanding men and women of the nineteenth century, from Raja Ram Mohun Roy to Rukma Bai laid solid foundations for further progress in the status of Indian women by their constant preaching and social work particularly in the field of education.

These efforts for women's emancipation and education found their climax and fulfilment in the return to India of Gandhiji and assuming leadership of the country with all the initiative and zeal.

Reading about Gandhiji's 'Hind Swaraj', Leo Tolstoy, the famous Russian writer, told Gandhiji, "I think the question you have dwelt with is important not only for Indians but for the whole of mankind."

His Satyagraha movement could attract many eminent men and women and this experiment proved to be a great success in the end, as we all know.

Women's Education: Further Progress Achieved

The progress of women's education remained slow in the early years of British rule. Very little was achieved till the end of 19th century. Modern movements of reform such as the *Brahmo Samaj* gave it a great impetus. Prominent members of the Samaj wrote journals for the promotion of women's education, for example the 'Brahman Pradhini' of Umesh Chandra Datta, the '*Mahola*' of Girish Chandra Sen and the *Suprabhat* of two graduate sisters Kamudini, and Basanti Mitra.

The *Arya Samaj* organised women's education through various institutions like the Mahakanya Vidyalaya in the Punjab. Primary and Secondary schools made their appearence all over India.

The *Prardhana Samaj* and the Deccan Education Society made strides in Women's education, and the Indian Social Conference passed resolutions regarding the extension of such education.

The Hindu Balika Vidyalaya was opened in Calcutta in 1849 due to the efforts of J.E. Drinkwater Bethune, legal member of the Governor General's Council of education and President of the council of education and of Iswarchandra Vidyasagar the great educationist and social reformer.

The Government made observation now and then on the importance of women's education. But practically did very little for it. Though Wood's Despatch of 1834, emphasised its importance, government felt that girls education should be mainly encouraged and supported by voluntary contributions.

There were only 1646 schools for girls in British India, as per the records of 1873. Between 1871 and 1882, there was slight improvement but it was confined only to primary education.

An education commission was appointed in 1882. The commission noting the unsatisfactory state of affairs observed that women's education should be taken as a legitimate charge on local, municipal and on provincial funds. This led to more liberal grants and consequently, the number of schools for girls increased. But the percentage of girls going to schools was only 2.2.

More progress was made in the 20th century. In 1911, literate women were 1.1 as against 11.3 of men, and in 1921, the figures were 1.8 and 13.0 respectively.

By 1937, number of girl's in school increased from 3810 to 10,315.

With the increase of education among women, co-education became inevitable. As observed by Radhakrishnan Commission, there were very few co-education colleges. There were only men's colleges which also admitted women.

As regards the curriculum, there were different opinions. Some felt that more emphasis should be on domestic Science, fine arts or handicrafts or industries for women. The All India Women's Conference on Educational Reform held at Poona in 1927 recommended such alternative courses for women.

Reforms Brought About in Educational Field

East India Company encouraged educated youth and gave them good jobs. With this move, more and more youth came forward to take up higher education and they could even aspire to go to London for studies. Some of them turned out to be great reformers, after their return to India.

Sir Thomas Monroe suggested a system of medicine to Madras presidency. They formed a department of education separately and began imparting training to teachers. They gave grants literally to private schools and formed certain schemes for the spread of primary education.

Lord Macaulay was entrusted with the responsibility of evolving a method of education. He submitted his report, keeping in view mainly the education system prevailing in England at that time. Sirdar K.H. Panikkar, a great intellectual, appreciated in his book that because of Macaulay's intellectual efforts only India could get modern educatioin.

In 1889, students of Elphinston College, started a school, specially for girls and taught them. They ran a paper specially for girls.

In 1847, Iswarchandra Vidyasagar and Drink Water Bethune, established a school in Calcutta. In 1851, Vidya Sagar took up the complete responsibility of running this school. Because it proved to be a success, many similar schools were established, all over India.

Through the sincere efforts of some eminent people like Pandita Rama Bai, Rama Bai Ranade, Francina Sorabji, and some others, Indian Education Commission was formed in 1882-83. Schools were started in every town and city for girls. People of higher families began to feel proud that their girls are educated.

In 1881, when there was only one woman educated among one hundred by 1886, there was at least one girl among every hundred. In course of time, education facilities for women were extended at college level also. From the records available there were six in the Madras Medical College, eighteen in Bombay, three in Calcutta Medical College studying medicine, in 1886. As many as 45 were studying in Arts colleges.

When Child Marriage Restraint Act came into implementation stage, several girls took to studying in different colleges. In 1932, Lady Irwin College was started in Delhi. Post-graduate courses were started in Home Management in Madras Province.

In 1951, as per census figures, 7.87 per cent girls were educated. In Travancore and Kochin, their percentage was 46.1. In Vindhya Pradesh, it was 1.4 per cent only.

The First War of Independence Led by a Woman

In Indian history, the period in between 1845 to 1863 is most important when because of the Sepoy Mutiny, the first battle for independence, took place. Rani of Jhansi, Lakshmi Bai, was the pioneer who led this war.

For great movements, sometimes small matters are responsible. Rani Lakshmi Bai banned cow slaughter in Jhansi. Dalhousie, the British ruler, called his army to Jhansi. Lakshmi Bai gave them a tough fight, disallowing the British army to enter into Jhansi. She is lavishly praised by British historians, saying that "among Indian rebels, she was very efficient."

Maharani Zindan, became the ruler for Punjab province after the death of Maharaja Ranjit Singh, on behalf of his minor son, Dilip Singh. Britishers wanted to convert Punjab state, which was hitherto independent, into their territory, by organising five thousand to twenty five thousand as soldiers.

As a ruler, she took three major decisions:

1. She increased the salary of her soldiers from Rs. 7 to 12. Britishers did not like this idea. Seven hundred Indian soldiers, came to Zindan, escaping from British army. Zindan absorbed all of them.
2. She appointed secret staff in Gwalior. Baija Bai was writing to Mysore to overthrow Britishers; Zindan issued an order to vacate Gwalior and to Chambal. This annoyed Britishers.
3. She appointed one 'panchayat' to every 'Regiment'. She gave independent status to these Panchayats and appointed a *Sardar*. That *Sardar* used to come to court and draw allowances from the treasury of the government. By this act of hers, she became popular among the army personnel. This was an eye sore for the Britishers.

Britishers wanted to disrupt every act of hers. Zindan also counter-acted. Britishers encouraged Tej Singh Lal Singh of Punjab army to come out, thus disrupting the discipline of the army, offering them high posts.

The first war took place in 1845 between Sikhs and Britishers. During the war, Zindan sent pieces of her saree to the Sardars, warning them that if they come back from war as cowards, they will have to wear such saree. But because of the deceipt of Tej Singh, British army could enter upto Lahore. Zindan had to endorse a compromise. After some time, she had to leave to Nepal disguised as a Buddhist nun, leaving the fort.

It was because of the antagonism she created towards the Britishers that the Sepoy Mutiny took place in 1857. In the end, Lord Canning sent her to London by the steamer. She finally died in 1863. Britishers never allowed for the construction of a "tomb" for her. The first woman, who inspired patriotism and led the war of independence, was therefore, Zindan. Her love for freedom was par excellence and never to be forgotten.

CHAPTER 12

Gandhian Era

Gandhiji's Personality

India had produced several great men and women. Our history bears eloquent testimony to the dedicated and selfless services of many. But a person like Mahatma Gandhi takes birth only once in an age. He was born in India, when she was suffering under the seige of foreign rule and slavery.

Gandhiji was a many splendoured personality, full of sincerity, honesty, seriousness of purpose, coupled with indomitable will and energy. His profound concern for human welfare places him on a high pedestal and reminds us of glorious person like Buddha.

He could create an era called Gandhian era, by his doctrine of 'Ahimsa'. Even the very Britishers against whom he fought and led the struggle admired the extraordinary qualities in him.

Albert Einstein said "Future generations may not believe that a person like Gandhiji in blood and flesh lived and walked on the earth as a human being." He led a bloodless recognition and transformed illiterate masses of Indian humanity into a fearless, non-violent and politically awakened people and literally "out of dust he made us into men."

(D.G. Tendulkar, *Mahatma Gandhi*, Vol. II, p. 57)

Writing a foreword to a book on Gandhiji, Kaka Kalelkar wrote "Gandhiji, with a woman's heart, could move the hearts of women." Such was the towering personality of Gandhiji.

Gandhiji had taken up a gigantic task of liberating women. "By sheer force of vicarious system" says Gandhiji, "even the most ignorant and worthless men have been enjoying a superiority over women, which they do not deserve and ought not to have. Many of our movements" continues Gandhiji "stop half-way because of the condition of our women. Much of our work does not yield appropriate results. Our lot is like that of the penny-wise and pound-foolish trader who does not employ enough capital in his business."

(D.G. Tendulkar, op. cit., Vol. I, p. 276)

Gandhiji seriously took up the unfinished task of the early reformers like Raja Ram Mohun Roy and Swami Vivekananda and began to work for its completion.

He said to women "The destiny of India is far safer in your hands than those of a Government, that has exploited India's resources that she has lost faith in herself.

(D.G Tendulkar, op. cit., Vol. I. p. 77)

His call for women had tremendous impact. There was a sudden enlightenment. Women seemed to have come out overnight and worked along with men for freedom.

Gandhiji's ambition was to plan for a society whose opportunities are given to every individual to grow in harmonious social relations with others and where everyone is free and independent, Gandhiji says "everyone is his own ruler".

Gandhiji: His Satyagraha Movement

Gandhiji's call to men and women for action in the name of *Satyagraha* had a tremendous response. Any number of students in government schools and colleges gave up their studies and many a government servants left their jobs. Distinguished lawyers like Motilal Nehru, Chittaranjan Das, Vallabh Bhai Patel, Babu Rajendra Prasad and Rajagopalachari gave up their lucrative practices and joined the movement. For the first time, in the annals of India, Indian women rallied around in untold numbers to fight for the common cause of freedom.

In 1920, Gandhiji launched his Satyagraha movement after getting resolution passed in Congress session. His innate faith in humanity had made him even appeal to every Englishman in India through *Young India* to join his Non-Cooperation Movement.

His appeal touched the hearts of women. Thousands of them started wearing Khadi and every home had a spinning wheel. It became a daily ritual with millions of people to spin this wheel.

Swadeshi became a way of life. "In burning my foreign clothes, I burn my shame .... nor is the scheme of non-cooperation, non-violence and *Swadeshi* an exclusive doctrine."

"India is a house on fire" he said "because his manhood is being scorched, it is dying of hunger becuase it has no work to buy food with."

Men and women, gave plenty of energy, time, and money to the cause of freedom and the movement became popular. Gandhiji's mass movements were a unique experiment not only in the history of India but in the whole world. Speaking about Congress under Gandhiji's aegis, Pt. Nehru says "it should be remembered that the nationalist movement in India like all national movements was essentially a bourgeous movement. It represented the natural historical stage of development and to consider or to criticise it as a working class movement is wrong. Gandhiji represented that movement to a Supreme degree and she became the voice of the Indian people to that extent." (*Nehru on Gandhiji*, The John Day Company, New York, 1948, p. 25).

Gandhiji's Call to Women

The impact of various movements of 19th century had been powerful enough on Indian society, especially on women. They brought about great awareness of the various social limitations that were standing in the way of progress of society. Yet, they have not penetrated into the ranks of Indian society.

Gandhiji said, "while travelling all over India, I have come to realise that all the existing agitation is confined to an infinitesimal section of our people who are really a mere speck in the vast firmament. Crores of people of both the sexes live in absolute ignorance of this agitation." (M.K. Gandhi, *Women and Social Justice*, Ahmedabad, 1954, p. 4).

In order to assist women to come into their own as early as possible, even before they are educated in the literal sense of the term, as that would take a long time, Gandhiji wanted women to be aware of their position and the actual hardships that they are facing.

"Our first attempt", he says "should be directed towards awakening in the minds of as many women as possible, a consciousness of their present condition. We can bring home to our women the sad realities of their present condition, without, in the first instance giving them any literary education."

So, he actually took up the unfinished task of the reformers of yester years; Gandhiji was keen on women joining the Congress and contributing their might to the promotion of its cause. But, to invite them to join the political struggle was not an easy task, because many women were living in seclusion and under the control of conservative men. Women were not permitted to participate in public activities.

So, Gandhiji had to go slow in the beginning. He began with the social reforms pertaining to women. He had the courage of conviction to question the religious leaders as regards the sanctity of child marriages. Enforced widowhood, which was retarding the progress of Hindu women, was not justified, he argued. He said "it was irreligion, not religion to give religious sanction to a brutal custom (child marriage). The Smrithies are full of contradictions. The only reasonable conclusion to be drawn from the contradiction is, that the texts must be rejected as interpolations. Inspiring verses on self-retraint could not be written at the same time and by the same pen, that wrote the verses encouraging the brute in man" Gandhiji concluded.

"The custom of child marriage is both a moral as well as a physical evil. For it undermines our morals and induces physical degeneration. By countenancing such customs, we recede from God, as well as *Swaraj*". (A.J. Hingorani, Ed., To the Women by M.K Gandhi, Law Journal Press, Allahabad, Vol. III, pp. 122-23).

When people suggested legislation to raise the age of consent to eradicate this obnoxious custom, Gandhiji said that "it might be good for bringing a minority to book, but then it is not legislation that will cure a popular evil. It is enlightened public opinion that can do it." Further he said, "I am not opposed to legislation in such matters but I do lay greater stress on culmination of public opinion" (M.K. Gandhi, *op. cit.*, p. 33).

So also, he deplored the treatment given to a widow in Hindu Society. While advocating for Hindu widow remarriage he said that "every widow has as much right to remarry as every widower voluntary widowhood is a priceless boon in Hinduism, enforced widowhood is a curse" (A.J. Hingorani, *op. cit.*, p. 132).

When a section of the people suggested legislation for stamping this evil, Gandhiji said, "no outside imposition can cure Hindu society of the enforced widowhood of girls, who don't even know what marriage is. The reform can come, first by the enlightened public opinion among the Hindus, secondly by parents recognising the duty of marrying their girl widows."

His fearless condemnation of this evil custom is seen in another statement "The curse of every widow, who is burning within is to remarry but dare not, for fear of a cruel custom descends upon Hindu society so long as it keeps the widow, under an unforgivable bondage (Hingorani, p. 159).

Thus his statements and his interest in the cause created a powerful impact on the public. There were many staunch reformers who were personally convinced of the need for reform. They strongly supported Gandhiji. Sir Gangaram in Lahore published an invaluable table giving facts and figures statewise about the widows in the country. He emphasised the urgency of the social reform and had put down his order of preference as

(a) social reformation,
(b) economic reformation,
(c) political emancipation.

While agreeing perfectly with the reformer, in regard to the urgency of social reforms, Gandhiji disagreed with him with reference to the last place he had given to political emancipation. "The fact is" said Gandhiji, "that political emancipation means the rise of mass consciousness. It cannot come without affecting all the branches of national activity. Every reform means an awakening. Once truly awakened, the Nation will not be satisfied with reform only in one department of life. All movements must therefore proceed, every one proceeding simultaneously."

Mrs. Dorothy Jinarajadasa, wife of Jinarajadasa, president of the Theosophical Society issued a circular letter upon a Bill before the Legislative Assembly to raise the age of consent to fourteen. She sent a copy of this letter to Gandhiji. He said "I am strongly in favour of raising the age of consent not merely to fourteen but even to sixteen ... I should heartily endorse any movement whose object is to save innocent girls of tender age from man's lust" Gandhiji continued.

A so-called marriage-rite ought no longer to confer legality upon an immoral and inhuman act, which consummation, even at the age of fourteen in my humble opinion, undoubtedly is."

He further said, "Sanskrit texts of doubtful authority cannot be invoked to sanctify a practice which is immoral. I have witnessed the ruin of many a child-mothers and when to the horrors of an early widowhood, added human tragedy becomes complete. Any sensible legislation in the direction of raising the age of consent will certainly have my approval." (M.K. Gandhi, *op. cit.*, p. 31).

Then Gandhiji realised how very difficult it was to get the members to support the Bill, because he knew public opinion had to be created in its favour. He knew conservation was rampant and that to break it, one had to work very hard. So, he advised the reformers,

"I am painfully conscious of the fact that even the existing legislation has proved abortive for want of public opinion to support it. The task before the reformer in this as in many other directions is more difficult. Constant and continuous agitation is necessary if any real impression is to be made on the Hindu public."

But Gandhiji knew well that a mere reform of these two evils will never free women in India. There was the traditional seclusion that kept the majority of women indoors and prevented them from taking any part in public affairs.

He knew that *purdah* was a real drag on women's social progress. So, he began to work incessantly against this custom also.

Following Gandhiji's interest in this issue, many of his followers took up the cause and started working for it. Some conservatives argued that "*purdah* was for preventing women from going astray and becoming immoral." Gandhiji's answer to them was "chastity was not hot housegrowth. It cannot be superimposed. It cannot be protected by the surrounding of the purdah. It must grow from within, to be worth anything. It must be capable of withstanding every unsought temptation." (A.J. Hingorani Ed, *op. cit.*, p. 214).

In course of time, agitation against purdah became a powerful movement that enrolled hundreds of staunch workers. There were organised demonstrations against the *purdah* and the results were spectacular.

Look into one of the reports sent to Gandhiji in this regard, "A unique spectacle was witnessed at the mixed meeting of men and women on 8th July 1928 at Patna in the Radhika Sinha Institute on Sunday last. In spite of heavy rains that fortunately stopped just at the time of the meeting, the gathering was unexpectedly large. In fact, half of the space in the hall of the Radhika Sinha Institute was crowded with ladies, three-fourths of whom were such as had been observing purdah a day before, nay, an hour before." (M.K. Gandhi, *Women and Social Justice* – 99).

In spite of his enthusiastic crusade against the general status of women, in view of these unhappy social customs, he condemned those, who were exaggerating the existing conditions.

When a women follower asked him "But you admit the treatment of women is as bad as the disease of untouchability itself? The attitude of the young nationalists, I have come in contact with, is beastly in ninety cases out of hundred. How many of the non-cooperators in India do not regard women as objects of enjoyment?

Is the essential condition of success—self purification—possible without a change of attitude towards women".

There was another unhappy issue, in regard to some women, that was causing great concern to Gandhiji. This was a group of women, who were compelled by circumstances to lead the life of prostitutes, whom he called "Fallen Sisters".

In the South, there was this evil well-rooted in society in the name of *Devadasis*, which Gandhiji called a euphemism for prostitution. Many did not even realise that it was a big issue. Gandhiji said "my whole soul rose in rebellion against the custom of dedicating minor girls for immoral purposes. By calling them *Devadasis*, we insult God himself in the name of religion and commit a double crime in that we use these sisters of ours to serve our lust and take in the same breath the name of God. To think that there should be a class of people given to this kind of immoral service and that there should be another who should tolerate their hideous immorality makes one despair of life itself."

It is no exaggeration to say that in those days, Gandhiji's word became more than a legislated law, many appealed to him, therefore, to address himself to the public and make men and women change their ideas in regard to these ill-conceived practices that were eating into the very vitals of society.

An Andhna Devadasi graduate, appealed to Gandhiji thus, "misery of a whole community consigned to a life of prostitution is great, young people here are trying their best to root out their evil. But they badly need help and guidance. Won't you kindly take up the matter as equally important and emergent as the Harijan movement? Please have this affair always in a corner of your heart and give it publicity. You have not only the Congress but the whole public opinion at your back. What the brothel Bills and IPC could not do, I am confident a word from your mouth would do."

Thus, Mahatma Gandhi was concerned with social reforms to get rid of the unfair customs that were concerning women and lowering her dignity. He gave a philosophical consideration to every aspect of the problem of women's emancipation and worked for it. His words were carrying much weight on the public. So, women began to write to him, asking for help to secure their rights. He actually believed in woman's ability, mental strength, will power and character to stand on her own. He always used to say that, woman is the companion of man, with equal mental capacities. She has every right to participate in every minute activity of man and she has an equal right for liberty.

On an occasion, he said, "I am uncompromising in the matter of woman's rights. In my opinion, she could labour under no legal disability not suffered by man. I should treat the daughters and sons on a footing of perfect equality." (A.J. Hingorani, *op. cit.*, p. 13).

Various problems concerning women were constantly discussed by him in his most popular and widely circulated newspapers, *Young India*, and *Harijan*. His speeches and writings on the question of women's freedom are voluminous. His ceaseless crusade was connected with his major task, the struggle for political freedom.

"The sooner it is recognised that many of our social evils impede our march towards *swaraj*" he said, "the greater will be our progress towards our cherished goal. To postpone social reform till after the attainment of *swaraj* is not to know the meaning of *swaraj*". (A.J. Hingorani, p. 217).

Gandhiji called upon women to join the Indian National Congress and work for the independence of the country. His appeal brought forth an amazing response. Women flocked to the organisation and threw themselves wholeheartedly into its work.

As an English observer said, "These was a breath-taking abruptness about the entry of Indian women into political life. One moment, they were not there, the next day they had sprung, like Athene from the head of Zews fully armed into the fore front of the scene." (Sir John Cumming, Ed. *Modern India*, Oxford University Press, London, 1931).

They had not merely entered the field of politics but played their role fully and freely. Every time, when Mahatma Gandhi launched political campaigns such as the Civil Disobedience, the Non-Cooperation, the expedition against the Salt Tax, women members and volunteers were there in good numbers to serve the cause. Their courage and energy contributed a great deal to the strength of the Congress.

By the end of the first decade of the century, womens formed a special organisation of their own, within the Congress, called the *Deshsevikas* and had pledged themselves to non-violent methods of popularising social reforms. These women were called upon by Gandhiji to undertake the difficult task of picketing foreign cloth and liquor shops, "a task carried through with such conspicuous devotion to peaceful methods that in some places, both the police and Congress called upon women to maintain order at times of dangerous rioting." (L.S.O Malley Ed, *Modern India and the West*, Oxford University Press, London, 1941, p. 476) The spirit of patriotism women showed during the periods of strife and struggle was admirable. Thousands of them swarmed forth from their sheltered homes and withstood bravely every hardship. "Their deeds bore witness to their faith," as an English Authoress said "But perhaps even more remarkable than the mass obedience to the nationalist call was the organising ability shown by the leaders. Women came upon the scene not merely as privates in the Congress army but as lieutenants and Generals and Mrs. Sarojini Naidu as Commander-in-Chief." (L.S.O Malley, op. cit., p. 476).

Referring to the part played by women in the historic *Dandi March* Mrs. Kamala Devi Chattopadhyay observes "women with pale eyes and blushing cheeks, they who had been nurtured behind silken curtains, women who had never looked upon a crowded street, never beheld a strange face, striped aside their silken curtains, threw off their gossamer veils, and flung themselves into the blinding glare of day, unshaded and unprotected; women whose feet were as velvet as rose petals, habituated to sink into soft Persian carpets, walked unshoed on hard stony paths. They who had been nurtured in the lightest of delicacies crunched bravely the tough sandy jail *rotis*. Their delicate limbs now reposed on the rough blankets; they faced perils and privations with a happy light in their eyes and a spring in their limbs. Almost overnight, their narrow domestic walls had given way to a new wide world in which they had a high place." (L.J. Venkateswaran, *Gandhi, Emancipation of Indian Women*, p. 6).

The following account further describes the hardships that women underwent during the political struggles.

"In Borsad .... one thousand five hundred women were going quickly along a street in a peaceful procession. The police met them with a 'lathi' charge. The woman leader was wounded but with blood-stained 'saree', she proceeded on again until disabled by further beating. At Wramgam, two hundred of them took water to the railway station to quench the thirst of volunteers, a simple act of human kindness. The police set upon them and beat them mercilessly." (All India Women's Conference Report, Lahore, 1931, pp. 165-172).

India saw many such scenes during the period of her struggle for independence. During the second non-cooperation movement the response of women was unprecedented. Over three thousand women had faced dangers of the most trying kind such as joining long and tedious processions, picketing liquor and foreign cloth shops, and suffering 'lathi' charge, standing painful trials at courts and serving long terms of imprisonment.

In praise of the hard work done by the thousands of nationalists, a *Resolution of Remembrance* at the instance of Pandit Motilal Nehru was passed on January 26, 1931 and hundreds of public meetings were called for the purpose all over India, despite the Government order prohibiting such meetings.

The following passage of the Resolution relates to women of India.

"We record our homage and deep admiration for the womanhood of India, who, in the hour of peril for the motherland, left the shelter of their homes and with unfailing courage and endurance stood shoulder to shoulder with their menfolk in the front line of India's national army to share with them the sacrifices and triumphs of the struggle."

This tremendous struggle continued and hundreds of women joined it courting suffering. Some had even laid down their lives, sacrificing their all for freedom.

Gandhiji's Women and Social Reforms

Discarding Foreign Clothes

"For India, craze of foreign clothes was a curse. Indian economy was not able to provide food to lakhs of people. So, unless the movement to boycott these foreign clothes is built up, the rulers will not realise" he felt. Who else can make it a success than women. So, he gave a clarion call to women to come and participate and make it a success and thus prove to the British government, the strength of the nation. "Take up this movement. Any movement which women can lead and women can participate will be a grand success."

"In this mighty movement, the educated and the uneducated can participate".

"If well-educated women can participate, they can give the moral courage and strength to the uneducated also" preached Gandhiji.

Burning foreign clothes took the turn of a great movement and it was considered to be honourable to wear *khadi* prepared in India. Women took it as a great opportunity to serve the cause of the nation and to participate in the non-violent movement. An estimate tells that as many as seventeen thousand women participated in salt *Satyagraha* of 1930 and more women participated in this boycott of foreign cloths. Thus the rural women got more recognition. When women began to weave, men also started weaving. Earlier men in Punjab treated wearing clothes as beneath their dignity. Wife of Deshbandhu Chittaranjandas and his widowed sister and niece were the first ladies who came forward to sell khadi in the Calcutta streets. Government arrested them, newspapers carried head-lines and there was so much of uproar, Highlighting this incident Gandhiji said,

"Bengal Government unmindful of racial discrimination, has given great respect to these three women. This is my message to the rest of the womenfolk in India. Prepare a list of women who are willing to join this movement. Tell Bengal women that there are more women to walk in their footsteps and walk in their ideological path. Let there be some sacrifice by some in the initial stages. The nation need not feel low of them". This was how Gandhiji encouraged women and gave them strength to move forward. Speaking of the importance of Khadi, Gandhiji said, "If the child is ugly, will any mother throw him out? So also shall we throw our clothes prepared by us? No, we must know how to respect our goods, prepared by us. They should be dear to us. Wear *khadi* that we prepare. For giving strength to Swadeshi movement this is essential". Taking que from his message, several women began to prepare *khadi*". They felt that the future of the nation depended on them.

Discarding Jewellery

Women donated their valuable jewellery for the cause of the nation. A 16 year old girl by name Kaumudi after his speech in Kerala, wanted to donate a gold bangle and asked for Gandhiji's autograph. 'What will you give, if I gave autograph Gandhi asked. She gave her second bangle also – did you take permission of your parents? He again asked. Even before giving a reply, she removed her necklace also and put it in the hands of Gandhiji. These jewels whom you removed, you should not wear again, Gandhjiji said and she promised not to wear. Again another question by him. "When you get married, if your husband compels you to wear them, are you going to oblige". She said quickly "I will never marry such a man", that is how women sacrificed and how they dedicated. (*Harijan* – Editorial – January 19, 1973)

Social Evils

Child marriage was considered to be a social evil by Gandhiji. So, he propagated against this evil because it would affect not only the mother but also the children to be born. In those days 181 out of 1000 were dead soon after birth as per some estimates and in some areas, this number was as high as 400, whereas in England such deaths were 60 and in Japan 124.

Gandhiji said "These figures say, that we must sink our heads in shame. What is required is awareness among rural women. We must be able to convince them." In a letter written to Gandhiji Mrs. Margaret Cousins wrote that a thirteen year old girl was burnt to death by her 26 year old husband. Moved by this incident, Gandhjiji wrote, "Child marriage is morally and physically a crime, a sin, a social evil. There is need to bring an act to ban these child marriages. But only Acts cannot bring about the change. Minds of the people should change. A girl below 18, should not be married. (*Young India*, August 26, 1926).

Widow Marriage

Hindu widows remained unmarried and remarriage was considered to be disrespectful. Those who married were looked down upon. Therefore Gandhiji took it as a cause and gave a call to end the evil practice of widowhood.

"There should be social renaissance firstly.

Secondly, the economic revolution and

Thirdly, Purna Swaraj" suggested Gandhiji, Ranade, Gokhale and Chandavarker also felt that even before achieving independence, social revolution is essential. Political awakening means *Jagriti*' among people. This awareness is not possible unless there is change in all fields. When once the nation is awakened, it will not be content with only social reforms, they felt.

"If we see several thousands of women amidst us, living in despair and helplessness, it means, we are sitting on a volcano. So, if we want to keep Hindu Dharma pious, we must put an end to this forced widowhood. Those who have widows in their houses, should start this movement and make it a success. They will automatically get cooperation from others. Widow remarriage is not a sin. Widowhood is not a religious practice. But all should not be compelled to marry also. It should be left to their free will." (*Young India* 5-8-1926).

Of course, today this is not a big problem. Sociologically, it is considered to be an evil also. But such a change was possible only because of the efforts of our elders, especially of the reformers.

Removal of Purdah

"*Purdah* is an uncivilised tribal tradition. This is bringing untold misery to the nation." Gandhiji felt. "By *purdah*, we cannot keep up piety. It cannot be imposed by anybody from above. A pious feeling should come from the depth of the hearts." Against this *purdah* system, there were several demonstrations in Bihar. Leaders like Babu Rajendra Prasad, Babu Vajra Kishori Prasad gave life to this movement. They were born in Hindu culture and had great respect for Indian tradition. Gandhiji said:

"*Purdah* should be a thing of the past" (*Young India* 26th July 1928).

No doubt, it is a thing of the past today mostly among the Hindus. Though not in all societies.

Women and Religion

Gandhiji had his own ideas on religious beliefs. "For us, religion means observing a code of conduct in eating and living. We also feel that one is superior and the other is inferior. Nothing else can be total ignorance than this. I want to appeal to you. To observe certain external practices cannot be called religion. Character is more essential. If we look down upon anyone, it is nothing but degrading God and truth. So, get rid of such false notions, said Gandhiji.

Do Boycott But Against What?

"All languages say that a woman is half of a man. English language goes a step further and says that "she is the better half of man. Man and woman are not separate. They are two parts of the same whole. Unless we add the other, it cannot be complete. Therefore, boycott all the senseless, useless customs. Observe those rules which you feel are genuine and useful. By this boycott, no one will come up. When piety is the basis or ideal for non-cooperation, nothing untoward happens." Telling about his image of independent India and the role of women in it, Gandhiji said, "Believe in giving good education to women. By competing and running with man, I don't think a woman can discharge her duties properly. She can lead the nation not by mere competition with man. She cannot reach a high level. She should work in an exemplary manner and in a way she can bring glory to man." Thus, Gandhiji spoke on several subjects concerning women on several platforms highlighting the evils in society and how to combat them. "Never seek patronage. I don't have any craze to tell that "Freedom" is wanted in all respects. It is dangerous to seek membership on the basis of discrimination of womanhood; on this base, never seek patronage, seek justice. It is the best policy to learn regional languages. The education would make you proper citizens but not English education or foreign civilisation."

Whatever may be the application or efficacy of such notions of Gandhiji, he took up the cause of women and in a way organised them under the banner of Congress.

Kasturba Gandhi

Mrs. Kasturba Gandhi and Mrs. Kamala Nehru were two of the foremost patriotic women, who had dedicated their lives to the cause of freedom and women.

Mrs. Kasturba Gandhi (1869-1944), the brave and courageous wife of Mahatma Gandhi, was the "world-famed heroine of a hundred noble sufferings in a nation's cause". As a devoted wife, Kasturba shared fully the eventful life of Gandhiji through joy and suffering and proved herself the very embodiment of all that is fine and pure in Indian womanhood. She had been in the forefront of the freedom struggle right from the South Africa *Satyagraha* days.

In a message to the country, immediately after the arrest of Gandhiji in the Non-Cooperation movement in 1922, Kasturba said,

"My dear countrymen and countrywomen, my dear husband has been sentenced today to six years of simple imprisonment. While I cannot deny that this heavy sentence has to some extent told upon me, I have consoled myself with the thought that it is not beyond our powers to reduce that sentence and release him by our own exertion long before his term of imprisonment is over."

"I have no doubt that, if India wakes up and seriously undertakes to carry out the constructive programmes of the Congress, we shall succeed not only in releasing him but also in solving to our satisfaction all the three issues which we have been fighting for the last eighteen months or more.

"The remedy therefore lies with us. If we fail, the fault will be ours. Therefore, I appeal to all men and women who feel for me and have regard for my husband, to wholeheartedly concentrate on the constructive programme and make it a success."

She was, as an English admirer puts it "a valiant participator in the fights in manifold causes which her great husband espoused ... Her smile lighted up with joy her little world around her husband.

Her eyes enveloped him with affectionate understanding. She kept company with the springy feet and was reminded of undying youth. She was a self-forged instrument of something above and beyond her. She was never a sorrowing wife seeking solace in a domestic tangle. She enlivened the dull moments with joyous jokes. In the welter of activities, she was the master of the situation. She applied the principle of non-violence to the fluctuating experiences of everyday life. She kept up the poise and pose of a yogi, she willed her body to perform her appointed task. She shaped the lives of those around her. Her courtesy was incomparable." (J.S. Bright, *The Women Behind Gandhi*, pp. 49-50).

She served many a term in jail and travelled with Gandhiji. During his last imprisonment, she addressed countless number of meetings and spoke to men and women about political struggle for Home Rule. She devoted her life to the service of her people and country. In short, her life had been one of saintly service and an inspiration to countless number of our women.

Mrs. Kasturba passed away on February 22, 1944 while serving her term in prison (Aga Khan Palace) at Poona. The country was moved to profound sorrow at the sad demise of Kasturba. Glowing tributes were paid to her. One of them said "Her death has placed the crown of martyrdom on a life of sorrow. She, who dedicated her life to the service of her husband and the ideals for which he strove all through, has been marked out for the Supreme honour of laying it down in the great cause.... in the illumined pages of the history of the struggle for freedom of our country, her name will occupy an honoured place and as years pass, it is sure to gain more imperishable renown." (J.S. Bright, *op.cit.*, p.72)

Eminent women like Mrs. Sarala Devi Chanda Rani of Tagore's family, Mrs. Annie Besant, Mrs. Sarojini Naidu, Mrs.Kamala Nehru, Mrs. Rameswari Nehru, Mrs. Kamala Devi Chattopadhyay, Mrs. Vijaylakshmi Pandit, Raj Kumari Amrit Kaur, and Mrs. Uma Nehru were some of the leaders who were in the forefront of the freedom struggle.

Sarojini Naidu

The dynamic genius among the galaxy of leading patriotic women was Mrs. Sarojini Naidu who was a poetess and a brilliant speaker with a powerful personality. She joined the Congress and worked ceaselessly for the freedom of the country. She went to prison a number of times and worked on various important committees set up for the cause of freedom. With her silver tongue, she moved vast audiences and she travelled through the breadth and length of the country. She also had the honour to serve as the President of the National Congress and in that capacity, she accompanied Gandhiji for the Round Table Conference at London. She is popularly known as the Nightingale of the East and her poetry is simple and heart warming.

Jawaharlal Nehru says this about her "Here was a person of great brilliance—vital and vivid. Here was a person in the so many gifts but above all some gifts which made her unique. She infused artistry and poetry into our national struggle."

Sarojini had her ideas about "The coming women of India." Today, we who dream dreams of the coming women of India, have our hopes centred round institutions like Kanya MahaVidyalaya, Jullunder, institutions like that of Prof. Karve in Pune .... the institutions that would send to the world women not merely brought up and fed in the dry pages of lifeless books rather women trained in the beauties and necessities of life. These women would go forth not bearing the burden of dead knowledge but culture transmitted in the services of humanity." It is in the comradeship of sexes that future India shall come out, men and women working hand in hand and supplementing each other."

The Bazaars of Hyderabad, the palanquin bearers, the weavers, the snake charmers, the wandering beggar minstrels – all inspired in the poetess a strange rich mood. She has portrayed all walks of Indian life in the glittering pages of her poetry. Her method of description is national. "June Sunset," "Indian Gipsy" poems like "Love and Death", "Caprice", "The Soul's Prayer", In salutation to My Father's Spirit "and Ode to H.H. The Nizam of Hyderabad" are Sarojini's poems, that could win for her lasting laurels. The imagery is so pretty, the expression so near, the rhymes so tidy even today that one is led to suspect the depth of spontaneous emotion.

In another poem "Sanctuary", she writes so beautifully.

"Take my flesh to feed your dogs if you choose,
water your garden trees with my blood, if you will.
Turn my heart into ashes, my dreams into dust,
Am I not yours, O Love, to cherish or kill,
strangle my soul and fling it into the fire!

Why should my true lover falter or fear or reb.
Love, I am yours, to lie in your
breast like a flower,
Or burn like a week for your sake in the flame of hell".

Such was her poetry! She was a remarkable personality even otherwise.

Her memory is honoured in India, not only great patriot and a fighter for just causes, but also as a great woman, at "once brave and tender" who brought cheer and courage into the loves of the big and the small alike by her laughter and her songs.

She spoke as a Governor from Lucknow thus "we are reborn today out of the crucible of our sufferings. Nations of the world greet you in the name of India, my mother whose name has a roof of Snow, whose walls are of living Seas, whose doors are always open to you ... I give the whole world the freedom of this India, that has never died in the past, that shall be indestructable in the future and shall lead the world to ultimate peace."

She often likened herself in that palatial establishment to a bird in a cage, a title particularly apt in the light of the one given by Mahatma Gandhi of "Bharat Kokila". She was the Superb hostess of this "gilded cage" making an official establishment into a beautiful home, a warm and welcoming official residence into a centre of importance and dignity and as many speeches and letters would show, her heart was heavy for the people.

"The older I grow, the more faith I have that the young people of the world will fulfil my dreams, my unfulfilled dreams .... let us speak of unity, not division. Let us speak of love, and not of hatred, let us speak of fellowship and not of rights. Let us speak of duty nobly and beautifully rendered. May we be the standard bearers of the new world."

Gandhiji in his a *Young India* wrote like this.

"I do not think any praise of Mrs. Sarojini Naidu is over done... She has wonderful charm of manner and is tireless in her duties"...I have compared her to Mira Bai ... She has such strength of mind and such love for her motherland that when occasion demands, she meets it. God alone knows from where she gets the strength."

By 1924, her leadership was acknowledged sufficiently for her name to be put forward for the presidentship of the Belgaum Congress. Though Gandhiji was eventually persuaded to preside, he made his views known in the issue of *Young India* of July 17, captioned "Sarojini the Singer". He wrote "Though I believe, I can contribute my humble share in the promotion of Hindu-Muslim unity, in many respects, she can do better. She intimately knows more Mussalmans than I do. She has access to their houses, which I cannot pretend to. Added to these qualifications, is her sex, which is the strongest qualification in which no man can approach her."

The impression made by her eloquence has been recorded in the History of Indian National Congress by Pattabhi Sitaramayya "Sarojini took charge with a few choice words. Her address was an expression of courage and hope."

Her eloquence gained worldwide attention. *New York Times* wrote, "A Joan of Arc, who rose to inspire India."

In her presidential address at the Kanpur Congress, Sarojini had called for a women's section of Congress.

A new adventure in 1928. She attended Pan-Pacific Conference in Honolulu (America) Miss Mayo's notorious book – Anti-Indian "Moher India" had attracted wide notice, Gandhiji asked her to visit America and Canada to rectify the wrong impressions that were created. She started her visit in a characteristic manner. "What do you think of Katherine Mayo?", "Who is she?", was her reply. Her humour, her eloquence and personality captured the journalists and her tour and speeches were widely reported.

"Mrs Naidu", commented the influential *New York Times*, "is a singular combination of personal qualities, her songs and poems reveal only love for the beautiful in nature and humanity."

In her letters to her daughter, during this hectic "Passage to America, she was wholly the mother giving warm and human accounts of the people she met. The annual poetry luncheon in New York, where she was the guest of honour – all the small intimate reactions to events to which she was the centre. Being so different from the popular image of an Indian woman, Sarojini's personality entranced and enthralled her audience. Working steadily from the East to the West Coast, she spoke not only on Indian womanhood, modern India renaissance and the spiritual ideals of India but also gave before select audiences recitations of her poetry.

She was feted wherever she went and many banquets were arranged in her honour. The famous New York International House, was the venue of one of the many and her speech on this occasion was "Better understanding between India, of the old world and America of the new". She described her mission as "the gospel of the mystic spinner" as interpreted by a "wandering singer". The intellectuals and the elite showered their attention on her; she took care to meet the American people at all levels.

She made a point to seek out all scholars, writers, politicians, preachers and especially men and women who had served humanity. She stayed in the midst of the slums of Chicago and wrote, "It breaks my heart to see the helpless, hopeless, silent and patient bitterness and the mental suffering of the educated Negroes ... They are so cultured, so gifted, some of them so beautiful, all of them so infused with the earnest and sensitive appreciation of all that is authentic in modern ideas of life .... and yet there is bar sinister upon their brow. They are the socially and spiritually outcast children of America."

Now I will quote a few of her poems:

1. *Let us rise, O my heart,*
   Let us gather the dreams that remain
   We shall conquer the sorrow of life
   With the sorrow of song.

2. *Where the Golden, glowing*
   Champak buds, are blowing
   By the swiftly flowing streams,
   Now, when day is dying,
   These are fairies flying
   Scattering a cloud of dreams.

3. *The hope of a bride or the dream of a maiden*
   Watching the petals of gladness unfold,

and looks towards the
.... timid future shrinking
there alone
Beneath her marriage veil of mysteries.

4. *Shall we in the midst of life's exquisite chorus*
Remember our grief
O heart, when the rapturous season,
is o'er us
Of blossom and leaf?
Their joy from the birds and the
streams let us borrow,
O heart! Let us sing
The years are before for weeping
and sorrow ...
Today it is spring!

5. *Weavers, weaving at break of day,*
Why do you weave a garment so gay?
Blue as the wing of a halcyon wild,
We weave the robes of a new-born child,
Weavers, weaving at fall of night,
Why do you weave a garment so bright?
Like the plumes of a peacock purple and green
We weave the marriage-veils of a queen
Weavers, weaving solemn and still
What do you weave in the moonlight chill
While a feather and white as a cloud
We weave a dead man's funeral shroud
And here is a little pretty poem.

6. *O mystic Lotus, sacred and sublime*
In myriad petalled grace inviolate
Supreme o'er transient storm of tragic fate
Deep-rooted in the waters of all time
what legions loosed from many a far-off clime
Of wile bee hord's twilips in satiate,
And hungry winds with wings of
hope or hate,
Have thronged and pressed round thy miraculous prime

To devastate thy loveliness, to drain
The midst rupture of thy glorious heart."

Thus quite a few of her songs of love and devotion are pretty, colourful and melodious. But power and passion are not the qualities associated with them.

She composed "The Gate of Delight", comprising a series of light songs—The Offering, The East, Ecstasy, The Lute Song, If You Call Me the Sins of Love, The Desire of Love and The Vision of Love.

Opening stanza of "Offering" reads as follows:

Were beauty mine, beloved, I would bring it
Like a rare blossom to love's glowing shine
Were a dear youth mine, Beloved, I would fling it
Like a rich pearl into Love's lustrous wine.

The stanza, as well as the whole poem is replete with the mystic ecstasy of the medieval saint poets and the well turned conceits of Persian poetry, with all its polished conventions.

She says in "Feast",

Bring no pearls from ravished seas
Gems from rifled hemispheres
Grant me Love in priceless boon
All the sorrow of your years
All the secret of your tears

The imagery is so pretty, the expression so near, the rhyms so tidy, that one is led to suspect the depth of spontaneous emotion.

Following is one of Sarojini's early poems:

To priests and to prophets
The joy of their creeds
To kings and their consorts
The glory of deeds and peace to the vanquished
And hope to the strong ...
For me, O my master,
The rapture of song!
Life of my life, death's bitter sword,
Hath rent us like a broken word,

Rent us in twain who are but one....
Shall the flesh survive, when the soul is gone.
Mother, O Mother, where fore doest thou sleep?
Arise, and answer for thy children's sake....
Waken O slumbering mother and be crowned,
Who once went empress of the sovereign past....
My proud soul shall be forgiven
For a passionate sin it will never repent,
And I shall be deemed, O Love and driven
and hurled from Heaven's high battlement
Down through the deep ages, alone, unfrightened
Flung like a pebble thro burning space
But the speed of my fall shall be sweet and brightened
By the memoried joy of your radiant face.
In the "Time of Roses", she cries:
Put me in a shrine of roses,
Drown me in a wine of roses ....
Bind me on a pyre of roses
Burn me in a fire of roses
Crown me with the rose of love.

Some women took part in the terrorist movement also about whom I shall write now.

Women Taking Part in Terrorism

Santhi and Sunithi

Stevens, Magistrate of Komilla District was known as a terrible fellow. So, to take vengeance on him, Santhi and Sunithi of 15 years age planned to enter into his bungalow, on the pretext of handing over applications in the month of December 1931. They could hide pistols in their half sarees. When Stevens entered the hall, pistols were fired and Stevens died. These two girls were arrested and police harrassed them a lot. The court imprisoned them for life. Sunithi's father had many children. Payment of his pension was stopped. The relatives and friends, who wanted to help him, were also harassed by the police. Sunithi's brother was prepared to work as a labourer. But, nobody was willing to take work from him. So, because of poverty and malnutrition, he died of tuberculosis. The whole family was shattered because of Sunithi's participation in terrorist activity.

Ujvala Majumdar

Ujvala Majumdar joined the guerilla movement in her fifteenth year. She participated in several struggles from 1930-35. Finally, when she fired at the Bengal Governor in the Race Course field of Darjeeling in 1935, she was caught red-handed. After much of harassment, she was sent to Andamans on life imprisonment.

Preeti Latha

Preeti Latha was head mistress of a girls school. She wanted to talk to Surya Sen and Nirmal Sen and so she reached Dhalghat village. On 13th June 1932, in the evening police encircled the whole village and tried to enter the house where Surya Sen was residing. But revolutionaries tried to fire at the police. A police officer died and Surya Sen and Apurva Sen also died. But Preeti Latha escaped.

There was a police club in a place called "Pahartali". Soldiers used to harass women and children of nearby villages. Sometimes, they were burning the houses of villagers. Preeti Lata assumed the leadership and under her guidance, another eight youth invaded the police club on September 24th at about 9 p.m. Sentries ran away. Some of those who were inside the club died. Some fired back. Along with Preeti Latha, her follower also returned after this incident.

Soldiers followed the revolutionaries and fired. After a long battle, a bullet pierced Preethi Latha. Immediately she consumed potassium cyanide available with her and collapsed. An appeal hidden in the wraps of her clothes read as follows:

"For the emancipation of our motherland, Indian women should fight against the British imperialists with arms. Death is a must even if we live for a long time. Instead of living for a hundred years, as slaves, it is better to die as heroes for the cause of independence."

Women's Organisations: Newspapers

In the year 1917, the first women's organisation was started by Mrs. Margaret Cousins. Mrs. Anne Besant was leading the Home Rule Movement.

On behalf of this organisation, a delegation of women representatives met Montagne and requested him to grant Voting right for women.

After 10 years, All India Women's Conference was started and this was the first people's organisation. Smt. Rama Bai Ranade, Pandita Rama Bai, Mrs. P.K. Ray, Lady Bose, Bhikajee Kama, Shireen Cursetji worked for creation of new opportunities for women.

As a result of their efforts, in the year 1928, two Indian women passed in "Medicine" and awarded degrees. During that time British Government with conservative ideas was not encouraging women's education and so there were not many educated women in the country.

In 1878, some Indian women studying at the universities went to America also for studies. Many "Seva Sadans" and "Widow Homes" came into existence. Some papers were also started for propagation of patriotism and love for India.

Women's Indian Association started a paper called *Streedharma*, All India Women's Conference started *Roshni* and National Council for Women started Bulletin. National Council of women was established in 1925 and was affiliated to the International organisation. All Indian Women's Conference could deal with the United Nations.

In addition to the above organisations, Kasturba Memorial Trust, Bharat Sevak Samaj, Bharat Scouts and Guides, Red Cross, Young Women's Christian Association began to work for the welfare of women.

In course of time, all the newspapers started several women's magazines. It is not easy to mention all of them as they were innumerable, circulated all over the country in all languages.

Women Shining as Writers, Journalists

By the time four decades passed in the 20th century, many women got educated and took to jobs also. Many joined government service as clerks, typists, teachers and nurses and did wonderfully well. In addition to medicine and education fields, women have began to shine in science and engineering fields also. Even before India achieved independence, many women got their economic independence.

Women began to shine as writers also. The first writer was 'Toru Datta'. She could write in English, which was a foreign language. She travelled all over Europe, and could attract the attention of intellectual community with her writings. She was born as the third daughter of Gobin Chander Dutta of Calcutta. Dutta's family happened to go to Europe in 1869 itself and so Toru Dutta could learn English and French. The delicacy and sweetness of French language appealed to her more and she developed taste for writing poetry in French. In 1875, English translation of 165 of her French poems, was brought out in a book form. Though she was suffering from ill health, she could translate some beautiful slokas of *Ramayana, Mahabharata* and *Sakuntala* into English and prepared a compilation (*Life and letters of Toru Dutta:* Harihar Das).

Due to acute illness she breathed her last, on 30th August in 1877, even before she completed her twenty two year of age. If she were to live for more time, she could surely have created wonderful works and could have won laurels as a great writer.

The best and most famous of all her writings is translation of Sanskrit *kavyas* which was a compilation. It was published in the name of "Ancient Puranic Songs of Hindustan. The famous English writer Edmond Ghouse, wrote its foreword.

In 1878, her translation of French poems into English had three editions. Her novel in Bengali *Biyana* was published serially in a Bengali paper. Another novel written in French and published in France created much sensation in France. In a short span of three to four years, she could win name and fame as a popular poetess and a famous novelist. God was unkind to her and she passed away at a very young age.

We have already noticed in the previous pages, the extraordinary talent of Sarojini Naidu, who got the appreciation of one and all, because of her writings. She came to be known as the "rose" of the nation.

Smt. Krishna Hathee Singh, the beloved sister of Pandit Nehru wrote "Shadows on the Wall", "We Nehrus" and "With no Regrets". Andal of Tamil Nadu wrote *Tiruppavai*, singing in a beautiful language the qualities of Krishna. Mukti Bai was a Marathi lady, she imagined Krishna as her lover and wrote good songs about him with great marvellous aesthetic sense. Madhayidasa was a worshipper of Chaitanya Maha Prabhu and a great Vaishnava singer.

In course of another 50 years we find many, many women in all languages, as poetesses and novelists.

In Music and Dance : Painting

Saint Tayagaraja was a Telugu man who settled in Tamil Nadu. M.S. Subhalakshmi, with her melodious voice, could sing his kritis with utmost devotion even in the United Nations and won laurels, not only to herself individually but also for the nation. She was very popular even before India got independence. She received "Padma Vibhushan" and also Magsaysay Award of Manila.

Several women like Rukmini Arundale who came from traditional families, took to dancing as a fine art and could shine as a great dancer. She brought name and fame to Bharata Natyam in the world and established Kalakshetra at Madras, which is doing wonderful work.

Mrinalini Sarabhai is another dancer with talent. Sarla Saigal, Tara Chowdhary, Shireen Roshan, Vazifdar, Vinu Indrani, Anjali Hora, Indrani Rehman, are some other outstanding dancers, who travelled all over the world and gave performances and could win fame for the nation. Kumudini of Ram Gopal Ballet, Savarthi, Amala of Udaya Sanker group are of great talent and could spread the fame of India abroad. Roshan Kumari, Damayanti Joshi, Rani Karna, are experts in Kadhak. Jhaveri sisters, Nyana Ranjan are good in Manipuri type of dance.

After independence, many could shine as great dancers. Yamini Krishnamurthy, Sobha Naidu, Swapna Kumari, Raja Reddy and Radha Reddy, Alekhya Punjala, Umabharati are some of the experts who are well known as good dancers.

Amrita Shergill is the first woman who took to painting. Sheela Aden, Annena Ahmed are good experts. Ratnala Kamala Bai, whom I personally know, was a good painter. Many women later on joined Santiniketan and learnt painting.

Voting Right for Indian Women

Whenever there was an upsurge of national unity, Britishers tried to suppress such move on the one hand and introduced some political reforms on the other.

On democratic lines, they introduced the system of election to *Panchayats* and Municipalities. They made Governor's responsible and answerable to the Viceroy and formed advisory councils. The members of these councils were nominated by them.

After the First World War, British Government felt that it is necessary to have elected members on these councils, instead of nominated members. So, they introduced for the first time in India, the system of elections in our country. Then they introduced 'right to vote', for the women also.

In England, in the yea. ..., the right of voting was introduced. But, it could be possible only after strong fight. Till that time, all the countries felt that it is not so good to grant voting right to women. But, in India, this sort of grant of voting right to women is really surprising. Before Montagul-Chelmsford reforms were introduced, there was so much of controversy about this, issue both in England and India. Some educated women argued vehemently that they should have a 'right to vote'. Some men with lofty ideals also supported this argument. Montague was Secretary of State in India. He came to India, to give a shape to the new constitution. Then a group of women met him as a delegation and submitted a memorandum. On 1st December, 1917, the delegation met him in Madras and made him to hear their argument. Montague wrote the following words in his diary.

'Some women came to meet me and told me interestingly, that women needed education, and they also want more hospitals. Sarojini Naidu is a poetess. She is an attractive and brilliant woman. But in her heart of hearts, she is revolutionary. She is the leader of this delegation. Another woman is Dr. Joshi, belonging to Bombay. They asked for 'voting right' to women. It was Mrs. Margaret Cousins, who originally wrote this memorandum. Mrs Cousins is a theosophist and a disciple of Anne Besant, a foreigner. They told me that Congress would pass a resolution, that it is necessary to grant voting right to women."

Montague listened to them patiently, politely replied to them and sent them giving farewell. But by the time Montague-Chelmsford reforms were prepared and published, voting right of woman, could not find a place in it. Everyone was surprised.

South Brea Franchise Committee also, did not show favour for the idea of granting voting right to women in India. Their conviction was, "So long Indian women are far away from social life, there is no advantage of giving them voting right."

The Committee members expressed the above idea openly. They actually came to India, to know about the people's opinion on the issue. Of course, women agitated but it was of no use.

Though there was voting right in electing Panchayat Raj bodies, many women were not utilising such right. So, there may not be any use by simply giving this right to vote, the members of the committee felt. But Indian women never felt desparately about this and did not stop their agitation. They continued the struggle.

In 1999, after the "Government of India Bill" was introduced in the parliament, they formed a "Jt Committee" on behalf of both the houses. Mrs. Cousins, Mrs. Sarojini Naidu and Miss Hirabai met the members of this Jt. Committee and made some proposals saying that voting right should necessarily be given to women in India. After that the committee members made some recommendations. Most important among the recommendations was that "the elected legislators should consider the proposal, and then decide."

Those legislators, who were Indians and duly elected, resolved that voting right should be given to women. In principle, the proposal was accepted in the end. In the year 1920, for the first time in India, voting right was introduced in Travancore. In 1921, in Madras voting right for women was granted. In 1922 in Bombay and in 1925, it was introduced in Punjab and in Central Provinces in 1927. Bihar was the last to introduce it in 1929.

But, by 1930, the voting right was introduced in all states.

Right to get Elected to Assemblies

Right to vote was achieved. But by that no tangible results were achieved. So, women continued their agitation. To give a right to women to participate in the assemblies, was not possible as the assemblies had no such power. Only the parliament has that power. So, women began to agitate that "those assemblies which have given the right to vote, should also give the right to women, to get elected as members of the assemblies." Thereupon, the Parliament introduced "Reforms Bill".

In 1926, when elections were held in Madras, Smt. Kamala Devi Chattopadhyaya and Mrs. Hannan Anjelo stood as representatives. No one got elected! While Kamala Devi got 4461 votes, her opponent got 4976 votes. Margin of defeat being very narrow, implies that people showed their willingness to elect her. After some more agitation for some more time, Smt. Muthu Lakshmi Reddy was 'nominated' as a 'member' by the Madras Government. So, that means, the first woman who stepped into the 'Assembly' was Smt. Muthu Lakshmi Reddy.

The number of women on the voter's lists was very less. In Madras state, there was one woman for every ten men; in Assam state, there was only one woman for every 114 men.

By this ghastly picture it appears that women did not possess the requisite qualifications or economic qualities, to remain as voters.

To remove this inequality, Britishers made some attempts.

They formed three committees:

(1) Lothian Committee,
(2) Statutory Commission,
(3) Franchise sub-committee.

They reserved many constituencies separately for women. But, there was no use even by this. At last, in 1937, Smt. Sarojini Naidu introduced the resolution that, "every adult should have the right to vote". Organisations like Women's Indian Association, All India Women's Conference, National Council of India for Women, led agitation asking for a right to vote for every adult Indian. Indian National Congress supported this "demand" of the women's organisations. Along with 'Declaration of Fundamental Rights of Citizenship", their 'right to vote' also should be granted to every adult. In fact this was the aim and ideal of Congress. In 1935, according to Government of India Act, Adult Franchise, was introduced in all states. But, even by that time, the number of women was very much less. One women for every seven men, was notified and included in the list of voters. Only fourteen per cent, out of the total population were shown as adults.

In the year 1937, Congress Governments were formed. In Bombay, Madras, Orissa, Central Provinces and Assam, several women got elected as members to the assemblies. Some women took over responsible posts like ministers and dy. speakers. Vijaylakshmi Pandit was elected as minister for local administration in U.P. She wrote a book entitled "So I Became a Minister in those days."

Smt. Achanta Rukmini Lakshmipathi, became a minister in Madras State. Smt. Malani got elected as a Dy.Speaker. Smt. Jyothi Venkatachalam became a minister later on. These ministries did not function for a long time. Except introducing some reforms for the prisoners in jails, these ministers could not bring about any change as expected. By 1939, these ministers had to submit resignations.

In 1949, after India became independent, every adult in India got a voting right So, every woman who was above eighteen, automatically got the right. With this, a new chapter was started and all the work done for the development of women became a success.

Congress, along with political resolutions, also passed resolutions for social justice, especially for the advancement of women. So, on account of their efforts and ideals, women also got voting right along with men and thus a political right to get elected to the assemblies also came to women alongwith men.

REFERENCES

1. Altekar, A.S. *The Position of Women from Pre-Historic Times to the Present Day* – Benaras Hindu University, The Culture Publication House, 1938.
2. *The Position of Women in Hindu Civilization*, Oxford University Press, London 1941.
3. *Education in Ancient India*, The Indian Bookshop, Benares City, 1934.
4. *All India Women's Conference Reports*, Lahore 1931 and Hyderabad 1946.
5. Andews, C.F. *Mahatma Gandhi's Ideas*, The Macmillan Company, New York 1930, *India and the Simon Report,* George Allen and Unwin, London, 1920
6. Asha Geoffrey: *Gandhi – A Study in Revolution 1969.*
7. Athawala Parvathi Bai: Mystory – *The Autobiography of a Hindu Widow*, Translated by Rev. Justin E. Abbot G P Putnams Sons, New York, 1930.
8. Banerji, Surendranath: *A Nation in the Making,* Oxford University Press, London, 1925.
9. Billington Mary Francos : *Women In India,* Chapman & Hall, London, 1895.
10. Butier Clementina : *Pandita Rana Bai Saraswati – Pioneer in the Movement for the Education of Child Widow*, Fleming H. Ravell Company New York, 1922.
11. Chapman, E.F.: Sketches of Some Distinguished Indian Women, W.H. Allan and Company, Calcutta, 1891.
12. Chattopadhyay and Others – *The Awakening of Indian Women,* Every Man's Press, Madras, 1939.
13. Cousins, M.E.: The Awakening of Asian Womenhood, Ganesh and Company, Madras, 1922.
14. Hingorani, A.T. Ed.: To the Women, By Mahatma Gandhi Vol. I and II *Law Journal Press* Allahabad 1941.
15. Sharma, A.N. : *Women and Society,* Padmaja Publication, Baroda, 1947.
16. Nehru Shyam Kumari Ed.: *Our Cause – A Symposium* Kitabistan, Allahabad, No date.
17. Sunderland, J.T : *India in Bondage Lewis* Copeland Company, New York, 1929.
18. Zacharias, H.C.E. : *Renascent India – From Ram Mohun Roy to Mohan Das Gandhi*, George Allan and Unwin, London, 1933.
19. S. Sree Devi : *Gandhi and the Emancipation of Indian Woman*, printed at Chary and Co., SPRD, Secunderabad, 1969.

CHAPTER 13

Post Independence Period

After India became independent, the status of women changed altogether. The laws in force were different in different provinces before 1947. Under the leadership of Pandit Jawaharlal Nehru, the first Prime Minister of India, B.N. Rao Committee was formed to work out the necessary changes in society. The members of the committee toured the four corners of the country and obtained the opinions of the people and based on their recommendationsm in 1955, some important Acts were passed. The Special Marriage Act, Hindu Marriage Act, Hindu Succession Act, Act of Maintenance were okayed by the Parliament. Hindu Minority Guardianship Act. Hindu Adoption Act were passed in 1956. Inequality of women was sought to be removed in all aspects. The woman was given, nationally equal status in all respects. The subordination of yesteryears was removed. But in practice laws remains on papers only even today. The most unfortunate thing is this awakening among women is limited, to urban areas only. Still millions and millions of women in rural areas remain uneducated and dumb.

To bring about change a much bigger effort is needed.

Social Reforms in Independent India

Social reforms in Independent India do not seem to be successfully carried out. Birth of girl in an average Indian family is not considered to be a rejoicing event, as the birth of a boy.

Forty-nine per cent of girls in the age group of 6-11 were enrolled in schools in 1975 as against 73 per cent of boys. In the High School Stage (12-17) these figures were 19 and 36 respectively. Thus education has not made great strides in respect of women.

Employment of women, also tells the same story. During 1961-71, number of working men rose by 15.2 per cent, the number of women workers fell by 41.4 per cent. Crimes against women have increased, over 4,000 cases of rape were reported in 1979. Dowry deaths, molestations eve-teasing etc. have increased considerably.Most of the post independence social reforms like the dowry abolition and the laws against child marriage have proved ineffective. Social welfare work is only on paper where it is acted upon seriously, there is corruption and mismanagement.

In the 19th century, western education and learning led to revival of Indian culture. In the 20th century, westernism has lulled it into sleep. In 21st century, we are witnessing our boys and girls wearing English dress and talking about world politics and Information Technology, rather than our Vedanta or philosophy or our Indian culture.

The transformation brought about is remarkable in the field of education.

Education After Independence

When the Nationalist government was formed, there were 25 universities in the country and 643 colleges attached to them. There were 1,34,866 primary schools at the eve of independence and there were only 10,525,943 students on rolls.

After independence, the first education commission was the University Education Commission of 1948, under the chairmanship of Dr. S. Radhakrishnan, the then President of India. Later on there were several commissions, but it cannot be said that any appreciable headway was made in free India. Still there were illiterates and education did not mean anything to them.

Newspapers and magazines hold much influence with decision makers and opinion formers. New ideas can be introduced or perpetuated based on what is read by a dominant section of people called intelligentsia. It is this middle class that is to be educated on the importance of education for girls and the utility of making them competent to hold their responsibilities, more efficiently in society. More stress should be laid on women's issues and more space to be allotted by the owners of these papers and magazines for women's problems. Portrayal of women in this media, which is very powerful, will be widely understood and awareness among society would be built up. Presentation of women as 'victims' of atrocities and implications of such portrayal should be prevented as it is a negative measure and its results would be alarming.

More Stress on Women's Issues

A positive portrayal of women in the media would definitely

yield good results and would lead to building up self-confidence among women. Social issues from women's perspectives might be put for open discussion by the public and solutions sought from them. Working journalists may help more in this aspect and more and more women may be added to this category. Though the women of India have undergone lot of bitter experiences in the previous history, they could not overcome some problems or raise their voice against these problems due to the peculiar structure of society that existed in India.

Dr. Veena Majumdar (Majumdar, 1956) says that the question of women as an issue started in India from 19th century onwards when social reformers began to question the growing inequalities and the major evils of social customs like prohibition of widow re-marriage, child marriage, discrimination of women towards education, purdah system, dowry etc. At that point of time, women were considered as only down trodden people who had to suffer for the well-being of society. The social problems they faced were considered to be the legacy, by the British rulers and a few Orthodox Indians. The 19th century reformers, who were concerned about women were not taking into consideration the sufferings of lower class women who were secluded by men and also by upper middle class.

During the struggle for independence, these women raised their voice not only against Britishers but also against the evils towards them. Women's movements were started effectively under the influence of Gandhiji. Women India Association (WIA) was formed in 1927, the National Council of Indian Women in 1926 and the All India Women's Conference in 1927, took active part in condemning evil social customs and practices which denied equal status to women. One of the activities was to create awareness about the plight of woman. This was done through debates, discussions and by writing articles in journals and newspapers. Anyway, the efforts made in pre-independence era only generated a climate which helped women to organise themselves. During 1970s, there was a global awakening on the issues of women and many efforts were taken to put an end to their discrimination. These efforts encouraged and inspired women of all levels and a new awakening and conscientisation came over. 1975 is an historic year so far women are concerned. UNO declared it as International Women's Year. In Mexico, a world conference was organised and a plan of action was adopted. With this, there were many debates and conferences held all over the world and women's issues were taken up as important by educationists, administrators and other decision making bodies. Women's issues could also attract the attention of social scientists especially women scientists.

Government of India, constituted a committee to study the status of women in India, under the leadership of Mrs. Leela Dave, which submitted its report in 1975. This document provided the necessary impetus to many people to undertake studies or researches on women. Earlier writings on women simply portrayed her as a meek and submissive person, who does not possess any individuality of her own, but only had to help man in his life.

A few writings before independence were on prohibition of widow-remarriage etc. Women writers were also very few in number. There were no women journalists to ventilate the grievances of women and papers also did not take much interest in women's issues though they maintained a column for women.

Women's movement in Post-independence India

The dawn of independence generated a new hope and a definite opinion in the hearts of the masses of India. Indian Constitution permitted equality of both sexes. While guaranteeing certain Fundamental Rights like freedom of speech and expression, our experts also provided certain safety measures, treating women as a weaker section of society.

As a matter of policy, from1950-70, i.e. for nearly two decades, women's movement was slow. Government adopted some welfare measures for the betterment of women.

The Central Social Welfare Board, under the able guidance of Dr. Durga Bai Deshmukh was started with a programme of grants-in-aid for some activities like adult education centres for women and *balwadis* for children. Centres were started in the districts also. Capable women, who participated in the freedom struggle were nominated to supervise these activities. Many active social workers and women leaders rallied round this organisation.

Five year plans were prepared and implemented by government. Order of priority upto the Fourth Five-Year Plan was on education, health, rural welfare services etc. Schemes were formulated for "Development of Women" and they were not treated as partners in development of women". It is only during the Seventh Plan that the planners realised that unless women are developed, it is not possible to develop the society. It is during the last decades of twentieth century that women's groups became active to fight against violence, dowry deaths, sati, alcoholism, trafficking in women, prostitution, Devadasi system and communal and class conflicts.

A sizable amount of literature on woman's issues was produced and many autonomous women's groups have come forward, to take up the responsibility of the women's movement.

A Recap of Performance

We know many women participated in the freedom struggle. But, they did not raise the issues that effected them as women. They never fought for their liberation from traditional constraints. The main objective was to fight for independence of the country only. Moreover, the struggle was led by male leaders and so they conformed to the prevalent ideologies on the status of women in society.

But the political struggles of nineteenth and early 20th centuries led to the movement for solving women's problems in the Third World. Dr. Mulk Raj Anand has remarked in an interview, "women in our society has been so much humiliated that there is no way in which you can restore her dignity. As the manager of the family and culture, a woman is on a ceaseless quest for a credible meaning to life. She is now seeking an intelligent purpose to live honourably along with her male counterpart."

The woman's issue in the western world is mostly on identity, job equality and sexism. But, in India, it is a question of survival. In spite of facilities for education and better opportunities women are compelled to submit to the indignities imposed on her, still, by a tradition-bound society, more so by a patriarchal society.

After 1960, a strong woman's voice is built up in the country. Some have generated their own experiences. The nature of writing by women is circumscribed by her relationship with other members of the family. She has to play many roles simultaneously; as a wife, as a daughter and as a mother. Thus she is split into several personalities and the woman writer has to shoulder the responsibility of transforming prevalent values and to rewrite culture.

Mary Helen Washington writes, "The search for a real self that often takes a woman back to her girlhood, the need for solitariness, a space and time for oneself, the fear of male domination, the need to be an angel in the house at the cost of one's creativity – these are the themes dominating the fiction of women writers".

Fully aware of the implications of self identity, a woman has to assert herself. She has to behave as an agent for social change.

What Needs to be Done

The need of the hour is not simply to criticise the social or cultural or political structure that was already existing. The woman should be empowered in all spheres of life to enhance her status.

There is also need to redefine her role in participation or giving a new shape to society. Keeping in view the realities, in which women has to survive, individual problems should be treated as community's problems.

Women Carriers of Social Revolution

Certain recent trends are indicative of the emergence of Indian women from traditional shackles. There is a growing realisation that any social revolution in the developing countries would only come from women. But, there is a gulf of difference between urban and rural women and in their requirements. So, special institutions are to be developed and a special task force has to be appointed to function under the control of women's commissions. All development plans must have specific programmes for woman on priority basis.

Last two decades have been spent by critical activity both "on women" and "by women". The literature produced or the agitation of the women's groups have brought 'Gender', to the centre-stage of all development efforts. So, it is essential to find out alternative or strategies suitable, to work out a satisfactory approach, to increase or enhance women's participation in public life. Though we have witnessed development in post-independence era, in several sectors, the invisibility of women in decision making bodies, is to be taken cognisance of. This can come only when women come out in large numbers in socio-political activities and also link up their status situation with it. There is thus a close interaction and relationship between women's empowerment and their role in politics and decision making. This would bring about qualitative change in the lives of women and also in the functioning of public institutions.

Exclusion of women from positions of power devices and deprives the society of the contribution of capable women and their intelligence. Women can have their distinctive values and priorities, perspective in public life, as they are traditionally associated with the family and home.

With the increasing demand for participation of women in the political process and decision-making bodies, their involvement at the grass root level acquires special significance. Institutional mechanisms and concrete measures for enhancing and ensuring better qualitative and quantitative participation of women, should be worked out. A deeper analysis and sustainable action to synthesize different experiences of women in different situations to develop a broad-based forum for women's development needs to be taken up.

Social Movement and the Media

In the modern era, when the whole world is coming closer, feminist organisation should think of the importance of mass media, in building up public opinion. With different orientations and ideologies, programmes prepared and broadcast are received by people belonging to different sections. The mighty middle class that is steeped in superstitions, to be brought out and enlightened.

Representation of women in illustrations is another major problem. This is one of areas, on which women have to protest strongly.

Many Radio and TV programmes are produced on social issues from women's perspectives. To improve the quality of the programmes, more and more women should be made to participate or produce these programmes, so that negative portrayal of a woman is prevented to a large extent. Many stories are about women who are victims of violence and accidents. Over eighty per cent of pictures of women appearing in media are obscene or vulgar. Women are also depicted as victims of violence and also as victims of disease or objects of sex. In most of the cases, she is shown as committing suicide or being raped. This is something very intolerable. Courage and conviction should be installed in a woman. Self-confidence is to be brought up as a force positively for social change.

Many success stories of women may be shown, to instil courage in the young minds. Women are playing very important part in all spheres of life including the judiciary. Their experiences, their convictions and success may be inspiration to the less privileged.

On a more positive note, it is encouraging that the space allocated to women has increased but the imbalance in favour of negative coverage of women has yet to improve. The abundant presence of women as artists in illustrations could be seen as a traditional role as women have been regarded as 'custodians of culture' and sources of entertainment throughout history. More women should be encouraged to take up the profession of journalism, so that they can express well on women's issues and about society's improvement. In a country where women are considered inferior it is necessary to redefine what it means to be courageous. Present position of representation shows that:

In spite of all the constitutional and legal provisions, the representation of women in Parliament is 8 per cent, 9.11 per cent in the State Assemblies and 12.6 per cent in the council of ministers.

The voting percentage of women from a minimum of 37.1 in the election of 1952, moved upto a maximum of 68.17 per cent in 1984. Thus the increase in the number of women as voters and the eager involvement in politics, has attracted the attention of all political parties, though this has not reflected in their reprevention.

Women are at a disadvantage because of their low numerical strength as true representatives of women.

Change of Attitude in Society

The Indian society is not static. It has been undergoing many changes throughout its history. The pace of change was also not uniform in all regions or among all sections of our society. Processes such as education, urbanisation and industrialisation, spread of political institutions specially after independence have induced the society to change. But the influence of age-old prejudices based on caste, community, have remained intact in spite of modernisation.

Indian masses are basically wise in orientation and they are tolerant towards diverse faiths and diversities. So, it may be possible that in change of attitude that is to be brought about in their cultural ethos towards understanding of gender issues may bear fruit in course of time. When we look back to the social attitude of society towards education of girls, we have travelled far and wide in three decades. Now, education for girls is considered to be a necessity and it is taken for granted that unless intelligence of women is utilised, the development of society is not possible.

Migration is effecting a systematic transformation of traditional occupational structure and so migration to the city involves not only a change in residence but a glaring shift in economic standards of the individuals. Thus rural way of life is slowly making way for urbanisation of individuals. It is a fact that the impact of urbanisation is leaving its imprint in all spheres of social life. Thus caste and family antecedents are undergoing change and an individual in the city is free from certain social constraints.

Traditional Values Undergoing Change

Cultural heritage of India was passed on from one generation to another, through women and women only. The traditional pattern of society which existed in India, remained unchanged for some centuries, in spite of foreign rule because most of the people lived in rural areas. Westernisation had little impact on the educated urban elite. Because of migration and the intermingling of uneducated rural people with the urban folk, rigid tradition may lose its weight as a whole.

How far the Hindu way of life or its value system would influence the modern educated children brought up by the nuclear families is a million dollar question. Evidently, they are witnessing two different cultures. How far the rigid traditional values would be respected and followed by the present younger generation is doubtful. Some of the professional children, who are brought up in the tradition-centred homes, are, now out of sheer necessity, changing their attitudes.

Aspects of the process of modernisation have been distinguished in different categories. Division of the world into advanced and unadvanced societies, in addition to easier methods of communication, have recognised education as a means of development. Education and modern communication facilities, thus create and encourage development of an intelligentsia. Women also are part of this newly created intelligensia and so, they have their own will and identity. This is a healthy phenomenon, so far the modern educated women are concerned.

Now let us examine the institutions that are having effect on modernisation—the school and the cinema.

Educational system in India, so to say, is in a state of uncertainty and so also the powerful medium of cinema. If only we can effectively use these two powerful instruments for improving the image of women, for facing the challenges awaiting us, it will do a lot of good to the society.

It is for us to build up a society, in which women are able to live up to their full potential and contribute freely and meaningfully to the society in which they live. "To pursue a development planning without women in development focus would be wasteful and defeating—wasteful because of impotential loss of the vital human resources and self-defeating because development which does not bring about its benefits to the whole of society is self-defeating." (US Aid, 1982; 2).

So, any development project, which neglects either of these dimensions runs the risk of allocating resources without due regard for the real structure.

Effects of Media

Our modern age is media-oriented. The print media as well as the electronic media have immense influence on the minds of people, as it is a unifying force and also leading to communication revolution in India.

Mass Communication Facilities—Their Impact

Mass communication is a very crucial factor, not to be ignored, if the nation's vision of society is to be realised. Role of broadcasting towards nation building is being appreciated by everyone. But we have not used this dynamic medium appropriately due to lack of understanding of 'it'. It should be used to serve as a vehicle of social awakening to open up the minds of people.

How far have we used this medium for development? Of course national consciousness is evoked. Similarly, Doordarshan has helped to familiarise its viewers with a composite image of India, with diverse cultures. In times of crisis, joy or sorrow, this electronic media has tried to promote courage and solace.

In the *print media*, there is a realisation that monopolies are building up. In addition, there are a number of challenges. The emergence of video and audio cassettes has created a distinct advantage to the audiences.

Thus, it has become easier, to reach out to people living in remote areas also. So, to bring about the required change, the above communication methods can be effectively used.

Television and Social Change in Rural Areas

The types of TV programmes and the values and ideas they convey are important, of course, in determining the influence of Television. Cooking habits and menus are undergoing change as a result of TV. Women have started including noodles and sliced bread in their family's diet.

There are men who say that they are open to the idea of female empowerment. Many have chosen to educate their girls on par with boys. Some men are accepting that their women are working more for the family. There is constant reference to changing times, when compared to the times of their fathers and forefathers. But though the gender roles are changing a little bit in the household works, many roles still remain rigid. Women are still treated on a lower level than their men in all aspects of household life. It is the man who makes all the decisions in financial matters. Men eat when women serve and watch.

What is more enterprising is that men and women are open to ideas of change more than ever before. With the arrival of TV in the home, men and women are spending more time together sharing each other's company. This improves inter-personal relationships, which may lead to better understanding between each other. People from all sections of the community are increasingly gaining access to TV including both men and women.

Ravindranath Tagore in his book entitled 'Personality' had said that "The responsibilities of Indian women have increased when compared to the previous years. Her field of activity has exceeded the limits of her house." Very true, Indian woman has stepped out her house and has entered the outside world. Hitherto her duty was to keep the house and to look after the children. But today, she is the symbol of modern civilisation. She is not only a wife and a mother, but a responsible citizen of the country. That is why her responsibilities have become manifold.

Lakhs and lakhs of women are now university graduates. Many are shouldering the responsibilities of very high and important jobs. There is no academic body, which has no women member in it. Many are judges, lawyers, engineers and principals. Many gold medalists are girls in any college or university. As per a rough estimate, by 1975, 20,000 girls were doctors, 94,000 were graduates, 23,450 were university lecturers and other employees. Telephone and telegraph departments are having many women employees as stenoes, typists and office assistants. Many are artists like announcers in All India Radio and Doordarshan. Some are civil servants, able administrators and some are even ambassadors in other countries. Some are in the army, some are majors of local bodies and some other are capable members of legislatures and parliament. When such was the status of women by the International Women's Year (1975), there is an ugly picture of the other side of the coin.

There is no dearth of laws or Acts, but still woman is not an active participant in the endeavours of the government, in the building of nation. She is not a decision maker in several fields she is still considered to be a second rank citizen. 81.28 per cent of women are still living in rural areas. They are denied the uptodate knowledge of everyday life. They are still far away from the modern civilization. Status of women labourers working in tea gardens and small factories is much lower. School drop-outs are many among girls and the girl child is looked down upon when compared to her brother. Some women are still steeped in utter ignorance of what is happening around them. Child marriages, are still rampant in some segments of society. Dowry is still a social evil, which nobody is able to combat and we read of dowry deaths or burning of brides in newspapers everyday, the girl has no free choice in the selection of her husband, and parents only preside over her fate. Her role in the family affairs is merely supplementary or secondary.

Every one talks of progress. But what is real progress? How far does welfare of the society depend on the welfare or development of women? We must find out answers.

Panchayat Raj and its Advantages

After independence, the Indian government with a view to decentralise administration, formed a new institution called *Panchayat*. This new actualization of an old concept was an attempt to democratise the village community. When the old *panchayat* system was limited to male-dominant caste males, the present system seemed to be more egalitarian.

This new institution with two reserved seats, one for woman and the other for a representative of the lower castes was an effort to empower people at the grass root level, to make development initiatives on their own.

If any change is desired in the village community, change should be brought about on three important aspects: (1) marriage and the family, (2) caste and (3) class relations.

All these are interwoven in the social structure of village life. A new social environment is created in the village because of developmental activities, economic change and political process. Power relationships and a multitude of other forces within the village are working, sometimes against development. So also, if women's issues are to be sorted in the village society, this favourable environment, should be properly moulded.

The village is undergoing tremendous economic and cultural transformation. On the way, a silent revolution is picking up.

Women in Panchayat Raj: Beginning of a Silent Revolution

"But you cannot draw the masses into politics without drawing the women into politics as well. For, the female half of the human race is doubly oppressed under capitalism ... (and) in "household bondage" – V.I. Lenin.

India is the first country to recognise this social fact, underlined by Lenin on the International Working Women's Day in 1921 and to have taken concrete measures to draw women into leadership position and thereby into politics.

73rd Amendment Act, 1992 (Article 243D(3)) has succeeded in drawing women from hearths and making them join the mainstream of village life. A berth in the Panchayat Raj System for women has no doubt empowered women to the extent envisaged by the advocates of 73rd Amendment.

It reads as follows:

"Not less than one third (including the number of seats reserved for women belonging to the Scheduled Castes and Scheduled Tribes) of the total number of seats to be filled by direct election in every Panchayat shall be reserved for women and such seats may be allotted by rotation to different constituencies in a Panchayat" and clause(4) of the Act has the following provision, ".... not less than one-third of the total number of offices of chairpersons in the *Panchayats* at each level shall be reserved for women provided also that the number of offices reserved under this clause shall be allotted by rotation to different panchayats at each level.

The above constitutional amendment providing one-third representation to women in elected bodies as well as reserving one-third of the offices of chairpersons for them, will have far-reaching consequences in Indian political and social life. This is a most welcome gesture, because, we cannot make democracy meaningful in a traditional society without full involvement of women.

But, for their dream of participation of women in public life and politics to become reality, much is to be done, in the present, socio-economic conditions.

Can this participation of women in the affairs of the society through the *Panchayati Raj* institutions remove the hurdles and handicaps that exist at present? There is no clear-cut answer to the question. But we must make a beginning somewhere. All said and done, this 73rd amendment provides us a great opportunity to improve the status of women.

Purdah is lifted in villages and this is a manifestation of the empowerment of women. Now, women are walking with their heads high and are able to interact with men of the village and others outside. In a way, their self-confidence has increased tremendously. This journey from "chulha to chaupal" (from the kitchen to the *Panchayat*) is a major achievement and we must be proud of this achievement as a first step for the betterment of the lot of women. Contrary to popular notion that it is the family which is preventing a women from coming out of the traditional mould, a survey conducted by a voluntary organisation showed that 95 per cent of the politically empowered women enjoy the support of their families. It is in fact the society, that is not encouraging woman's empowerment. Actual participation of women is decision making process is needed and this is provided by reservation of 33 per cent of seats for women in Assemblies and the Parliament.

Of course, a sizeable number of women are still illiterate. Leadership needs more than literacy. With resolve and integrity, all the hurdles posed by illiteracy can be surpassed. Measures are also being taken to make women cent per cent literate and that day of achievement of this goal may not be far off.

Modern educated women are making their presence felt in all walks of life, with an inherent instinct and sixth sense. We are able to see women heading big industrial concerns and working as pilots of aeroplanes as well.

A social transformation aimed at the woman's changing role can be achieved undoubtedly by these *Panchayat Raj* institutions. Women have to face certain challenges bravely in the early stage and overcome some difficulties.

Women should be given their due share one day or other, as members of society. Social awareness should be built up on this issue. I don't think that it will be a hard task as we have crossed many barriers in the past. It is only required that mindset of people be changed and new orientation is given to certain values of life, in the changed set of conditions of modernism.

To make democracy genuine and meaningful, it should be brought nearer to the people and women at the grass root level, who are well aware of the problems locally, should come out to hold positions. In fact a silent revolution is picking up in the rural areas. When once, a jolt is given to the masses, hitherto unaware of curtain values, they wake up and begin to think of the realities. This would help them to prepare their minds in tune with the changed circumstances. A strong political will, will be developed automatically, for achieving better results.

Role of Religion Too Undergoing Change

Role of religion in rural society occupies an important place. It is now at the cross roads. Because of the new political and economic environment people are becoming secular, democratic and oriented to scientific ethics. The battle line between religiosity and secularism has been drawn. Women, who were previously observing festivals and festivities are no more orthodox in the true sense.

Modern Legislation: Attitudinal Change

Modern Indian legislation helped in establishing the position of women and freeing them from Independence on men. The Hindu Code Bill of 1954-55 made Hindu marriage monogamous, permitted divorce and made women equal partners with inheritance of property. It also legislated against dowry. But how many of these rights are being exercised by women in present day India, is a different matter. However, their existence itself is a matter of great importance.

The social barriers that prevented women from taking advantage of their education and participation in public activities began to lift with the beginning of this century. The attention of all social reformers was directed towards improving the status of women and they endeavoured to abolish the myth that women are inferior to men. It should be the aim and objective of the women's movement, to strive for a society based on individual and social dignity, in which, women feel strong, active, creative and empowered; where diverse abilities and talents are valued; where women can make decisions and choices, express freely and move about freely and confidently without fear of any violence. The lack of political will to empower women beyond statements of policy and legislation and to truly redress systematic and structural imbalances, which is reflected in insufficient resources allocations and support mechanisms to achieve these objectives and too frequent reliance on micro-schemes and initiatives to address macro-structural problems. We must recognise the challenges posed by new trends that perpetuate injustices, threaten world justice and impede women's empowerment. The inadequate attention given to the needs of women and girls, who are marginalised because of their disability or because of their race, language, culture, religion, or socio-economic status should be removed.

Lack of educational policies, that would contribute to the elimination of attitudes towards women that would limit the role of women in society, should be considered as top priority issue. The culture of violence against women and the escalating exploitation of women and girls should be put an end to.

To sum up, I would like to caution about the forces in society working against development, such as age-old attitudes, lack of management skills, lack of healthy competition, political interferences, etc. over and above everything women's intelligence is not taken into consideration, while planning for the success of any programme. Still women are considered to be only caretakers of the families and children and not executors of any public industries or concerns. But how far the rural society would encourage and appreciate woman's participation is to be observed. Reorientation of certain values of the existing system and a broader perspective for over-all development of women is necessary.

Anyhow, it will be a big experiment in India, from which many lessons can be drawn. By increased involvement of women in administration, policy-making as a process of decentralisation, may spread more confidence among women. But, programme should be chalked out properly. Impending barriers should be removed in the implementation of major policies. Women should play important role in monitoring, evaluation and promoting needs of women.

REFERENCES

1. Gupta S.P.: *Modern India and Progress in Science and Technology*, Vikas, 1979.
2. Madan I.N.: *Modern Indian Literature* 1930.
3. Raysmith W.: *Nationalism and Reform in India.*
4. Raghuvanshi V.P.S.: *Indian National Movement and Thought* 1959.
5. Natarajan S.A.: *Century of Social Reform in India.*
6. Aijazuddin Ahmed: *Social Geography.*
7. Rama Mehta: *The Western Educated Hindu Women.*
8. Kirk Johnson: *Television and Social Change in Rural India.*
9. M.K. Joseph: *Mass Media and the Challenge of Change.*
10. A.K. Majumdar and Bhanwar Singh: *Political Sociology.*
11. Suchitra Deshprabhu: *Sociological Research Approaches, Techniques and Applications.*
12. Dr. Susheela Kaushik: *Empowering Women for Politics.*
13. *Women 2000; Women in Public Life*, No. 2, 1992, p. 4.
14. *History of Brahma Samaj* Vol. I (1911), p. 1876.
15. R.K. Prabhu & U.R Rao: *The Mind of Mahatma Gandhi.*
16. *Harijan* Editorial: Jan. 19, 1934.
17. Jawaharlal Nehru: *India Today and Tomorrow.*
18. D.N. Majumdar: *Races and Cultures of India.*
19. Smita Gate: *Development of Women (Maharashtra Experience).*
20. A. Rane Gonda: *Gender Inequality.*
21. Maitreyi Dixit: *Women and Achievement: Dynamics of Participation and Partnership.*
22. Bernd Hanm, Pandurang K. Muttagi (Eds): *Sustainable Development and Future of Cities.*
23. Tripat Taneja and Kadambari Sarma: *Sustainable Society.*
24. Duncan Melaren, Simon Bullock and Nusrat Yousuf: *Tomorrow's World.*
25. K.K. Varma, Rajan Varma and Saboohi Kazim: *Towards Gender Equality.*
26. Vijay Kaushik and Bela Rani Sarma: *Women in Developed World.*
27. Latika Menon: *Gender Issues and Social Dynamics.*
28. Raj Mohini Sethi, *Globalisation, Culture and Women's Development.*
29. Santi Jaya Surya and D.C. Jaya Surya: *Women and Development: The Road from Beijing.*
30. Dr. Mukherjee: *Nationalism in Hindu Culture*, pp. 20-22.

Index